A Case for
H I S T O R I C
Premillennialism

A Case for
HISTORIC
Premillennialism

An Alternative to "Left Behind" Eschatology

EDITED BY

Craig L. Blomberg
and Sung Wook Chung

Baker Academic
a division of Baker Publishing Group
Grand Rapids, Michigan

Published by Baker Academic
a division of Baker Publishing Group
P.O. Box 6287, Grand Rapids, MI 49516-6287
www.bakeracademic.com

Printed in the United States of America

Library of Congress Cataloging-in-Publication Data
A case for historic premillennialism : an alternative to "left behind" eschatology / edited by Craig L. Blomberg and Sung Wook Chung.
       p.   cm.
    Chiefly proceedings of a conference held in 2007 at Denver Seminary.
    Includes bibliographical references and indexes.
    ISBN 978-0-8010-3596-8 (pbk. : alk. paper)
       1. Millennialism—Congresses. 2. Tribulation (Christian eschatology)—Congresses.
    I. Blomberg, Craig, 1955– . II. Chung, Sung Wook, 1966–
    BT892.C37 2009
    236′.9—dc22   2008034926

In keeping with biblical principles of creation stewardship, Baker Publishing Group advocates the responsible use of our natural resources. As a member of the Green Press Initiative, our company uses recycled paper when possible. The text paper of this book is comprised of 30% post-consumer waste.

For Bruce A. Demarest

biblical scholar, systematic theologian,
spiritual director, mentor,
colleague, friend

Contents

Acknowledgments

The idea of editing and publishing this collection originated with Sung Wook Chung. Craig Blomberg came on board as a coeditor when Dr. Chung was sidelined for several months for health reasons. Most of the contributions are papers given at a conference sponsored by the Biblical Studies division of Denver Seminary. We are grateful to all of those who wrote and presented these papers as well as to the two contributors who wrote their essays later. They were almost entirely on time, and at times even early, with both their first drafts and their revisions, for which we are profoundly thankful. Mrs. Jeanette Freitag graciously turned all of the essays into the Baker house style and format. Jim Kinney, editorial director for Baker Academic, a division of Baker Publishing Group, persevered with us even after the original form of our book proposal seemed unworkable and even after our final submitted manuscript was about a month late. Thanks, Jim, for your faith in, and patience with, us!

For the last thirty-four years, Bruce A. Demarest has played a central role in the life of Denver Seminary. Trained as a New Testament scholar, with a doctorate under F. F. Bruce at the University of Manchester, Bruce quickly added theology to his repertoire of skills and for years was the one full-time systematic theologian on our faculty, working closely with Gordon Lewis, who split his time between theology and philosophy. In midlife and midcareer, Bruce added a passion for spiritual formation and soul care. Upon the reduction of his teaching role to a half-time faculty load as Bruce neared standard retirement age, he insisted on continuing to teach spiritual formation. A prolific author, Bruce's largest work is his coauthored three-volume *Integrative Theology*, completed in 1994. Working with Gordon, he was able to agree on positions about every major doctrine except eschatology, at least when it came to dispensationalism versus historic premillennialism (or, perhaps better put, pre- versus posttribulationism). Bruce found himself clinging to the latter in both instances; Gordon, to the former. The diplomatic and judicious language of their section on eschatology is a tribute to how devout Christian scholars can work together. It is to Bruce, therefore, that we would like to dedicate this book—a friend who throughout his career has modeled exemplary scholarship, interdisciplinary expertise, and Christian character and conduct. As a new cadre of younger theologians takes up the torch for Denver Seminary, they will long be indebted to you, Bruce, in these and numerous other wonderful ways. We offer this short book to you, therefore, as a small token of our many thanks for your ministry, past and present, in our midst. *Ad multos annos.*

Sung Wook Chung

Craig L. Blomberg

Introduction

CRAIG L. BLOMBERG AND SUNG WOOK CHUNG

Walk into one of the largest Christian bookstores in the Denver metropolitan area, and the first and largest display that visually confronts you is an attractive arrangement of the sixteen volumes of the Left Behind series.[1] Much like Hal Lindsey's *Late Great Planet Earth* and subsequent volumes in the 1970s and 1980s, Left Behind by Tim LaHaye and Jerry B. Jenkins has received countless hours of attention from readers in the last decade of the twentieth century and the first decade of the twenty-first.[2] To the uninitiated, these books might appear as if they were the most important items for Christians to read, perhaps even more so than the Bible.

In fact, they are simply the latest in a long line of prophecy "manuals," purporting to teach, through either didactic or narrative forms, how biblical apocalyptic literature is being fulfilled in the current generation of world history. Bernard McGinn's fascinating survey of all the candidates for the "antichrist" that have been confidently put forward throughout church history demonstrates one fact unequivocally: to date, 100 percent of all the attempts to

---

1. Tim LaHaye and Jerry B. Jenkins, Left Behind (Wheaton: Tyndale, 1995–2007). Also available are, e.g., "kids' editions," packaged sets, study guides, and DVDs.
2. Hal Lindsey, *The Late Great Planet Earth* (Grand Rapids: Zondervan, 1970). See also esp. idem, *There's a New World Coming* (Santa Ana, CA: Vision House, 1973); idem, *The Liberation of Planet Earth* (Grand Rapids: Zondervan, 1974); idem, *When Is Jesus Coming Again?* (Carol Stream, IL: Creation House, 1974); idem, *The Terminal Generation* (Old Tappan, NJ: Revell, 1976); idem, *The 1980's: Countdown to Armageddon* (King of Prussia, PA: Westgate, 1980); idem, *The Rapture: Truth or Consequences* (New York: Bantam, 1983); idem, *The Road to Holocaust* (New York: Bantam, 1989).

correlate biblical prophecy with current events have been wrong![3] This in itself should inspire enough humility in Christians that we stop assuming that if we just tweak one or two details, the next published scenario will get it right.

Moreover, not only does Jesus insist that "about that day or hour no one knows, not even the angels in heaven, nor the Son, but only the Father" (Mark 13:32 TNIV); he later admonishes his followers that it is not for them "to know the times or dates the Father has set by his own authority" (Acts 1:7). Although a few date setters have avoided literally violating Mark 13:32 by predicting "merely" the month or year of Christ's return,[4] the Acts passage utilizes the two broadest words in Hellenistic Greek for "time" (*chronos* and *kairos*). Any claim to be able to pin down end-times events to any definable period of time violates Jesus's word in the Scriptures.

How, then, should Christians interpret biblical prophecy and apocalyptic, particularly with reference to the events surrounding Christ's return? Four broad approaches have developed and taken turns in the limelight throughout church history: historic or classic premillennialism, amillennialism, postmillennialism, and dispensational premillennialism. Numerous good resources introduce the interested reader to the interpretive grids of each of these perspectives in detail;[5] some of the best are those in which each view is described by an advocate of that perspective and followed by a brief response from the other contributors to the volume.[6] In its simplest form, premillennialism refers to the conviction that Christ will return at the end of human history as we know it, *prior* to a long period of time, depicted in Revelation 20:1–7 as a thousand years, in which he reigns on earth, creating a golden era of peace and happiness for all believers alive at the time of his return, along with all believers of past eras who are resurrected and glorified at this time. Postmillennialism takes this thousand-year period, or millennium, as the final period of time during this present era, in which believers, yielded to the power of the Holy Spirit, facilitate a Christianizing of the earth to an unprecedented extent, thereby creating the idyllic earthly conditions described in Revelation 20 and

3. Bernard McGinn, *Antichrist: Two Thousand Years of the Human Fascination with Evil* (San Francisco: HarperSanFrancisco, 1994).

4. E.g., Edgar C. Whisenant, *88 Reasons Why the Rapture Will Be in 1988* (Nashville: World Bible Society, 1988); recalculated to have been a year off in idem, *The Final Shout: Rapture Report, 1989* (Nashville: World Bible Society, 1989).

5. E.g., Stanley J. Grenz, *The Millennial Maze: Sorting Out Evangelical Options* (Downers Grove, IL: InterVarsity, 1992); Millard J. Erickson, *Contemporary Options in Eschatology* (Grand Rapids: Baker Academic, 1977).

6. Esp. Craig A. Blaising, ed., *Three Views on the Millennium and Beyond* (Grand Rapids: Zondervan, 1999); Robert G. Clouse, ed., *The Meaning of the Millennium: Four Views* (Downers Grove, IL: InterVarsity, 1977).

in numerous Old Testament passages (particularly in the closing chapters of a number of the Prophets). In this scheme, Christ then comes back *after* the millennium. Amillennialism has typically understood the entire church age, symbolically, as the millennium, during which believers *spiritually* reign with Christ but does not look forward to a literally transformed earth or literal millennium in the way that both premillennialists and postmillennialists do.[7]

Although representatives of all three millennial perspectives may be found in almost every era of church history, premillennialism appears to have commanded a majority of proponents in the first four centuries, amillennialism dominated from the time of Augustine's major writings in the fifth century onward, and postmillennialism found its greatest support in the modern missionary movements of the eighteenth and nineteenth centuries. The nineteenth century also saw the development of a new form of premillennialism with the founding of the Plymouth Brethren denomination in Great Britain and Ireland by J. Nelson Darby. To distinguish this branch of premillennialism from its predecessor, scholars today speak of the newer development as dispensational premillennialism and the older form as historic or classic premillennialism.

Dispensationalism, in fact, represents an entire system of interpreting the Bible, not just an approach to eschatology or the study of future events.[8] An analysis of most of this system need not detain us here. Of particular interest, however, is its characteristic view on the relationship between the rapture (in which believers are reunited with the incarnate Jesus when he descends to earth to gather them together; see esp. 1 Thess. 4:16–17) and the "great tribulation" (apparently an era of unprecedented distress on the earth just before Christ's public, visible second coming to judge all the peoples of the earth; see esp. Rev. 7:14). Nineteenth-century dispensational premillennialism developed the first unambiguous articulation of a "pretribulational" rapture, thereby separating the rapture and Christ's second coming into two discrete events.

The twenty-first-century church worldwide is becoming increasingly a potluck of Christian doctrines that individual believers and entire denominations are combining in unprecedented ways. Not long ago it would have seemed incongruous for Presbyterian or Christian Reformed churches to advocate anything except the amillennialism so consistently supported by John Calvin

---

7. Occasionally, however, amillennialists have tried to equate the millennium with the new heavens and the new earth, as in esp. Anthony A. Hoekema, *The Bible and the Future* (Grand Rapids: Eerdmans, 1979).

8. For a standard explanation of its classic form, see Charles C. Ryrie, *Dispensationalism* (Chicago: Moody, 1995), which was a substantially revised and expanded edition of idem, *Dispensationalism Today* (Chicago: Moody, 1966).

and his theological successors in the Calvinist and Reformed wing of the Protestant Reformation. And it would have seemed anomalous for Pentecostal churches to embrace dispensational distinctives, since one of the bases for separating church history into different ages was the conviction that the charismatic gifts ceased within the end of the apostolic era. Today, at least at the grassroots level, one can find in both of these traditions many believers whose eschatology is largely or entirely determined by Hal Lindsey, Tim LaHaye, Jerry Jenkins, and other writers of similar bent and who are oblivious to how contrary those traditions are to their church's own heritage. And with the proliferation of nondenominational churches (sometimes forming their own quasi-denominations) founded by visions and missions not primarily theological (other than broadly evangelical) in nature, many churchgoers do not even have an eschatological tradition to forget.

Only a few decades ago it was commonplace for eschatology to be overemphasized in evangelical church and parachurch settings. Seminars, conferences, and preaching series regularly featured as-yet-unfulfilled biblical prophecy. Pretribulational premillennialism could be made a litmus test of correct doctrine and/or fellowship. Many younger Christians have recognized that these trends assigned these concerns to a much more central place in Christian theology than they deserved, and they have, understandably, swung the pendulum in the other direction, sometimes to the point of almost disregarding eschatology altogether. In other cases, a healthy balance has been struck by removing a requirement that a particular view on the millennium or the rapture form part of a church or parachurch ministry's doctrinal statement that all of its members must affirm, even as teaching continues periodically on these topics and people are guided to see what is and is not at stake in the debates.

Today three of the four major eschatological perspectives are comparatively well known, both in the academy and among rank-and-file Christians. Each has undergone significant development and enjoyed new arguments in its defense. In dispensational circles, a majority of practicing academics, at least in North America, have embraced what has been dubbed progressive dispensationalism—a movement that closely resembles historic or classic premillennialism by, for example, recognizing significant continuity between the Testaments and important overlap between the biblically defined roles for Israel and the church, by identifying many of the Old Testament prophecies concerning Israel's restoration as events that will occur in the millennium rather than as signs of Christ's impending return, by recognizing the partial presence of the kingdom of God already in this "church age," and even by including at times certain sociopolitical, not just spiritual, dimensions. Progressive dispensationalism sees the church as God's intention for this age all along and not a parenthesis or "plan B" implemented only because Israel as a whole rejected the kingdom offer at the time of Christ's first coming, and it holds that Jesus's teaching to his Jewish disciples (classically in the Sermon on the Mount) applies to all believers, Jew and Gentile alike, now and in the future.[9] For the most part, however, progressive dispensationalism still affirms a pretribulational rapture.

Classic Reformed or covenant theology has also experienced significant shifts in recent years, allowing for important discontinuities between the Testaments and the different covenant eras in salvation history. In a different kind of development, preterism has taken on a higher profile in some Reformed circles. This view sees all biblical prophecy about the events leading up to Christ's second coming as fulfilled in the first century. At times it even argues that the second coming itself was fulfilled in Jesus's invisible coming in judgment on Israel in AD 70, when the Romans squelched the Zealot rebellion, razed the temple, and burned large parts of Jerusalem.[10]

Even postmillennialism, whose demise many were trumpeting in the 1960s and 1970s after two world wars, Korea, Vietnam, the liberal-leaning churches of many mainline Protestant denominations, and the rapid secularization of the Western world, particularly outside the United States, has made a comeback. The spectacular growth of the church, at least numerically, in many parts of Latin America, Africa, China, and Southeast Asia in the 1980s and 1990s led some people to revive a more chastened form of postmillennialism.[11] Although these postmillennialists might not have penned the lyrics to classic hymns with the triumphalism of previous centuries (e.g., "Jesus shall reign where e'er the sun doth his successive journeys run; his kingdom stretch from shore to shore, till moons shall wax and wane no more"), efforts to at least give everyone on the planet the opportunity to hear and respond to the gospel proliferated. The arrival of the new millennium gave many people hope that it might mark a significant new stage in the progress of the gospel.

9. See esp. Craig A. Blaising and Darrell L. Bock, *Progressive Dispensationalism: An Up-to-Date Handbook of Contemporary Dispensational Thought* (Wheaton: BridgePoint Books, 1993); Robert L. Saucy, *The Case for Progressive Dispensationalism* (Grand Rapids: Zondervan, 1993). Cf. Herbert W. Bateman, ed., *Three Central Issues in Contemporary Dispensationalism: A Comparison of Traditional and Progressive Views* (Grand Rapids: Kregel, 1999).

10. See esp. Kenneth L. Gentry, *He Shall Have Dominion* (Tyler, TX: Institute for Christian Economics, 1992). Agreeing with this interpretation for the parousia passages in the Gospels, though not for the rest of the New Testament, is N. T. Wright, *Jesus and the Victory of God* (Minneapolis: Fortress, 1996).

11. See esp. John J. Davis, *Christ's Victorious Kingdom: Postmillennialism Reconsidered* (Grand Rapids: Baker Academic, 1986). Cf. Keith A. Mathison, *Postmillennialism: An Eschatology of Hope* (Phillipsburg, NJ: Presbyterian & Reformed, 1999).

Arguably, the eschatological perspective that has received the least formal attention in the last twenty-five to thirty years is classic premillennialism. The scholar, professor, and writer who was by far more responsible than any other individual in the twentieth century for resurrecting this approach, for tirelessly promoting it throughout his career, and for convincing a generation of students and readers of its validity was George Eldon Ladd at Fuller Seminary. But Ladd passed away in 1982, and most of his major works on the topic spanned the 1950s through the 1970s.[12] No one has since emerged as his successor in championing classic premillennialism, even though countless evangelical biblical scholars and theologians have adopted his views. New generations of students, however, do not automatically follow their teachers, and since every other branch of eschatology has received sustained attention and developed new permutations, it is past time for a new look at classic premillennialism.

This collection of essays emerged from precisely this conviction. Beginning in February 2000, the Denver Seminary Institute of Contextualized Biblical Studies has sponsored an annual conference exploring a branch of biblical scholarship worthy of contemporary contextualization. The first seven conferences addressed, respectively, the topics of contextualized biblical studies in general, the Messiah in the Bible, the family in the Bible, methodologies for translating Scripture, war from biblical and ethical perspectives (including contributions by contemporary Christian military leaders), the integration of biblical studies and Christian counseling, and worship (both ancient and modern). The papers from the conferences on the Messiah, on the family, and on war have been published in book form, while those on translation and on the integration of the Bible and counseling have appeared as entire fascicles of journals.[13] The very first conference, though including some of the finest presentations in the eight-year history of these conferences, was not woven tightly enough around an attention-catching theme to garner the necessary interest among the publishers that were approached. The worship conference,

---

12. See esp. George E. Ladd, *Crucial Questions about the Kingdom of God* (Grand Rapids: Eerdmans, 1952); idem, *The Gospel of the Kingdom* (Grand Rapids: Eerdmans, 1959); idem, *The Presence of the Future* (Grand Rapids: Eerdmans, 1974); and idem, *A Theology of the New Testament* (Grand Rapids: Eerdmans, 1974).

13. Richard S. Hess and M. Daniel Carroll R., eds., *Israel's Messiah in the Bible and the Dead Sea Scrolls* (Grand Rapids: Baker Academic, 2003); idem, *Family in the Bible: Exploring Customs, Culture, and Context* (Grand Rapids: Baker Academic, 2003); *Bible Translator* 56.3 (2005); James R. Beck and M. Daniel Carroll R., eds., special edition, *Journal of Psychology and Christianity* 25.2 (2006); Richard S. Hess and Elmer Martens, eds., *War in the Bible and Terrorism in the Twenty-first Century*, Bulletin for Biblical Research Supplements 2 (Winona Lake, IN: Eisenbrauns, 2008).

because of the very nature of the topic, was not intended to produce academic essays, although its presenters possessed the caliber and the credentials to do so had the conference been packaged differently.

This brings us to the conference of 2007 and to this volume. Conference format has varied slightly over the years, but usually six presentations spanning a Friday evening through early Saturday afternoon, with time for discussion after each and with interaction of the presenters in panel format at the end, has proved optimal. In order to round out the published collections, we have often invited one or two supplementary essays on the theme of the conference, and this year proved no different. Thus the chapters by Don Fairbairn and Tim Weber do not reflect oral addresses from the conference; the remaining chapters do, even if in slightly revised form. Unlike the previous conferences, we began lining up participants for the one on premillennialism by looking solely in-house. Sung Wook Chung, Craig Blomberg, Rick Hess, Hélène Dallaire, and Don Payne all teach at Denver Seminary. As it turns out, Fairbairn and Weber also have close connections with Denver Seminary. Fairbairn received his master of divinity degree here, and Weber taught church history here for many years, and so we were doubly grateful to have them participate in this project. Finally, one of the goals in every conference has been to afford representation to women and minority participants. Because of our partnership, in recent years, in several endeavors with our peer institution for theological education in Guatemala City, the Seminario Teológico Centroamericano (SET-ECA), we invited Oscar Campos to round out our program. Campos is the one contributor to this collection who would identify himself as a progressive dispensational premillennialist rather than as a classic or historical premillennialist, but, as is clear from his chapter, his positions within that interpretive community prove far closer to those held by the rest of us in this volume than to classic dispensationalism.

What, then, is the content of this volume? It begins with Tim Weber's overview of millennial positions throughout church history, culminating in the rise of dispensationalism in the last 180 years or so. This essay reflects on the reasons dispensational premillennialism has become much better known and more frequently adopted than historic premillennialism at the Christian grassroots level during the centuries since its conception. Weber offers the in-depth but very readable kind of survey that only one who has done most of his major scholarly work in this arena can produce. In short, dispensational approaches to biblical eschatology have proved so popular because they have consistently addressed the *populace* and at a *populist* level to a degree that historical premillennialists have never approached.

Two essays related to the Old Testament follow. Both branches of premillennialism have typically believed in the literal fulfillment of a variety of Old Testament prophecies about the end times, but the relationship of the rapture to the tribulation in view of these prophecies often remains comparatively neglected, understandably so because it could appear that the Old Testament teaches nothing explicit on this topic. Hess, however, shows a recurring pattern according to which God's people have to experience tribulation before restoration in a fashion that in fact supports posttribulational premillennialism. Nonpremillennialists often point to early stages of Israelite religion, where eschatology seems altogether absent, and to later branches of Judaism, in which hope for a millennium or even a bodily resurrection seems unimportant, in order to dispute the viability of premillennial eschatology for a religion (Christianity) that grew organically out of Jewish roots.[14] Dallaire, who reexamines a broad sweep of Old Testament, intertestamental, and early rabbinic thought on this subject, demonstrates that there was a much greater diversity of perspective than is often acknowledged. Blomberg rounds out the three biblically based chapters by arguing that posttribulational premillennialism is the consistent teaching of the New Testament.

Most scholars today recognize that all exegesis functions with various preunderstandings and presuppositions and within conscious and unconscious interpretive grids.[15] What, then, are the most important hermeneutics of premillennial thinking that its adherents must recognize, and how defensible are they? Payne tackles this topic in the first of this volume's theological and historical essays. Though claiming that dispensationalism is the natural result of a straightforward, literal reading of Scripture, its adherents ignore certain tensions with the results of this method with which historic premillennialists find it easier (and important) to live. Dispensationalists in fact make important appeals to tradition, reason, and experience as well, which are actually more amenable to broader premillennialist hermeneutics.

Is it indeed true that classic premillennialism finds significant precedent in the early patristic writers instead of being a fringe movement, as some nonpremillennialists have argued, or instead of supporting dispensational and/or pretribulational premillennialism, as some supporters of those positions have alleged? Fairbairn's study of Irenaeus in detail and of other early patristic millenarians helps to show that there is significant precedent. But what

14. From a Jewish perspective, Jon D. Levenson (*Resurrection and the Restoration of Israel: The Ultimate Victory of the God of Life* [New Haven: Yale University Press, 2006]) presents and debunks this consensus perspective among more liberal Christian and Jewish scholarship.

15. See, e.g., William W. Klein, Craig L. Blomberg, and Robert L. Hubbard Jr., *Introduction to Biblical Interpretation*, rev. ed. (Nashville: Nelson, 2004), 142–68.

of the Reformers, especially Calvin? If Reformation and Reformed theology recovered much of genuine biblical teaching on so many doctrines, and given the interrelationship among all of the major doctrines of systematic theology, must not amillennialist eschatology necessarily follow? Chung shows how the traditional Reformed covenant theology has spiritualized the biblical teachings on the material and institutional dimensions of redemption. For Chung, amillennialism is the product of a gnostic reading of Revelation 20:1–6. Indeed, much like Paul Jewett, who made a compelling case for believer's baptism as the proper outgrowth of covenant theology,[16] Chung argues that classic premillennialism flows naturally from this theology.

Finally, we return to the present and sample an important non-American perspective and set of insights. What were premillennialism's influences on the mission field, especially in the Majority World? What is the lasting legacy of this influence, and how are things changing today? If the answer is not always the same, how should things be changing, both at home and abroad? Perhaps historic premillennialism or its very close cousin, *progressive* dispensationalism, is better poised to meet the challenges of the twenty-first century than classic dispensationalist premillennialism. Guatemala's Campos reflects on these questions from several different angles. A brief conclusion, like these opening remarks from the pens of the editors, concludes the collection of studies. But enough of introduction; it is time to turn to the texts and to the presentations themselves.

---

16. Paul K. Jewett, *Infant Baptism and the Covenant of Grace* (Grand Rapids: Eerdmans, 1978).

1

Dispensational and Historic Premillennialism as Popular Millennialist Movements

Timothy P. Weber

America has always been fertile ground for millennialism. Given the American free-market religious economy, people are free to believe what they want, organize as they please, and spread their ideas as best they can. Sometimes such efforts pay off nicely, but sometimes they do not. In a relatively few cases, millennialist ideas have generated large and hard-to-ignore movements. When this happens, millennialist ideas can even seep into the popular culture.

A 2002 *Time*/CNN poll reported that since 9/11 more than one-third of Americans have been thinking more seriously about how current events might be leading to the end of the world. Even though only 36 percent of those polled said they believe that the Bible is the Word of God, 59 percent thought that events predicted in Revelation were being fulfilled. Almost one in four Americans thought that 9/11 had been predicted in the Bible, and almost one in five expected to live long enough to see the end of the world. Finally, more than one-third of those who expressed support for Israel said they based their views on the belief that the Jews must have their own country in the Holy Land for the second coming to occur.[1]

One could credibly maintain that the poll merely uncovered the views of many American evangelicals, who now constitute somewhere between one-quarter and one-third of the population and among whom Bible prophecy still resonates. But as historian Paul Boyer has argued, many other Americans who usually ignore the Bible are willing to listen to teachers of Bible prophecy when world events reach crisis levels.[2] We probably all know biblically illiterate and religiously unaffiliated people who have somehow picked up rudimentary notions of the rapture, the antichrist, or Armageddon. It is clear, then, that one way or another, someone's millennialist beliefs have made their way into nonevangelical territory. And we know who they are. From Hal Lindsey's *Late Great Planet Earth* to Tim LaHaye and Jerry Jenkins's Left Behind series, dispensational premillennialists have made impressive forays into the popular culture, often combining their views of the future with well-organized right-wing and pro-Israel political action.[3] No American millennialist group has received more attention or reached further into mainstream culture than dispensationalism. But despite its successes, dispensationalism is not the only kind of premillennialism current.

How does historic premillennialism—the subject of this book—measure up as a popular millennialist movement, especially when compared with its biggest rival, dispensationalism? As we shall see, comparisons are difficult because these are two very different kinds of movements. Nevertheless, the relationship between the two is interesting and revealing. This study will explain how and why.

The place to begin is a definition of what we mean by "popular." When used to describe a millennialist movement, the word can have two quite different meanings. "Popular" can refer to the *size of its following*, to the extent of its acceptance. In this sense, then, a popular millennialist movement has a large clientele with recognizable leadership, supporting institutions and organizations, and a clear set of identifying beliefs. This "popular" refers to a movement's popularity.

The word "popular" can also refer to the *kind of following* a movement possesses. Does it appeal to common folks or to a more elite audience? Does it consciously position itself over against the so-called experts? Where do its

1. Nancy Gibbs, "Apocalypse Now," *Time*, July 1, 2002, 41–48.

2. Paul Boyer, *When Time Shall Be No More: Prophecy Belief in Modern American Culture* (Cambridge, MA: Harvard University Press, 1992).

3. Hal Lindsey, *The Late Great Planet Earth* (Grand Rapids: Zondervan, 1970); Tim LaHaye and Jerry B. Jenkins, Left Behind (Wheaton: Tyndale, 1995–2007).

leaders come from, how do they make their case, and what is the nature of their appeal? Does it come across as a highbrow or a lowbrow movement? In this sense of the word, "popular" can mean that a movement is populist rather than elitist.

In a nutshell, this study will show that historic premillennialism does not qualify as a popular millennialist movement in either sense of the word, at least not yet.

Labeling Millennialist Movements

Christian eschatology includes a large number of end-times issues—death, the end of the world, divine judgment, and heaven and hell. Some Christians have paid special attention to the end of history and whether there will be a golden age of peace connected to Christ's return. The key biblical passage for such speculation is Revelation 20, in which Christ returns to earth, defeats Satan, and sets up a thousand-year kingdom on the earth, a millennium (from the Latin *mille*, "thousand"). This passage in particular and the book of Revelation in general have been interpreted in vastly different ways, which has led systematic theologians and historians to provide labels to identify various millennialist positions.

Most early Christians interpreted Revelation 20 quite literally and expected a millennial age following Christ's return. Such views are called *premillennialist* because they place the second coming *before* the millennium. After the fifth century and Augustine's enormously influential *City of God*, most Christians adopted a more figurative interpretation of Revelation 20. They concluded that the "millennium"—a spiritual kingdom characterized by Christ's reign—actually began with Christ's resurrection and will continue to expand in both the church and in heaven until Christ's return. Because they do not expect a literal millennium on the earth, they are called *amillennialists* (literally, "no-millennialists"). A third, more recent group of Christians argues that the second coming will follow the world's conversion to Christ and the rise of a Christian golden age. Because they place Christ's return *after* this millennium, they are called *postmillennialists*.

Differences extend beyond the interpretation of Revelation 20. Interpreters have also disagreed about the way to approach Revelation as a whole. Most modern scholars choose between a *preterist* and an *idealist* reading of Revelation. Preterists believe that the book reflects late-first- or early-second-century conditions and was written to bring hope to persecuted believers at that time. Thus preterists understand Revelation more in political than in prophetic terms. Idealists set aside all chronological or predictive issues in order to treat the book as an artistic exposition of the ongoing battle between good and evil; in short, Revelation is a drama that speaks to the longings of the human heart.

Others (mainly those holding millennialist views) utilize either a *historicist* or a *futurist* approach. Historicists believe that Revelation contains a prophetic overview of the entire church age. Thus they look for prophetic fulfillments in past, present, and future historical events. Futurists believe that Revelation's prophecies are scheduled to occur in the future, just before Christ's return, which leads them to develop elaborate future scenarios and look for current "signs of the times" that point ahead to expected events. If a core sample is taken of Christian thought almost any time in the last two thousand years, advocates of these positions can be found.[4]

Although such labeling helps in distinguishing one group from another, many millennialist movements are difficult to classify. History is messy, and most prophetic movements do not consult with theologians before putting together their belief systems. Consequently, historians who trace these movements over time often find it very difficult to fit them into neat categories.[5] Nevertheless, for the people within these movements, even small distinctions can have big consequences. For example, the premillennialist revival that began in Great Britain in the late eighteenth century and moved in waves to America in the nineteenth produced not only advocates of historicism and futurism but fierce divisions within the ranks of the futurists, as the comparison below between dispensationalists and historic premillennialists will show.

So Many Millennialist Choices

Dispensationalism and historic (not historicist) premillennialism were relative latecomers to a religious culture already replete with millennialist successes and failures. In the first half of the nineteenth century, evangelical Protestantism was overwhelmingly postmillennial. Historians have called antebellum America an "evangelical empire" characterized by optimism, growth, and democratic ideals. Religious and political leaders alike viewed the new nation in millennial terms, as a "city upon a hill" with a special role to play in the world.

4. Steve Gregg, *Revelation, Four Views: A Parallel Commentary* (Nashville: Nelson, 1997).
5. Historical surveys of Christian millennialism include the following: Frederic J. Baumgartner, *Longing for the End: A History of Millennialism in Western Civilization* (New York: St. Martin's, 1999); Stephen Hunt, ed., *Christian Millennialism: From the Early Church to Waco* (Bloomington: Indiana University Press, 2001); and Eugen Weber, *Apocalypses: Prophecies, Cults, and Millennial Beliefs through the Ages* (Cambridge, MA: Harvard University Press, 1999).

The dominance of postmillennialism came as a surprise. Most of the Protestants and Catholics who settled colonial America were overwhelmingly and "officially" amillennialists; however, most Puritans who settled New England held historicist premillennial views that had grown popular in England in the early/mid-seventeenth century, especially among the radical Fifth Monarchy Men. Colonial Puritans believed that they were in the last days, that the work of the antichrist was already evident all over the world, and that signs of the end were everywhere. Then the unexpected happened: the First Great Awakening of the 1740s generated thousands of conversions and hundreds of new churches. Jonathan Edwards, borrowing heavily from the prophetic writings of Daniel Whitby, concluded that God was using such ordinary means of grace to Christianize the world and bring in a golden millennial age *before* Christ's return. Although the results of the First Great Awakening faded fast, these postmillennial expectations were revived and validated by the even more impressive Second Great Awakening in the early nineteenth century. Popular commentaries throughout these periods by Matthew Henry, Thomas Scott, and Adam Clarke articulated a postmillennial understanding of the Bible that became deeply rooted in the evangelical churches.

Postmillennialism joined forces with the surge of democratic ideals to make American Protestantism boldly evangelical and activist. Operating with the certainty of prophetic promises, evangelicals built schools, churches, publishing houses, and missionary agencies in order to carry out God's plan to Christianize America and the world. Their strategy included both religion and politics. Evangelists such as Charles Finney told their converts to apply Christian principles to social and political causes and predicted that if they did so, the millennium was just around the corner.

Along the margins of this culture-shaping postmillennial juggernaut were a number of other distinctive and often controversial millennialist movements. In the 1770s an Englishwoman called Mother Ann Lee brought the United Society of Believers in Christ's Second Coming to America. More popularly known as the Shakers for their distinctive worship style, her followers believed that Mother Ann was a female incarnation of Christ who intended to bring in the millennium by forming distinctive communities. Eventually the Shakers established nineteen such communities from Maine to Florida, where they attempted to reproduce primitive Christianity. Shakers adopted simple lifestyles; husbands and wives lived apart and turned their children over to be raised by the community; and no one had sex. Because of the latter restriction, the Shakers prospered only as long as the Second Great Awakening provided a stream of new converts or as orphans found their way to the Shaker communities. But once the revival peaked, the Shaker communities started their slow decline. On their best day, the Shakers numbered no more than five thousand.[6]

John Humphrey Noyes, a Yale graduate and convert of Charles Finney, formed another millennialist group. He taught that the second coming occurred in AD 70 but that Christ decided not to establish his millennial kingdom because of the lack of Christian love among his followers. Noyes believed that it was up to him to set things right. In 1838 he started a small Christian commune in Vermont where he promoted his notion of sinless perfection and "complex marriage." Under his careful supervision and control, community members were encouraged to have sex with each other's spouses, which he thought would facilitate greater love within the community and counter the selfish tendencies of traditional marriage. Noyes maintained that such practices marked the arrival of the kingdom of God, but outraged neighbors saw things differently. Fierce opposition forced Noyes to move the commune to Oneida, New York, where in time his followers tired of the unavoidable and disruptive complications of complex marriage and Noyes's millennial schemes. Their numbers, which never exceeded three hundred, dwindled, but those who remained found a new calling in successful business ventures.[7]

In the 1830s Joseph Smith founded the Church of Jesus Christ of Latter-day Saints after he discovered and translated the Book of Mormon. The Mormons believed that through them God was restoring the authentic apostolic gospel and reestablishing the Aaronic priesthood. As a modern-day prophet, Joseph called all Mormons to relocate ("gather") to Jackson County, Missouri, to begin the work of establishing the new Jerusalem to which Christ would shortly return. When anxious and angry Missourians drove the Mormons out of the state in 1839, Smith led them across the Mississippi River to Nauvoo, Illinois, where he built a new temple, revealed new "endowments" (i.e., temple rituals), and began preaching the plurality of gods and wives. After the prophet's murder in 1844, Brigham Young led the church to a temporary Zion in Utah. Unlike the Shakers and the Oneida Colony, the Mormons survived and prospered. In the twentieth century, Mormon leaders talked much less about Joseph Smith's prophetic teachings, but faithful Mormons still await a new prophet's call to move back to Missouri just before Christ returns.[8]

6. Stephen Stein, The Shaker Experience in America (New Haven: Yale University Press, 1992).

7. Spencer Klaw, Without Sin: The Life and Death of the Oneida Community (New York: Penguin Books, 1994).

8. Grant Underwood, The Millenarian World of Early Mormonism (Urbana: University of Illinois Press, 1993).

Reflecting more-typical evangelical Protestant beliefs and practices were the followers of William Miller, a Baptist preacher from Vermont and upstate New York. A skeptical deist, Miller was converted after the War of 1812 and began reading the Bible with the critical eye of a former rationalist. Using a historicist and premillennialist approach to the study of Bible prophecy, he studied the numerology of Daniel and Revelation. Once he established past prophetic fulfillments as a starting point, he used "millennial arithmetic" and the "year-day theory" (by which he converted days to years in prophetic texts) to set a date of the second coming "in about 1843." Although Miller claimed that he came to these conclusions on his own, as we shall see, they were nearly identical to those held by other historicist premillennialists in Great Britain at about the same time.

Miller arrived at these findings in 1818 but waited about fifteen years before making them public. Thanks to new advertising and promotional techniques, his message generated a large following (estimates range from thirty thousand to one hundred thousand) drawn from the evangelical denominations, more or less where the Shakers, John Humphrey Noyes, and the Mormons obtained their followers. But the Millerites were different. They never questioned traditional marriage or practiced unconventional sex or altered the church's historic teachings about the Godhead. Miller did not claim to be a prophet, only a careful reader of Scripture who invited others to check his calculations and come to their own conclusions. In time, however, he grew tired of his critics and instructed his followers to separate from "Babylon," by which he meant the dismissive evangelical denominations, in order to spread the word of the "Advent near." As the predicted time approached, Miller felt pressure to be more precise about the date for Christ's return. He eventually settled on October 22, 1844, which set him and the Millerites up for the Great Disappointment. Some Millerites returned to their former churches, but others established a number of new Adventist denominations. The largest was the Seventh-day Adventist Church, which made a few necessary adjustments to Miller's historicist premillennialism and in time became famous for other characteristics, such as worshiping on Saturday, vegetarianism, medical care, and missions.[9]

In comparison to the other millennialist alternatives discussed above, the early Millerites were the most orthodox and traditional premillennialists before the Civil War. But their very public failure dealt a serious blow to the credibility of premillennialism and confirmed most evangelical Protestants

9. Ronald L. Numbers and Jonathan Butler, eds., *The Disappointed* (Bloomington: Indiana University Press, 1987).

in their postmillennialist ways. Nevertheless, postmillennialism's days were numbered. Instead of the coming millennium, America experienced a series of unprecedented social, political, intellectual, and religious crises in the second half of the nineteenth century. By almost any measure, the world was growing worse, not better, and demographic studies proved that Christianization was not keeping pace with world population growth. What did devoted postmillennialists do when events ran counter to their eschatological expectations?[10] Some held on, convinced that the golden age was still coming, despite the temporary setbacks. Others dropped their postmillennial expectations for other forward-looking causes, such as the Social Gospel, the Progressive movement, and, later on, the New Deal. Still others traded one kind of millennialism for another, a new kind of premillennialism that eventually gained unprecedented success in the United States.

The Rise of a New Kind of Premillennialism

The premillennialism that gained a following in late-nineteenth-century America differed significantly from the teachings of William Miller. It was futurist, not historicist, which made it virtually incapable of date setting, the Millerites' undoing. In addition, futurist premillennialism introduced a number of new elements into the millennialist mix and offered a much more realistic view of current conditions, about which postmillennialism seemed obviously mistaken.

This new prophetic option came out of a British revival of premillennialism that began in the late eighteenth century and reached its zenith in the 1830s and 1840s. The French Revolution was the catalyst for this revival. Something so momentous had to fit into God's prophetic plans, but how? In the beginning, leadership in the movement came from clergy and lay leaders of the established churches (Anglican and Scots Presbyterian). At first, interested persons found each other through Bible studies, new books and journals, and missionary groups, but eventually the revival took shape in three weeklong study conferences at Henry Drummond's Albury Park estate in 1826, 1827, and 1828. Using a more-or-less literalistic hermeneutic, participants agreed on a number of bedrock convictions: the present age (or "dispensation") will end in cataclysmic judgment; the Jews must be restored to Palestine before this judgment takes place (something never taught by William Miller); divine judgment will begin with an apostate Christendom; the millennial age will follow God's judgment on the earth and

10. James H. Moorhead, *World without End: Mainstream American Protestant Visions of the Last Things, 1880–1925* (Bloomington: Indiana University Press, 1999).

the second coming of Christ; and the second coming is imminent, a view based on a particular way (strikingly like Miller's) of connecting prophecies in Daniel 7 and Revelation 13 to current events.[11] In short, like the Millerites, these British millennialists believed they had cracked the prophetic code by using a historicist and premillennialist approach to the Bible.

Not all British millennialists, however, were historicists. There was a small group of futurist premillennialists as well. Futurism did not originate in the British revival but came from sixteenth-century Roman Catholic scholars who tried to repudiate the common Protestant assertion that the present pope was the antichrist. The Catholic futurists argued that since Revelation's prophecies were meant for the future, not the present, the current pope could not possibly be the "man of sin." In the 1820s and 1830s, some premillennialists found in futurism a connection to early-church teachings about the end times and began to promote it; examples are S. R. Maitland, James H. Todd, and William Burgh. These futurists used the prophetic teachings of the early church to refute historicist premillennialism's approach to prophetic texts, especially the year-day theory.[12]

One early futurist leader was the charismatic Scot, Edward Irving. Like most other British millennialists, he used a literalistic approach to prophetic interpretation, affirmed the restoration of the Jews, expected (and saw current evidence for) the apostasy of the churches, and preached the imminent return of Christ to establish his millennial kingdom in Jerusalem. He had read Catholic futurists and agreed with them: Revelation's prophecies pointed to the future, just before Christ's return. He preached futurist views after he accepted the pulpit of a London congregation, and he began attracting large crowds. But his standing among British evangelicals and premillennialists declined when his church experienced an outbreak of glossolalia and divine healing. Even though many evangelicals expected a restoration of apostolic gifts shortly before Christ's return, the experience of it in Irving's church proved to be extremely controversial. When he started preaching that Christ had a fallen nature, the Scots Presbyterians defrocked Irving, who then helped to establish the Catholic Apostolic Church as an alternative to the religious apostasy he saw in his former denomination.

The Plymouth Brethren, who had left apostate Anglicanism in order to meet regularly for Bible study, fellowship, and the Lord's Supper, likewise championed futurist premillennialism. At first the Plymouth Brethren lacked direction and a clear identity despite the emergence of two powerful leaders

11. Ernest R. Sandeen, *The Roots of Fundamentalism: British and American Millenarianism, 1800–1930* (Chicago: University of Chicago Press, 1970), 3–22.
12. George E. Ladd, *The Blessed Hope: A Biblical Study of the Second Advent and the Rapture* (Grand Rapids: Eerdmans, 1956), 35–40.

and teachers, Benjamin Wills Newton and John Nelson Darby. During a series of study retreats first held at the estate of Lady Theodosia Powerscourt in 1831, the Brethren defined their eschatology: they took a futurist approach to Revelation, rejected the year-day theory, and declared the established churches already apostate. This challenge to the dominant historicist perspective also closely followed Irving's views.

The Plymouth Brethren received a shock at the third Powerscourt Conference in 1833, when Darby introduced his teachings on the pretribulation rapture of the church and the postponement theory, which argued for a "great parenthesis of prophetic time" between the sixty-ninth and seventieth weeks of Daniel 9. Most Brethren as well as other futurists initially considered both ideas complete novelties. The ensuing argument drove a deep wedge between Darby and other Brethren leaders, especially Newton and Samuel P. Tregelles, another respected Bible teacher, and eventually split the Plymouth Brethren. Futurist premillennialism has never been the same.

Darby's mind remained open on these new ideas for another decade, but by 1840 he had constructed an elaborate dispensational system that supported and explained them. Darby's version of futurist premillennialism divided history into distinct eras or dispensations in order to keep track of God's changing redemptive plan. But even more fundamental to his interpretation of the Bible was the conviction that God had two completely separate plans and peoples in the divine plan of redemption, one "earthly" (Israel) and one "heavenly" (the church). Thus, "rightly dividing the word of truth" meant keeping the passages that applied to the two plans clearly delineated. This interpretive rule of thumb led Darby to his striking innovations. Because he believed that God could work with only one of his peoples at a time, he insisted that Jesus must rapture the church before he can restart the prophetic clock and resume his dealings with the Jews. In practical terms, this required Darby to divide the second coming into two parts—Christ coming *for* his saints before the tribulation and *with* his saints after it, when he will defeat the devil and the antichrist and establish the millennial kingdom. Darby also taught that since the church, as God's heavenly people, had no earthly prophecies of its own, there was no prophesied event between the present and the rapture of the church; thus it might occur at any time. In short, Darby's view of the any-moment, pretribulation rapture allowed him to avoid "the pitfalls both of attempting to predict a time for Christ's second advent and of trying to make sense out of the contemporary alarms of European politics with the Revelation as his guidebook."[13] Darby was not deterred by the fact that before

13. Sandeen, *Roots of Fundamentalism*, 64.

him no millennialist, British or otherwise, had taught anything like his view of the rapture.[14] He continued to teach his version of futurist premillennialism in Britain, throughout Europe, and, most significantly, in the United States, where it had its greatest success.[15]

The New Premillennialism Comes to America

John Nelson Darby made seven trips to North America between 1862 and 1877. At first he worked among Canadian Plymouth Brethren, but eventually he shifted his attention to non–Plymouth Brethren evangelicals in Chicago, St. Louis, Boston, and New York. His initial forays into the American churches were disappointing. He was appalled by the worldliness of American Christians and their still overwhelmingly positive view of their denominations. Most American evangelicals found the separatist views of the Plymouth Brethren too crabby and schismatic. Darby quickly discovered that although some American Christians were interested in his eschatology, the overwhelming majority rejected his ecclesiology.

Darby's reception in America was clearly mixed. Writers in some Protestant journals warned readers of the dangers of dispensationalism, but Darby's views found an outlet in the premillennialist *Prophetic Times*, edited by the Lutheran Joseph Seiss. Its leading contributors were denominationally diverse (Lutheran, Episcopalian, Presbyterian [Old School and New School], Dutch Reformed, Moravian, and Baptist) and advocated both historicist and futurist positions. Without mentioning its origin among the Plymouth Brethren, which would have put most readers off, some writers promoted the pretribulation rapture, which the journal's "creed" was broad enough to allow. Another journal, James Inglis's *Waymarks in the Wilderness*, took an unapologetic pro-Darby stance. This journal's readership was a fraction of that of the *Prophetic Times*, but many of the people associated with Inglis's journal were

14. The origins of Darby's rapture view remain cloudy. He claimed that it just came to him once he understood God's two peoples and plans. Other explanations—that the idea arose during a tongues-speaking outburst in Irving's church or that it came from a teenager named Margaret MacDonald in Scotland during another Pentecostal outbreak—seem far-fetched and unproven. See John Nelson Darby, *Collected Works*, ed. William Kelly, 34 vols. (London: G. Morrish, 1967), 11:56; Samuel P. Tregelles, *The Hope of Christ's Second Coming* (London: Samuel Bagster & Sons, 1864), 35; and David McPherson, *The Incredible Cover-Up: The True Story of the Pre-trib Rapture* (Plainfield, NJ: Logos International, 1975).

15. Sandeen, *Roots of Fundamentalism*, 59–80; H. A. Ironside, *A Historical Sketch of the Brethren Movement* (Grand Rapids: Zondervan, 1942); Clarence Bass, *Backgrounds to Dispensationalism* (Grand Rapids: Baker Academic, 1960). For Darby's views, see Darby, *Collected Works*.

influential in starting the Bible conference movement, which spread dispensationalism far and wide.

Inglis organized the Believers' Meeting for Bible Study in the late 1860s. After his death and a brief hiatus, the Believers' Meeting was restarted in 1875 and eventually located at Niagara-on-the-Lake, Ontario. The Niagara Conferences, which met for a week or two each summer, offered a packed schedule: two speakers in the morning, two in the afternoon, and one in the evening. For two decades the Niagara Conferences were led by James H. Brookes, for thirty-nine years the pastor of the Walnut Street Presbyterian Church in St. Louis, author of *Maranatha* (1878), and editor of *The Truth*. Niagara became a gathering place for traditional Protestants, an outpost against the spread of liberal theology. Ironically, although Niagara stood fast in support of the old doctrines, it also welcomed advocates of the new premillennialism. Under Brookes, then, Niagara became a kind of boot camp for emerging premillennialist leaders and the launching pad for the dispensationalist movement in America.

In 1878 Brookes composed a fourteen-point statement of faith to mark theological boundaries for speakers and attendees. The Niagara Creed was typically evangelical but obviously Calvinist-leaning. It began with an article on biblical inerrancy and ended with a rather generic article on millennialism. The latter took no stand on futurism or Darby's rapture doctrine, but it did affirm the restoration of the Jews to the Holy Land, the worsening of world conditions in the present age, and Christ's personal and premillennial return to establish his earthly rule.[16] With such wiggle room in the creed, dispensationalists pushed their views hard. Given the makeup of evangelicalism at the time, many Niagara regulars objected to the creed's premillennial statement and complained that such prophetic views were getting far too much attention at the summer sessions. Wanting to keep their clientele happy, Niagara leaders decided to organize another series of Bible conferences that focused solely on prophecy.

The first American Bible and Prophetic Conference was held in New York City in 1878. Six more followed: Chicago in 1886; Allegheny, Pennsylvania, in 1895; Boston in 1901; Chicago again in 1914; and Philadelphia and New York in 1918. At the beginning, speakers and hearers represented a variety of premillennialist views, but over time these prophetic conferences came to be dominated by dispensationalists, who were quickly discovering how to get their message across.[17]

---

16. Sandeen, *Roots of Fundamentalism*, 141–42; for the entire Niagara Creed, see 273–77.

17. Timothy P. Weber, *Living in the Shadow of the Second Coming: American Premillennialism, 1875 to 1982* (Chicago: University of Chicago Press, 1987), 28–29.

Niagara had the same experience. Once those in charge developed a clear preference for dispensationalism, they pushed to the forefront those who taught it. Rapidly the differences within the new premillennialism became apparent for all to see, and the ties that initially held futurist premillennialists together began to break. In 1897 the Niagara Conference was nearly torn apart over whether the rapture will occur before or after the tribulation. The arguments were repeated over and over in the decades to come. Dispensationalists insisted that by "rightly dividing the word of truth," the pretribulation rapture became obvious. For them, dispensationalism was the key to understanding the whole Bible, not just prophecy, and it was a bulwark against liberalism and the guarantee of orthodoxy. They held that all other approaches were seriously defective. The other premillennialists argued that Darby's view of the rapture was not explicitly taught in the Bible and was merely an inference based on other mistaken notions. They maintained that dispensationalism was a theological novelty created by Darby out of thin air and that, in short, its claims were pretentious and unsubstantiated by either the Bible or the history of Christian theology. With so little room for compromise, no one was able to resolve the dispute, and Niagara closed down for good in 1900. In the story of Niagara's demise we can see something of the future of American premillennialism.[18]

By the twentieth century, then, futurist premillennialism had divided into two warring camps. Many of dispensationalism's strongest critics were veterans of Niagara and the prophetic conferences. Some of them had even been dispensationalists themselves, early devotees who changed their minds later on. Nathaniel West, one of the founders of Niagara, wrote the highly regarded but nondispensational *Thousand Years in Both Testaments* (1880). A. J. Gordon was an early follower of Darby but repudiated his teachings in *Ecce venit* (1889). Two men who are listed as contributing editors of the *Scofield Reference Bible* later repudiated dispensationalism: William J. Erdman and William G. Moorehead. Robert Cameron also disavowed his earlier dispensationalist convictions in *Scriptural Truth about the Lord's Return* (1922).[19] These men appealed to a more venerable premillennialist tradition that was rooted in the early church's eschatology, which contained no reference to a pretribulation rapture.[20]

18. Ibid., 132–61. William Trollinger, "Niagara Conferences," in *Dictionary of Christianity in America*, ed. Daniel G. Reid et al. (Downers Grove, IL: InterVarsity, 1990), 824–25.
19. His personal explanation of this shift is found in Sandeen, *Roots of Fundamentalism*, 278–81.
20. Ladd, *Blessed Hope*, 45–49.

Such a list constitutes only some of the leading voices of the nondispensationalist, futurist premillennialism in late-nineteenth- and early-twentieth-century America. Others who should be included are Charles Erdman, Philip Mauro, Rowland Bingham, G. Campbell Morgan and Oswald J. Smith (both leading dispensationalists at one time), and Harold John Ockenga, the Boston pastor who called for a "new evangelicalism" after World War II.[21] Their views have often been called historic premillennialism because they claimed to be following the legacy of earlier premillennial perspectives stretching back to postapostolic times. The term "historic," however, must be qualified, since futurism in its present form is in fact a post-Reformation perspective or at best a late medieval one.

Although it is certainly true that modern-day futurists can find similar views of prophetic chronology in the first three centuries, the eschatology of the early church is hard to fit into modern categories and contained features that futurists have never accepted. For example, *Epistle of Barnabas* 15 and Irenaeus, *Against Heresies* 5.28, use a "days of creation" motif to understand the flow of history: just as God created the world in six days and then rested on the seventh, so the world will last six thousand years, then be followed by a millennium of peace ("with the Lord a day is like a thousand years," 2 Pet. 3:8). Interpreters in the third and fourth centuries employed this theory to predict Christ's coming about three hundred years beyond their own time (Hippolytus, *Commentary on Daniel*; Lactantius, *Divine Institutes*).[22] Nevertheless, on the question of the rapture's timing, posttribulational historic premillennialists have many allies in the early centuries, whereas pretribulational dispensationalists have none.[23]

Comparing Dispensational and Historic Premillennial Movements

By the end of World War I, dispensationalists had clearly eclipsed their rivals in size and influence. How did this happen? How do dispensationalism and historic premillennialism compare as popular millennialist movements? In

21. Ibid., 50–60.

22. Timothy P. Weber, "Millennialism," in *The Oxford Handbook of Eschatology*, ed. Jerry L. Walls (New York: Oxford University Press, 2007), 365–83. As the year 2000 approached, a few dispensationalists (e.g., Jack Van Impe) resurrected the "days of creation" approach. To make the six thousand years of human history work as a predictor of Christ's return ca. 2000, they had to date the creation of the world to 4000 BC, which even many fundamentalists found difficult to accept.

23. When I was teaching the History of Millennial Thought at Denver Seminary, I made my students read the eschatological writings of the early fathers; they likewise could not find the pretribulation rapture.

a nutshell, dispensationalism developed into a robust popular millennialist movement, whereas historic premillennialism did not. By the end of the nineteenth century, dispensationalists were collecting supporters and institutions the way speakers at the Niagara Conferences used to pile up Bible passages for a Bible reading.

Darby appealed to successful evangelical pastors with big churches, good reputations, and large followings. Such leaders used their pulpits and their sizable clergy networks to open doors for dispensational teachings. Other early adopters were the professional revivalists who found in the teaching of the any-moment rapture an important tool to shake sinners from their lethargy: Jesus may come at any time, even before I finish this sermon; are you ready? D. L. Moody became an early but not always consistent convert to dispensationalism, and virtually every major revivalist from him to Billy Graham has preached a gospel message anchored in premillennialism.[24]

At a time when conservative evangelicals were building new coalitions to do battle against liberalism, dispensationalists often maintained a nondenominational and sometimes even cooperative ethos. This was certainly true at places such as Niagara and the prophetic conferences, but although everyone was welcome, not everyone came. Dispensationalism did not spread evenly through American Protestantism. Lutherans, Methodists, the German and Dutch Reformed, and Congregationalists seemed especially impervious to dispensational teaching. There were exceptions: Joseph Seiss was a prominent Lutheran; L. W. Munhall, E. F. Stroeter, Arno C. Gaebelein, and W. E. Blackstone were Methodists; W. R. Gordon and George S. Bishop were Dutch Reformed; and Edward P. Goodwin, Reuben A. Torrey, and C. I. Scofield were Congregationalists. But most pastors and laypeople from such churches remained indifferent or opposed. Dispensationalism enjoyed its greatest success among the Baptists, the Reformed Episcopalians, and especially the Presbyterians. Even so, denominational arguments over eschatology could become fierce. For example, James H. Brookes often complained that even fellow conservative Presbyterians made his life difficult; these included fellow biblical inerrantists A. A. Hodge, B. B. Warfield, and J. G. Machen, who were outspoken opponents of dispensationalism, which they considered close to heresy, even though they found much to admire among dispensationalists on other issues. Since dispensationalists saw themselves as thoroughly orthodox and fierce defenders of the Bible, such criticism hurt.[25]

24. Weber, *Living in the Shadow*, 13–28. See also William McLoughlin Jr., *Modern Revivalism: Charles Grandison Finney to Billy Graham* (New York: Ronald, 1959), 167–530.
25. Weber, *Living in the Shadow*, 29–31.

Although dispensationalism did not gain majority status in any of the existing mainline evangelical denominations, its impact on new churches was more pronounced. For example, many immigrant groups were deeply influenced by the revivalism of D. L. Moody. Some Scandinavians adopted both his style and his dispensationalism; what eventually became the Evangelical Free Church certainly did so, but the Swedish Mission Covenant (now Evangelical Covenant Church) did not. The new Pentecostal denominations adopted dispensationalism wholesale, although Pentecostals rejected the view, held by most other dispensationalists, that the apostolic gifts of tongues, divine healing, and prophecy ceased with the closing of the New Testament canon. Thousands of new independent and Bible churches included dispensationalism in their statements of faith, and almost all the self-identified fundamentalists who left their old denominations to start new ones were dispensationalists also; these included the General Association of Regular Baptists, the Conservative Baptists (with exceptions), and the Bible Presbyterians. Although historical generalizations are often foolhardy, this one is not: by the end of World War I, dispensationalism was nearly synonymous with fundamentalism and Pentecostalism.[26]

In the early days of the fundamentalist movement, it often seemed that dispensationalists had to force their way into the newly forming conservative coalitions. But once it became clear that fundamentalists were not going to regain control of the older evangelical denominations, dispensationalists were quite willing to go their own way. During the 1930s and 1940s, they completed the construction of a large and sophisticated subculture that had been decades in the making. In many ways dispensationalists operated like a typical denomination: they developed a full complement of goods and services and founded numerous institutions to support and perpetuate their movement. The Bible institutes, which began in the 1880s with the founding of schools such as the Moody Bible Institute, quickly fell into dispensationalist hands.[27] Some of these Bible institutes transformed into Bible colleges and then liberal arts colleges. Dispensationalists founded a few seminaries, starting with Dallas Theological Seminary in 1924, and gained control of a few others. They also founded a number of "faith missions" (e.g., the Central American Mission, the Sudan Interior Mission, and the African Inland Mission), which soon were taking the lead in the American foreign missionary movement after mainline

26. Martin E. Marty, *Modern American Religion*, vol. 1, *The Irony of It All, 1893–1919* (Chicago: University of Chicago Press, 1986), 208–37; Grant Wacker, *Heaven Below: Early Pentecostals and American Culture* (Cambridge, MA: Harvard University Press, 2001), 251–65.

27. Virginia L. Brereton, *Training God's Army: The American Bible School, 1880–1940* (Bloomington: Indiana University Press, 1990).

Protestant missions began cutting budgets and bringing their missionaries home during the Great Depression.[28] They had their own publishing houses; Zondervan, Baker, Eerdmans, Scripture Press, David C. Cook, and others were established to serve a dispensationalist clientele. In short, their networks of institutions were fully capable of sustaining and expanding their movement without help from anyone else.[29]

For much of their history, dispensationalists kept their subculture hermetically sealed. Reflecting Darby's view of the coming apostasy and the need to separate from unbelief, they kept their walls high and their contacts with the outside world few and far between. But as many historians have noticed, while they condemned the world, they also became masters of the world's media. They knew how to write best sellers to spread the word beyond their boundaries. The first was W. E. Blackstone's *Jesus Is Coming* (1878), which broke down the complicated dispensationalist system for the average reader and identified the "signs of the times." It was followed by C. I. Scofield's *Rightly Dividing the Word of Truth* (1888) and the *Scofield Reference Bible* (1909), published by Oxford University Press no less. *The Late Great Planet Earth* (1970) and the Left Behind series (1995–2007) are more recent examples of this old dispensational tradition.

In addition to the printed word, dispensationalists also made use of music and films. With the rise of popular Christian music came a number of "second coming songs"—for example, Larry Norman's "I Wish We'd All Been Ready" (1969). Churches used "rapture movies" to attract outside audiences—for example, *A Thief in the Night* (1972), *A Distant Thunder* (1977), *Image of the Beast* (1981), and *Prodigal Planet* (1983). There has been a steady stream of such movies since then, including the four-film Apocalypse series (1998–2001) and the three Left Behind movies (2000–2005). One can hear and see dispensationalism being preached on cable television all day every day, and it is a rare televangelist who does not keep his or her prophecy charts handy.

To some extent at least, these efforts have been successful at spreading the dispensational message, even into the crevices of the popular culture. Why? The basic answer lies in dispensationalism's ability to link prophecy with current events. With the Bible in one hand and the morning newspaper in the other, dispensationalist teachers have been able to make a case for their view of the world and what is going to happen next. No millennialist movement retains its audience for long unless it is able to do this consistently or else

28. Joel A. Carpenter and Wilbert R. Shenk, eds., *Earthen Vessels: American Evangelicals and Foreign Missions, 1880–1980* (Grand Rapids: Eerdmans, 1990).

29. Joel Carpenter, *Revive Us Again: The Reawakening of American Fundamentalism* (New York: Oxford University Press, 1997).

adjust its system when history takes an unexpected turn. Dispensationalism has always been able to do both.

From the early days of their movement, dispensationalist Bible teachers worked out an amazingly detailed scenario for the end times, then stuck to it: the decline of human civilization, the growing apostasy in the churches, the refounding of the State of Israel in the Holy Land, the rapture of the church, growing pressure on Israel and the rise of a peace-promising antichrist, the building of a third temple in Jerusalem, the revelation of the antichrist as the "man of sin," the great tribulation, the battle of Armageddon, and the return of Jesus. Although they did not expect to be here to see these events take place, they expected to witness history move in discernible directions. Since the mid-nineteenth century, the Bible teachers have kept their story straight but also stayed flexible enough to change their interpretations when necessary. Sometimes all that was needed to keep the dispensationalist rank and file happy was a good second edition. Dispensationalists have proven themselves to be quite willing to forgive and forget their teachers' mistakes, and they seem eager to accept new explanations.[30]

Since the founding of Israel in 1948 and especially the Six-Day War of 1967, dispensationalists have taken the lead in promoting U.S. support for the Jewish state. For most of their history, they sounded and acted like people who had completely given up on the world, and so they surprised nearly everyone by taking up politics and becoming major players in the new Christian right. At one time dispensationalists believed that their job was to teach the Bible and explain the end times, but by the 1980s they were becoming active in the political fray, evidently convinced that they could keep the devil somewhat restrained until the rapture. They took up various causes, formed political-action groups, and began lobbying Congress and the White House for Israel and a strong military. Given all this activity, they are hard to miss and evidently love being in the middle of things.

It is easy to conclude that no American millennialist group has been larger or more successful than the dispensationalists. By almost any measure, they are popular, although it is impossible to determine with certainty how many dispensationalists there are. They would have everyone believe that their views are held by most American evangelicals, but no serious observer believes it, although there is no scientific or reliable poll to settle the issue one way or the other. Probably the best guess is that no more than one-third of American evangelicals are dispensationalists. Or perhaps it is two-fifths or one-quarter.

30. Timothy P. Weber, *On the Road to Armageddon: How Evangelicals Became Israel's Best Friend* (Grand Rapids: Baker Academic, 2004).

Who knows for sure? Whichever fraction is correct, it still represents a very large number of dispensationalists. If there are seventy-five million evangelicals in America, then there may be anywhere from eighteen to twenty-five million dispensationalists. Darby would be both pleased and astonished.

Where does this leave historic premillennialists? They never developed anything like the dispensationalist network or numbers. As we have seen, it did not take long for dispensationalists to take charge. As people who lived along the margins of a larger movement, historic premillennialists had few options other than to argue for tolerance and maneuver for a place at the table. But it was not easy. Once fundamentalists put dispensationalism on their list of orthodox nonnegotiables, they in effect hung out a sign: "Nondispensationalists need not apply."[31]

Dispensationalism maintained its hegemony as long as the fundamentalist movement stayed strong and united. But maintaining unity was not a fundamentalist strong suit. By the 1940s many second-generation fundamentalists began calling for reforms, and by the 1950s many openly advocated a new evangelicalism that toned down some of fundamentalism's less appealing features, such as its separatism, legalism, anti-intellectualism, and general bad manners.[32] The new evangelical adjustments frequently included the reconsideration of eschatology, which opened the door for people such as George Eldon Ladd, probably the greatest historical premillennialist of them all. Raised a dispensationalist Northern Baptist in New England, Ladd graduated from Gordon College and Divinity School, earned a doctorate at Harvard, pastored for nearly fifteen years, and joined the faculty of Fuller Seminary in 1950. Within six years he published *Crucial Questions about the Kingdom of God* and *The Blessed Hope*, which started historic premillennialism's comeback in American evangelicalism.[33]

Ladd paid a price for his views; for the next three decades, he told his Fuller students about the recriminations and condemnations sent his way by angry dispensationalists.[34] But Ladd's books had broken the ice, and other scholars

31. George Marsden, *Fundamentalism and American Culture: The Shaping of Twentieth Century Evangelicalism, 1870–1925* (Oxford and New York: Oxford University Press, 1970); Martin E. Marty, *Modern American Religion*, vol. 2, *The Noise of Conflict, 1919–1941* (Chicago: University of Chicago Press, 1991), 155–214.

32. George Marsden, *Reforming Fundamentalism: Fuller Seminary and the New Evangelicalism* (Grand Rapids: Eerdmans, 1987).

33. George E. Ladd, *Crucial Questions about the Kingdom of God* (Grand Rapids: Eerdmans, 1952); idem, *Blessed Hope*.

34. People at Conservative Baptist Theological Seminary also paid a price. From its founding, the seminary allowed its faculty to hold various premillennialist views, which produced intense outside opposition for decades. Having a theologically mixed faculty also made things

found it easier to take dispensationalism on. In the 1960s a new generation of historic premillennialists began publishing scholarly books on eschatology to make their case historically, biblically, and theologically.[35] Soon it became clear to dispensationalists that the rules of the game had changed. And since the 1970s, a number of books have been published that bring together representatives of various eschatological views to discuss them side by side, on what seems almost a level playing field.[36]

Despite this intellectual resurgence, historic premillennialism has never come close to becoming a *popular* millennialist movement, and I am not aware of any reliable study that even estimates how many historic premillennialists there are. Part of the problem is that its advocates do not write best sellers (fiction or nonfiction), produce movies, or write songs. They do not organize politically or lobby Congress. They believe many of the same things about the future that dispensationalists do, but they do not spend their energy figuring out elaborate scenarios or creating prophetic charts or battle maps of future wars. They host not a single *Post-tribulational Prophecy and the News* program on cable television, nor do they sell board or video games based on their view of the future. In comparison to dispensationalists, they do not seem to be trying very hard.

If historic premillennialism is not popular in the sense of having a large (or at least discernible) following, how does it measure up on the populist/elitist scale? One is tempted to say that historic premillennialism rates high as elitist because its leadership tends to be school-based. Most writing on historic premillennialism is not intended for the masses; most of it is written by scholars for scholars. In contrast to most dispensationalist writing, it aims high and thus misses a more popular audience. Every successful millennialist movement has both highbrow and lowbrow elements. Dispensationalism certainly has its share of smart and well-trained defenders who lack neither sophistication nor the ability to elaborate. It has schools and scholars who remain committed to research and high-level academic discourse. The new wave

---

interesting on the inside. Well into the 1970s and 1980s the faculty and students at Denver Seminary sometimes argued over the merits of dispensationalism and historic premillennialism.

35. A short list would include Bass, *Backgrounds to Dispensationalism*; Robert H. Gundry, *The Church and the Tribulation* (Grand Rapids: Zondervan, 1973); Millard Erickson, *Contemporary Options in Eschatology: A Study of the Millennium* (Grand Rapids: Baker Academic, 1977); Stanley J. Grenz, *The Millennial Maze: Sorting Out Evangelical Options* (Downers Grove, IL: InterVarsity, 1992).

36. Robert G. Clouse, ed., *The Meaning of the Millennium: Four Views* (Downers Grove, IL: InterVarsity, 1977); Gleason L. Archer et al., *The Rapture: Pre-, Mid-, or Post-tribulational* (Grand Rapids: Academie Books, 1984); Darrell L. Bock, ed., *Three Views of the Millennium and Beyond* (Grand Rapids: Zondervan, 1999).

of "progressive dispensationalists" have doctorates from Oxford, Cambridge, and other impressive universities. This is true also for some more traditional dispensationalists, but most tended to stay close to home and take their degrees at "insider" schools. Nevertheless, even some of dispensationalism's best scholars have been wary of highbrow academic theology. Lewis Sperry Chafer, by far dispensationalism's most influential mid-twentieth-century theologian, left Oberlin College after three years to become a pastor. He saw his lack of formal academic study as a distinct advantage: "The very fact that I did not study a prescribed course in theology made it possible for me to approach the subject with an unprejudiced mind to be concerned only with what the Bible actually teaches."[37] Such a populist statement plays well among common folks but not among academic elites.

The biggest names in popular dispensationalism have never needed highbrow academic credentials to attract and keep a popular following. They know their material and are very good at communicating it to common people. It is very significant that the best-selling dispensationalist books of all time are *fictionalized* accounts of the end-times scenario: no careful exegesis there, no laborious comparisons with other alternatives, just a ripping good story told well. This is exactly what one would expect in a populist millennialist movement. In comparison to dispensationalism, historic premillennialism scores low in "lowbrow."

Perhaps, in the end, what separates the two versions of futurist premillennialism is that dispensationalists simply have a better story to tell. Laying all matters of truth aside, in a popularity contest the pretribulation rapture is always going to easily beat the posttribulational rapture. No matter what they do, historic premillennialists have a hard sell: going through the tribulation is not nearly as appealing as escaping from it. Years ago, while teaching an adult Sunday school lesson on pre- and posttribulation rapture positions, I was stopped cold in my pedagogical tracks by a class member who exclaimed, "But I really don't *want* to go through the tribulation." Case closed.

What does the future hold for these two versions of futurist premillennialism? Clearly, dispensationalism is not what it used to be. "Progressives" have tweaked the system in ways that concede major points to historic premillennialists. While maintaining their insistence on a distinct future role for the Jews in God's prophetic plan and the pretribulational timing of the rapture, they affirm, among other things, Ladd's argument that the coming kingdom is also present now and that there are hermeneutical dangers in overplaying one's

---

37. Quoted in Mark Noll, *Between Faith and Criticism: Evangelicals, Scholarship, and the Bible in America*, 2nd ed. (Grand Rapids: Baker Academic, 1986), 59–60.

prophetic hand in interpreting current events.[38] Furthermore, dispensational-ism's hold on institutions has declined considerably. Old-line dispensationalists have detected slippage at, for example, Dallas Seminary and the Moody Bible Institute, once bastions of dispensational truth, and many schools that once defined themselves in dispensational terms now recognize that their own sur-vival depends on appealing to a broader kind of evangelicalism. As separatist fundamentalism has lost ground to a more inclusive evangelicalism, so has dispensationalism to historic premillennialism. When once fervent dispensa-tionalists tire of their movement's lowbrow excesses or can no longer accept its exegetical arguments, they move to historic premillennialism, which is the most logical fallback position for those who want an alternative. More and more evangelicals are coming to the conclusion that dispensationalism is not the only way of being premillennialist.

38. Craig A. Blaising and Darrell L. Bock, *Progressive Dispensationalism: An Up-to-Date Handbook of Contemporary Dispensational Thought* (Wheaton: BridgePoint Books, 1993); Robert Saucy, *The Case for Progressive Dispensationalism* (Grand Rapids: Zondervan, 1993).

2

The Future Written in the Past

The Old Testament and the Millennium

RICHARD S. HESS

Personal Reflections

The questions that the study of Bible prophecy seeks to answer have always been intriguing to many of us. I remember as a teenager seeing the local church I attended unable to contain the crowds who appeared night after night through the week during the ministry of a well-known Bible prophecy teacher. He would connect Scriptures with the events of the newspaper and weave a synthesis that was at once frightening and reassuring. It was frightening because the wrath of God was about to be poured out on our country and civilization for our wickedness and corruption. But it was reassuring because those of us who were believers were guaranteed salvation before it all happened. We would be raptured away from this and not have to face all the wickedness that was coming.

Several experiences in my life moved me away from this fascination with, and focus on, the details of Christ's return. First was the fact that some of the predictions of these prophecy teachers fell short. Thus I learned that unless

America repented, Communist Russia was planning to march down the main street of what was then nearby Philadelphia and declare the country under its control on July 4, 1976. As far as I know, no one made the march nor did America repent. I suppose one could argue for a spiritual fulfillment of one of these things, but no one did, and that was not the tenor of the prophecy speaker when he made this prediction a few years earlier. I was disillusioned. Then too my college and seminary years were spent moving about in circles with a strong posttribulationist view. By the 1970s the premillennial wing of evangelicalism and many of its scholars and seminaries had come to the opinion that the next event on the prophecy calendar was not Jesus's return to rescue his church from the coming great tribulation. Instead it was the coming great tribulation itself. For me, awaiting possible martyrdom generated a lot less enthusiasm than seeing my Lord. A third experience grew out of my study of 1 Peter in Greek exegesis class with Murray Harris. When we came to 1 Peter 4:7, we read, "The end of all things is near. Therefore be clear minded and self-controlled so that you can pray." Dr. Harris reminded us that the purpose of prophecy was to receive encouragement to live faithfully and not "to satisfy idle curiosity." I was not certain what, exactly, idle curiosity was, but I determined to avoid it. The ensuing years occupied me with the study of the Hebrew Bible in its original context and kept me safely away from the prophecy wars in evangelicalism. Or so I thought.

In fact, the issue has never disappeared entirely. It was there at the Jewish rabbinic school where I received my doctorate. I learned that these Reform Jews looked with uncertainty at conservative Christianity's support of Israel. The issue was there when I first visited Israel in the 1980s. I met Christian Zionists who were convinced that the state of Israel was a fulfillment of biblical prophecy. I also met Christian Palestinians and their champions who were equally convinced that the state of Israel was not God's gift to Israel. Skipping to this past year: taking a Denver Seminary group to Israel, where we listened to speakers who continued to represent both sides of the debate, I learned once again that these questions of prophecy will not die. Am I going to side with Gershon Nerel and the Jewish Believers in Yeshua, for whom the church has not replaced Israel and thus all the prophecies of the Old Testament await literal fulfillment in the Holy Land? Or am I going to side with Naim Ateek and the Palestinian Christian Sabeel organization, for whom the Christians have replaced Israel in God's plan and the Holy Land belongs to God and not to the current states that occupy it?

The question takes on political significance that has ramifications beyond just my personal life and questions as to how I can live so that I will be prepared for the ever-imminent return of Jesus Christ. It also speaks to the question of how I regard my denomination, the Presbyterian Church U.S.A., and its decisions about divestment from companies that build machinery for use by Israel in its punishment of Palestinians. It is a question of how I regard my nation's policies with respect to the states of Israel and Palestine and the search for a just and secure peace. This, then, is my past and the importance I have given and do give to questions about the Bible and the future.

So, what are those questions? There are a lot of them, and they are more than this essay can or will answer. Here I want to examine what the Old Testament of the Protestant Christian Bible has to say about the future and especially about the events that people refer to as the great tribulation and the millennium. Neither of these terms appears in the Old Testament in any of the Bible translations that I checked. By itself, the term "tribulation" occurs in specific cases of distress and is used as a synonym for the latter term rather than as the name of a specific time. This is its usage in 1 Samuel 26:24 in the Revised Standard, King James, and American Standard versions. The translation "tribulation" also appears in Deuteronomy 4:30, where it describes the tribulation for the people of Israel. Although still not identical to the great tribulation, it is of interest and I will return to this text later.

Are there other ways in which the Old Testament might address these questions of the future? I would like to spend the remainder of this discussion examining two aspects. The first question considers the overall structure that may be common to the major biblical prophets. Do we see something here that might suggest a consistent pattern regarding the method in which God works? Are patterns present that might provide some indication as to the customary way in which God relates to his people? The second concerns the manner in which the writers and readers of Old Testament prophecies would have understood many of them, especially those envisioning a future restored Israel. To what extent were these prophecies intended to be understood in terms of temporal and spatial fulfillment? For example, would the early generations who first read and heard of the prophecy of a restored temple in Ezekiel 40–43 have understood this temple as something resembling a physical temple that one could visit and at which one could worship in Jerusalem? I propose to consider these aspects of Old Testament prophecy.

A Prophetic Pattern

My first consideration has to do with the structure of the books of the major biblical prophets and what this might teach us about the future. To begin with, we look at Isaiah. The book opens with an announcement of judgment against the nation of Judah. The first twelve chapters are occupied with this theme, although it is not an exclusive concern. Judgment against another land, Assyria, is promised in Isaiah 10. Further, the famous prophecies of hope in Immanuel and a future child (Isa. 7–9) form additional significant exceptions to the negative theme. Nevertheless, the overall tone is one of judgment against God's people. There follows a collection of oracles against surrounding nations in chapters 13–23. This expands to general expressions of universal judgment and oscillates back and forth with texts addressing specific nations in chapters 24–35. As always, there are some exceptions in which judgment and deliverance are promised to Jerusalem (chap. 22) and to Judah and Israel (chaps. 26–28). Still, the overall tenor is one of judgment for the nations. After a historical section of four chapters (36–39), the second half of the prophetic scroll of Isaiah turns to consider the message of promised comfort and hope (chaps. 40–66). Indeed, "Comfort, comfort" are the first two words of the first verse of chapter 40. Return from exile, restoration, and universal dominion and blessing are major themes throughout this section. Here and there are apparent exceptions, such as the oracles of judgment against Babylon (chaps. 46–47) and the Suffering Servant poem of 52:13–53:12. But even these are incorporated into a greater message of hope. The oracles against Babylon contrast that city's doom with Jerusalem's resurrection. The Suffering Servant lives on to "see his seed" and to "divide the spoils with the strong." Thus the major structure of this prophetic text begins with judgment against the people of God, moves on to judgment against the nations, and culminates with future redemption and blessing.

The book of Jeremiah has a somewhat different structure in its Hebrew Masoretic form. Still, many themes recur. The historical and biographical notes of the first twenty-nine chapters intersperse an unremitting warning of the coming judgment and destruction. Jeremiah 30–33 provides a brief interlude in which future peace and prosperity for the people of God are envisioned. Chapters 34–45 return to a message of condemnation and destruction that has as its backdrop the historical fall of Jerusalem to the Babylonians. Chapters 46–51 develop the theme of the judgment against the nations. Although the Greek Septuagint repositions this last section to the middle of the book, in keeping with the structure of Isaiah and Ezekiel, its position here follows the much larger message of judgment against God's people. This, after all, is the dominant concern of this prophet. The final chapter of Jeremiah appears to return to a message of judgment regarding the historical destruction of Jerusalem, as in chapter 39. It concludes with a note regarding the life of the last king of Judah in captivity and the mercy shown to this king by the Babylonian ruler. These final verses in the book, 52:31–34, are identical to the final verses in the books of Kings, 2 Kings 25:27–30. These verses thus conclude the primary and major ("Deuteronomistic") history as found in Deuteronomy, Joshua, Judges, Samuel, and Kings. Their message may be understood as a message of anticipated hope. God is not finished with the line of David or with the people of God. They continue in exile and come to flourish there. There will be a restoration, as promised in Jeremiah 30–33. As in Isaiah, we find an initial section of judgment against God's people followed by judgment toward the surrounding nations. This is followed by a message of hope and restoration. It is far shorter, however, than that found in the entire second half of the book of Isaiah. A more detailed message of hope is found earlier in the book, in the midst of the lengthy sections on judgment. The final verses of Jeremiah only hint at the earlier promises.

Ezekiel is the third great prophet. Ezekiel 8–11 depicts the sins of idolatry in the temple and God's departure. These are part of the larger themes, developed throughout chapters 1–24, of judgment and destruction against Jerusalem and Judah. As in the other two prophetic scrolls, Ezekiel follows these statements with oracles against other nations of the world in chapters 25–32. Chapters 33–48 conclude the book with Israel's promised restoration and blessing. Prominent and central in this section is the new temple. As in Isaiah and Jeremiah, so in Ezekiel the prophet begins with judgment against God's people, which is followed by judgment against the surrounding nations. Promises of a blessed future to come conclude the scroll.

As is true of virtually every literary structure in the Bible and the ancient Near East, this form is not rigid and deviates in many different ways in the Minor Prophets. In Amos, for example, the judgments against the nations open the book and are followed by the judgment against Israel. An oracle of restoration concludes the final chapter (Amos 9:11–15). Daniel also has a hybrid form in which the punishment of Israel is embodied in the stories of Daniel and his friends and the persecutions they endure. These are interspersed with dreams and visions addressing other nations of the world and their eventual downfall. The mixture of these elements occurs in the first eight chapters. Chapters 9–12 conclude the book with the promised success of God's people over persecution and their victory against their enemies.

Nevertheless, the dominant structure of the major prophetic books is tripartite, with condemnation and judgment of God's people followed by judgment against the surrounding nations and culminating with future salvation and blessing for God's people.[1] One wonders if, in his epistle encouraging Chris-

---

1. While the three-part pattern proposed here is distinctive, the awareness of judgment and blessing (as hope after the judgment) in the prophets has been noted previously. Most recently,

tians to endure through persecution, Peter did not have in mind something of this order when he concludes, "For it is time for judgment to begin with the family of God; and if it begins with us, what will the outcome be for those who do not obey the gospel of God?" (1 Pet. 4:17).

And indeed this is more than merely a literary structure. These prophets, especially Isaiah and Ezekiel, who follow this structure most closely, organized their messages in a generally chronological fashion. They understood this sequence to apply to both the past and the future. It was and is the manner in which God acts. Therefore, they would have expected that any major persecution in the world that was divinely ordained by God would begin with the suffering of God's people. Although the Old Testament does not mention the great tribulation explicitly or discuss it in detail, it does presume an order to God's plans according to which such a tribulation would necessarily include a time of testing for God's people. In account after account, God preserves his faithful people through suffering and trials, but there is no evidence that they are preserved from or out of such experiences. If today we are blessed with an absence of severe testing here in this country, we must know that this is not the case with many Christians throughout the world, whether in this generation or in each and every previous generation extending back to the beginning of Christianity. Given the dominant structure of the Old Testament prophetic messages, the example of Jesus Christ, and the consistent experience of God's people throughout history, it is difficult to believe that any future great tribulation will not also include God's people.

A Restored Temple

When we look at Old Testament prophecies, we must ask the question, What did the writers intend and what did the readers find there? This must be distinguished from what we might think should be the appropriate expression of prophecy. For example, does the restored temple in Ezekiel's vision truly speak of an anticipated future event when this will take place, or is it a vision that portrays an ideal of holiness and purity that the people of Ezekiel's time are to seek? Although it might be argued that such a question bristles with issues that are specific to the particular text mentioned, this would be true of every biblical example. Rather, the question is one that

---

see the following quote from John Goldingay: "Indeed, each of the prophetic books as we have them associates a message of hope with the declaring of the nightmare—beginning with the vision that closes Amos. There are limits set to punishment" (*Old Testament Theology*, vol. 2, *Israel's Faith* [Downers Grove, IL: InterVarsity, 2007], 344).

must be asked in terms of what Ezekiel saw and intended for his readers/ listeners to understand.

In order to interpret prophecy, it is important to understand that prophecy is not unique to Israel. We may think of the presence of false prophets among God's people, but prophecy is more widely attested than this. Prophets at the ancient north Syrian city of Mari in the eighteenth century BC made predictions concerning the king and when he should go to war in order to achieve victory. More of interest to us are prophets who ministered during the time of many of the Old Testament prophets. These prophets were part of the Neo-Assyrian Empire, which destroyed the northern kingdom of Israel in 722 BC and would threaten the southern kingdom of Judah during the century after that disaster. They prophesied in what is modern-day Iraq and spoke only of the king and national matters; at least all twenty-nine of the prophecies preserved contain such messages. These prophets were mainly or exclusively female, and their messages are short in comparison to the scrolls of biblical prophets such as Isaiah, Jeremiah, and Ezekiel. They are even shorter than the Minor Prophets. While there are differences with the biblical prophets, a brief consideration of some of their messages will provide insights into what was expected of prophetic messages in the time of the biblical prophets.

These prophets were concerned with the future. They saw it as a time of restoration. Thus more than once they assure the king, "The future will be like the past."[2] The implication is that the future events will resemble those that have taken place in the past. The world will not be so strange or different that only symbols and metaphors can be used. Consider this prophecy to the king of Assyria, Esarhaddon:

> Safe food you will eat.
>> Safe water you will drink.
>> In the midst of your palace you will remain safe.
>> Your son and your grandson will exercise kingship in the lap of the goddess Ninurta.[3]

Here we see a prophecy extending over several generations and concerning the well-being of the royal family. There are also prophecies that describe the future destruction of nations that are enemies of the Assyrians:

2. Simo Parpola, *Assyrian Prophecies*, State Archives of Assyria 9 (Helsinki: Helsinki University Press, 1997), 6, 14. See also Martti Nissinen, *Prophets and Prophecies in the Ancient Near East*, Society of Biblical Literature Writings from the Ancient World 12 (Atlanta: Society of Biblical Literature, 2003), 105, 112.
3. Parpola, *Assyrian Prophecies*, 10; Nissinen, *Prophets and Prophecies*, 110–11.

Words [about the Elam]ites:
    The [god] says: "I have [come and go]ne."
    Five or six times he spoke.
    He then said,
    "I have come from/with the weapon.
    The snake in its midst I have torn out and cut up.
    I have destroyed the weapon.
    I will destroy Elam.
    Its foreign force will be cast down to the ground.
    So I will bring Elam to its end."[4]

This prophecy uses pictorial forms, a weapon and a snake, as metaphors for Elam and its army. Yet it is clear where the word pictures stop and the explicit mention of Elam begins. No one would interpret this prophecy as referring to any nation other than the historical Elam.

From this brief survey we learn that specific events and matters were mentioned in prophetic texts and were intended to have a literal fulfillment. For our purposes it does not matter that one may classify these prophecies as non-Israelite and as coming from a god other than Yahweh. The point is that prophecies were known in the ancient world and that people who spoke them and those who heard them expected a kind of literal fulfillment, where the prophecies touched upon known events in the real world in which they lived. Thus the prophecies in the Old Testament are best interpreted in a manner that would agree with a one-to-one historical correspondence. Those who listened to the prophets and who read their words would not have instantly assumed a metaphor when the future was being described.

Now, it is true that some texts in the Old Testament were meant to be taken symbolically. For example, there is the picture of the valley of dry bones in Ezekiel 37:1–14. The fantastic vision of bones coming back to life does not demonstrate, however, the symbolic nature of this text. Rather, the evidence for a metaphor in these verses is made clear by verses 11–14, which begin, "Then he said to me: 'Son of man, these bones *are* the whole house of Israel.'" There follows an explanation in which the details of the vision each correspond to something in the resurrection of Israel as portrayed here. The statement "these bones *are* the whole house of Israel," or, more generally, "X *is* Y," is a formula that identifies the allegory. This formula does not appear in the chapters that precede or those that follow Ezekiel 37, and these chapters would therefore not have been understood as allegorical. Thus Ezekiel 35 prophesies the destruction of Edom. No ancient Israelite took this in any

4. Parpola, *Assyrian Prophecies*, 40; Nissinen, *Prophets and Prophecies*, 129.

way other than as a literal conquest of that land, as would happen with the Babylonians. Chapter 36 describes the punishment and restoration of Israel. Ezekiel's own contemporaries and the generations after him lived through this chapter and understood the prophet's words as a real punishment and a restoration in the land of promise. Ezekiel 37 uses images and pictures to describe this key event in Israel's history. Ezekiel 38 and 39 refer to the people of Gog, probably a Semitic word related to the roof of a house or, in this case, the roof of the world, that is, the high mountain range of Lebanon and especially Ararat, far to the north of Israel. From this region fierce hordes would come, as they had in the past, and threaten Israel. This could refer to the Assyrians and Babylonians as well as other historical groups named in this chapter. It could also refer to the Scythians and others emerging from central Asia and threatening God's people. Certainly Israel did not see this as allegorical, and there is no "X is Y" formula in these chapters.

We come now to the description of the new temple in Ezekiel 40–43, which is followed by descriptions of a renewed religious order and a new land in the remaining five chapters of the book. We may also consider the tabernacle description and construction in Exodus 25–40 and that of Solomon's temple in 1 Kings 6–8 and 2 Chronicles 2–7. Granted, there is a difference in the form of the revelation. For the tabernacle, divine words are followed by obedience. For the temple of Solomon, King Solomon supervises the details of the construction. For Ezekiel's temple, no one is described as building it. Nevertheless, the same sort of detail is present. Indeed, of all the temple descriptions in the Old Testament, Ezekiel's description is the most detailed in terms of the measurements and specifics of the rooms. When it is compared with other contemporary temple descriptions in Assyria and Babylonia, these sorts of detailed description appear to prevail. Such description is to be distinguished from earlier temple-building inscriptions where less concrete detail and more praise and laudatory expressions seem to have occurred.[5] In every comparable description in both the Bible and the ancient Near East, it was understood that the description of a temple for the gods was to be interpreted as providing a detailed essay about a real building. Thus both temple descriptions and

---

5. See the extensive discussion by Victor Horowitz, *I Have Built You an Exalted House: Temple Building in the Bible in Light of Mesopotamian and Northwest Semitic Writings*, Journal for the Study of the Old Testament Supplement Series 115 (Sheffield: Sheffield Academic, 1992), 224–59. Despite the details of the temple of Ezekiel, its architectural feasibility has been disputed. See Hermann Weidhass, *Wörter und Sachen aus 1. Regnum 6 und II. Chronica 3*, ed. Wolfgang Zwickel, Kleine Arbeiten zum Alten und Neuen Testament 3 (Waltrop: Spenner, 2001). Whether Ezek. 40–48 is architecturally correct is, however, irrelevant to its intended effect on its readership.

prophetic texts within and outside Ezekiel point toward the expectation that a real building was intended.

Does recent scholarship support this view of a real temple?[6] The major evangelical commentary by Daniel Block argues for an "ideational" interpretation in which the temple vision describes "spiritual realities."[7] Thus Block seems to argue for a symbolic temple. But like Jon Levenson, he compares the structure of this vision and its context in Ezekiel with that of the construction and function of the tabernacle in Exodus, Leviticus, and Numbers.[8] The readers of Ezekiel understood the tabernacle as an architectural reality. Even if the pentateuchal tabernacle were to be understood as a postexilic invention of the ruling priesthood—and I am not convinced of this—it would nevertheless be necessary for this artificial creation to have been accepted widely among the postexilic community as an authentic description from the beginning of Israel's history. By inference, the same would be assumed of the temple foretold by the prophet Ezekiel.

In line with redaction criticism, recent scholarship on Ezekiel 40–48 focuses on its editorial history as a sequence of multiple redactional layers beginning in the exilic or postexilic period and extending as late as the third century BC.[9] Of greater interest are studies suggesting that various specifics of temple area and architecture that occur only in Ezekiel are also found in the archaeology of the Persian-period Samaritan temple on Mount Gerizim, in Josephus's description of the second temple, in the area of the Herodian Temple Mount, and in the future temple envisioned in various writings of the Dead Sea Scrolls.[10] All

6. See a review of recent scholarship in Paul M. Joyce, "Temple and Worship in Ezekiel 40–48," in *Temple and Worship in Biblical Israel*, ed. John Day, Library of Hebrew Bible/Old Testament Studies 422 (London: T&T Clark, 2005), 145–63.

7. Daniel I. Block, *The Book of Ezekiel*, New International Commentary on the Old Testament (Grand Rapids: Eerdmans, 1998), 2:505–6.

8. Block (ibid., 498–500) follows Jon Levenson, *Theology of the Program of Restoration of Ezekiel 40–48*, Harvard Semitic Monographs 10 (Missoula, MT: Scholars Press, 1976).

9. Michael Konkel, *Architektonik des Heiligen: Studien zur zweiten Tempelvision Ezechiels (Ez 40–48)*, Bonner biblische Beiträge 129 (Berlin: Philo, 2001); idem, "Die zweite Tempelvision Ezechiels (Ez 40–48): Dimensionen eines Entwurfs," in *Gottesdienst und Gottesgarten: Zur Geschichte und Theologie des Jerusalemer Tempels*, ed. Othmar Keel and Erich Zenger, Quaestiones disputatae 191 (Freiburg: Herder, 2002), 154–78; Thilo Alexander Rudnig, *Heilig und Profan: Redaktionskritische Studien zu Ez 40–48*, Beihefte zur Zeitschrift für die alttestamentliche Wissenschaft 287 (Berlin: de Gruyter, 2000).

10. For the Dead Sea Scrolls, in addition to such similarities as are found in the *Temple Scroll*, see the comparison with *Songs of the Sabbath Sacrifice* in F. García Martínez, "L'interprétation de la Torah d'Ézéchiel dans les MSS. de Qumrân," *Revue de Qumran* 13 (1988): 527–48. For the other examples of the application of Ezek. 40–48 to existing temple areas and structures, see the summary of Michael Konkel, "Paradies mit strengen Regeln: Die Schlussvision des Ezechielbuches (Ez 40–48)," *Bibel und Kirche* 60 (2005): 167–72.

of this demonstrates that wherever it can be checked—among Samaritans and Second Temple mainstream Jews and in the separatist Jewish community of Qumran—the vision of Ezekiel was understood as intending a real, physical temple in the centuries after the prophet wrote.

Finally, I would turn to the overall structure of the book of Ezekiel and the context of the temple within that structure. One of the most dramatic pictures of the book is found in chapter 8. Here Ezekiel is taken in a vision from his home in the exiled land of Babylon to Jerusalem. There he sees the temple. As he visits room after room, he finds the worship of all sorts of spirits and deities other than Yahweh. This leads to the scene of marking those who grieve over these practices in chapter 9 and the departure of the presence and glory of God from the temple and Jerusalem in chapters 10 and 11. This description becomes the justification for God's allowing the Babylonians to destroy Jerusalem and the temple. It was not that God was not strong enough to protect his temple and defeat Jerusalem. God was gone because the sins of the people had so polluted the temple and the city that God's holy presence could no longer remain in them. The key point for us is that however the vision took place, there can be no doubt that it was intended to be interpreted at face value. Ezekiel wanted his readers to believe that he actually did see the temple in the last days of its existence. The worshiping of other deities and related practices really did take place in the temple precincts. There really was a presence of God that Ezekiel saw, and it really did depart from the temple. This was necessary to explain how God could allow the temple of Solomon to be destroyed, a historical fact concerning which all of Ezekiel's early readers were keenly aware. Although parts of this vision may be miraculous or even impossible to believe, it remains a fact that the intention was for Ezekiel's readers to believe that what he described actually took place.

When we then consider Ezekiel 40–48, especially the first part of this final section of the scroll, we find the vision of another temple. It, too, is in Jerusalem. As in the first scene that Ezekiel sees, here again he visits the many rooms of the temple precincts. In the new temple there is no worship of other deities. Instead it is prepared for the restored nation of Israel to worship in it. Here God returns to the temple (43:1–9). As in his departure, there is much emphasis in these chapters on the gates and thresholds. The picture, however, is a mirror image of chapters 8–11. In place of sin followed by divine departure and judgment, there is a pure and holy house followed by the return of God and blessing for the people. If the first vision was to be understood as realistic—and it has to have been so understood in order to justify God's role in the events of judgment that occurred in 587 and 586 BC—then the second vision at the end of the book should also be understood as realistic. Certainly this is how the readers and listeners of the prophet would have understood what was said. Given the traumatic events of that generation, the reality and promise of seemingly impossible miracles in the future temple and the surrounding land would not have been impossible to accept. To the contrary, the expectation would have been that this was exactly what was necessary. So dramatic and complete a defeat and destruction required a miraculous resurrection of the temple and its service.

In every manner in which it can be considered in its original context, then, this temple is described as realistic: (1) the ancient Near Eastern prophetic and temple description parallels; (2) the immediate context of the difference with, for example, chapter 37, where the "X is Y" formula indicates an allegory, whereas the other nearby chapters appear to describe expected events with named adversaries; (3) the role of the temple in the overall structure of the book; and (4) the conscious attempt to compare and parallel real and ideal temples in mainstream and sectarian Judaism and among the Samaritans, all during the Second Temple period.

If the restoration of the temple is to take place, how can this portrayal by the prophet Ezekiel function for the Christian in the light of New Testament texts? In particular, where does this temple fit into God's plan? It is clear that the pure and magnificent temple of Ezekiel was not fulfilled by the construction of the second temple, whether we consider the one constructed immediately after the return from the exile or the one that Herod the Great began building and that was destroyed by the Romans in 70 AD. Herod built a temple that could perhaps be compared to the one in Ezekiel in terms of its splendor but hardly in terms of its purity. This is true despite the intentional comparisons already made by Josephus and perhaps even by the architects of the sacred structure. Thus the Dead Sea Scroll community of Qumran created their own version of the future temple, supplementing the text of Ezekiel with their own *Temple Scroll*. In the New Testament, Jesus drove the money changers from the temple and condemned it as an impure house (John 2:16). Stephen and others looked to a God who would not live in a temple made by human hands (Acts 7:48–49). There has been no temple in Jerusalem since AD 70. Nor does the New Testament understand or expect a temple in the future new Jerusalem, where God and "the Lamb" are the temple (Rev. 21:22). If the words of the prophet are to be realistically fulfilled, as the early generations of readers of, and listeners to, the prophet certainly expected, then in its canonical context, it must take place sometime in the future but before the final appearance of the new heavens and the new earth. For various reasons, it seems best to describe the time of the restored temple as millennial or as the millennium. It will be an ideal time in which many of the prophecies that occur elsewhere in the Old Testament will find their fulfillment.

Now, this may raise many questions regarding Jesus and his own claims to be the temple (John 2:19–21) and the manner in which other New Testament writers emphasized the important role of the church as the new Israel (Rom. 9–11; Gal. 6:16). And indeed I cannot easily harmonize the two streams of teaching in the New Testament. But both are found already in the Old Testament. Thus Stephen quotes Isaiah 66:1 in his speech in Acts (7:49): "Heaven is my throne, and the earth is my footstool. Where is the house you will build for me? Where will my resting place be?" (7:49). The writer of Kings describes Solomon as declaring a similar sentiment at the dedication of the first temple: "But will God really dwell on earth? The heavens, even the highest heaven, cannot contain you. How much less this temple I have built!" (1 Kings 8:27). Yet as Ezekiel was aware, there was an understanding in which the glory of God did indeed inhabit the temple. These two aspects were present to the people of God in the Old Testament, and the writers of the New Testament did not deny them. If we cannot completely flatten out all the bumps in this picture, I will not worry. The future is a long time, and there is plenty of opportunity for God to demonstrate his presence in a purified and magnificent temple on this earth as well as in the expected glorious presence of the Father and the Son in the life of the world to come.

Concluding Reflections: Faith and Faithfulness

Were I to look at the Old Testament and hear it as the prophets and their first audiences seem to have understood it, I would be forced to conclude that many elements specific to the restoration of Israel are yet awaiting fulfillment. A future temple is just one of these. Nevertheless, it is not only the promise of future restoration that awaits the people of God, according to the Old Testament. There is also an expectation of judgment in this world and of suffering in that judgment. This principle is found already in the first books of the Bible. The Israelites experienced God's miraculous salvation and his judgment against the nation of Egypt and later other nations in Exodus and Numbers. But they experienced this only after enduring their own suffering in Egypt. Deuteronomy 4:30, mentioned earlier, and the following verse read, "When you are in distress and all these things have happened to you, then in later days you will return to the LORD your God and obey him. For the LORD your God is a merciful God; he will not abandon or destroy you or forget the covenant with your forefathers, which he confirmed to them by oath." God will allow his people to go through tribulation but will bring them through such suffering and employ it as a means to demonstrate his own faithfulness. If we do not expect our faith to be tested, we do not know the God of the Bible and we cannot testify to his faithfulness and holiness. Only through such experiences will God's people then find the millennial promises fulfilled just as they were made so long ago and just as the first generation who heard them looked forward to them.

3

Judaism and the World to Come

HÉLÈNE DALLAIRE

Introduction

The topic of this essay belongs to the larger field of Jewish eschatology, with its debates on messianism, Jewish apocalypticism, immortality, resurrection, divine retribution, the end of days, paradise, the netherworld, and other related subjects.[1] These topics overlap in great measure, and consequently, it is difficult to address one topic without referring to the others. But for the purpose of this

---

1. For further study on these topics, see Matthew Black, *The Scrolls and Christian Origins: Studies in the Jewish Background of the New Testament* (New York: Scribner, 1961; repr., Chico, CA: Scholars Press, 1983); Louis F. Hartman, "Eschatology," in *Encyclopaedia Judaica*, ed. Fred Skolnik and Michael Berenbaum, 2nd ed. (Detroit: Macmillan, 2007), 6:489–503; Rifat Sonsino and Daniel B. Syme, *What Happens after I Die? Jewish Views of Life after Death* (New York: UAHC Press, 1990); Jacob Neusner, *Rabbinic Judaism: The Theological System* (Leiden: Brill, 2002); E. Earle Ellis, *The Old Testament in Early Christianity* (Grand Rapids: Baker Academic, 1991); J. Julius Scott Jr., *Jewish Backgrounds of the New Testament* (Grand Rapids: Baker Academic, 1995); Emile Puech, "La croyance à la resurrection des justes dans un texte qumranien de sagesse: 4Q418 69 ii," in *Sefer Moshe: The Moshe Weinfeld Jubilee Volume*, ed. C. Cohen, A. Hurvitz, and S. M. Paul (Winona Lake, IN: Eisenbrauns, 2004), 427–44; L. H. Schiffman, *The Eschatological Community of the Dead Sea Scrolls* (Atlanta: Scholars Press, 1989); A. F. Segal, *Life after Death: A History of the Afterlife in Western Religion* (New York: Doubleday, 2004); F. Rosner, trans. and ed., *Moses Maimonides' Treatise on Resurrection* (New York: KTAV, 1982); J. D. Levenson, *Resurrection and the Restoration of Israel* (New Haven: Yale University Press, 2006); Bruce Chilton and Jacob Neusner, *Classical Christianity and Rabbinic Judaism: Com-*

essay, I will limit the discussion to the themes of millennialism, the afterlife, and resurrection in the Jewish literature of the biblical, intertestamental, and rabbinic periods.[2]

Before exploring the literature of the ancient Jewish sages, it is important to note that in modern Judaism, a millennial kingdom, the afterlife, and bodily resurrection are not the most central topics in a discussion about life and death. Modern Judaism is much more conscious of the here and now than it is of a world beyond this earthly realm. Consequently, as Simcha Raphael maintains,

> When asked "What do Jews believe about life after death?" individuals respond with a variety of answers that invariably demonstrate both confusion and a paucity of information available on the hereafter in Jewish tradition. "Jews believe in life after death, but there are no details to speak of" is a common answer. Or "Jews believe that the soul is eternal, and after death one lives on as a soul." Another recurring theme frequently expressed is "Jews believe that there is a resurrection of the dead that will take place after the Messiah comes."[3]

These ambiguous answers to the question "Does Judaism believe in an afterlife?" are not uncommon in this day and age. Modern Judaism is much more concerned with the fulfillment of *mitzvoth* (the commandments of Torah) and with *tikkun olam* (the mending of the world) than it is with life after death.

In a nursing course, Bio-Medical Ethics: The Jewish Approach, a lecturing rabbi was asked if Judaism believes in an afterlife. The rabbi promptly answered that "Judaism celebrates life and the living. It dwells on life here, rather than on the hereafter as other religious faiths do. Life is precious in the here and the now."[4]

In a 1991 interview by Israeli students, the prominent Orthodox Israeli scientist, philosopher, and historian Yeshayahu Leibowitz (1903–94) was asked

paring Theologies (Grand Rapids: Baker Academic, 2004); S. P. Raphael, *Jewish Views of the Afterlife* (Northvale, NJ: Jason Aronson, 1994); E. P. Sanders, *Paul and Palestinian Judaism: A Comparison of Patterns of Religion* (London: SCM, 1977); H. Küng, *Judaism: Between Yesterday and Tomorrow* (New York: Continuum, 2002); A. Levine, *The Misunderstood Jew* (San Francisco: HarperSanFrancisco, 2006); S. J. D. Cohen, *From the Maccabees to the Mishnah* (Louisville: Westminster John Knox, 2006); L. R. Helyer, *Exploring Jewish Literature of the Second Temple Period: A Guide for New Testament Students* (Downers Grove, IL: InterVarsity, 2002).

2. By "rabbinic period" I mean the period of the Tannaim (Jewish scholars of the Mishnah during the first two centuries CE) and the Amoraim (Jewish scholars of the Gemara and Talmud during the third to fifth centuries CE).

3. Raphael, *Jewish Views of the Afterlife*, 12.

4. Jean Herschaft, "Patient Should Not Be Told of Terminal Illness: Rabbi," *Jewish Post and Opinion*, March 13, 1981, 12.

about his personal view about an afterlife and about Judaism's attitude toward death. Leibowitz answered,

> Death has no significance . . . only life matters. . . . *In the entire Torah* there is not the slightest suggestion that anything happens after death. All the ideas and theories articulated on the subject of a world to come and the resurrection of the dead have no relationship to religious faith. It is sheer folklore. After you die, you simply do not exist.[5]

Although the rabbi and the scientist expressed a common modern Jewish worldview on the subject of life after death, one cannot deny that Judaism has a long and extensive tradition on the topic, a theme that is addressed in the Hebrew Bible, the Apocrypha, the Pseudepigrapha, the Dead Sea Scrolls, the Mishnah, the Talmud, rabbinic and medieval midrashim, medieval Jewish literature, the Kabbalah, and other Jewish texts.

Judaism and the Messianic Age

On many fronts, Judaism and Christianity find common ground in their discussion on issues related to the last days. Both communities speak of hardships and tribulation, of a messianic age, of a judgment day, of resurrection of the dead, and of a world beyond this earthly realm. Although long-standing debates continue in Christianity and in Judaism regarding the accurate interpretation of each of these themes, the Christian versions of events are fewer than those found in Jewish literature, especially on the topic of a messianic age.

The notion that the Messiah will rule and reign on earth for a specific amount of time went through major developments in the Jewish literature of the intertestamental and rabbinic periods. One of the important developments related to our study is reflected in the rabbis' opinions on the amount of time allotted for the messianic age.

Jewish literature confirms the enduring belief that a day will come when Israel will experience redemption from sin and deliverance from oppression during a messianic age, followed by a resurrection of the dead, a day of final judgment, and life in the world to come. According to some Jewish authors, during the messianic age, everyone will worship one God and will live in a perfect, harmonious, and peaceful society. According to others, the era between this worldly existence and eternal bliss for the righteous in the world to come

5. Yeshayahu Leibowitz, interview by Israeli students, *Sof Shavua*, weekend supplement of *Maariv*, February 8, 1991.

will find the earth desolate with God highly exalted over his creation. Both of these views, along with numerous others, appear in rabbinic literature. The proponents of the various interpretations defend their positions with texts from the Hebrew Scriptures, as will be shown below.

Jewish literature does not address in such unequivocal terms the Christian debate over premillennialism, postmillennialism, and amillennialism. The thousand-year reign of Christian millennialism appears in a variety of formats in Judaism. The time frames attributed to the messianic age vary greatly, from forty to seven thousand years, depending on the authors' interpretations of canonical and noncanonical texts.

For example, in *Sanhedrin* 97a, a tractate of the Babylonian Talmud, Rabbi Kattina speaks of a *thousand-year* period in which God alone will be exalted while the earth will lie desolate.[6] This interpretation, based on Isaiah 2:11[7] and Psalm 90:4,[8] promotes the notion that each day of creation represents a thousand years and that the last days, the Sabbath (the messianic age), will extend over an equivalent period of one thousand years. According to this view, the existence of humanity before the messianic age lasts six thousand years, which means the beginning of a one-thousand-year messianic reign would be virtually upon us. Included in the same talmudic text is the conflicting opinion of Rabbi Abaye, who, on the basis of Hosea 6:2,[9] advocates a *two-thousand-year* messianic period followed by a resurrection of the dead and an existence in the world to come.

Sanhedrin 99a provides a variety of additional rabbinic propositions. First, Rabbi Hillel denies the possibility of a future messianic age. To the question "When will the Messiah come?" he answers, "There shall be no Messiah for Israel, because they have already enjoyed him in the days of Hezekiah." This position echoes in part the Christian amillennial view of the last days, a position that advocates that the church is currently living in the millennial age and will continue to do so until the final (second) return of Christ and the final day of judgment.[10]

---

6. "R. Kattina said: Six thousand years shall the world exist, and one [thousand, the seventh], it shall be desolate, as it is written, And the Lord alone shall be exalted in that day." See also *1 Enoch* 33.1–2 and Ps. 90:4.

7. "The eyes of the arrogant man will be humbled and the pride of men brought low; the LORD alone will be exalted in that day."

8. "For a thousand years in your sight are like a day that has just gone by, or like a watch in the night."

9. "After two days he will revive us; on the third day he will restore us, that we may live in his presence."

10. Amillennialism is also called present or realized millennialism by Reformed theologians.

Sanhedrin 99a presents additional rabbinic positions. In the same text, rabbis offer the following alternative scenarios:

- Rabbi Eliezer advocates for a *forty-year* messianic age (based on Ps. 95:10).[11]
- Rabbi Eleazar ben Azariah proposes a period of *seventy years* (based on Isa. 23:15).[12]
- Rabbi Dosa suggests a *four-hundred-year* messianic age (based on Gen. 15:13).[13]
- An unnamed rabbi, intimating that the number of years of the messianic kingdom will reflect the number of days in the calendar year, advocates for a period of *three hundred and sixty-five years* (based on Isa. 63:4).[14]
- Abimi the son of Rabbi Abbahu declares that Israel's Messiah will reign for a period of *seven thousand years* (based on Isa. 62:5).[15]
- Rabbi Judah said in Samuel's name that the messianic age would endure the length of time *between creation and his day* (based on Deut. 11:21).[16]
- Rabbi Nahman ben Isaac adjusted Rabbi Judah's view slightly by asserting that the messianic age would extend *from Noah's day until his day* (based on Isa. 54:9).[17]

Additional early Jewish views include that of *4 Ezra* (end of first century CE), where the author describes a messianic kingdom of peace that will last *four hundred years*.[18] According to the text, this extended period of peace will be followed by seven days of silence after which a resurrection of the dead will occur, followed by a day of reckoning known as "the final judgment." Those

11. "For forty years I was angry with that generation; I said, 'They are a people whose hearts go astray, and they have not known my ways.'"

12. "At that time Tyre will be forgotten for seventy years, the span of a king's life. But at the end of these seventy years, it will happen to Tyre as in the song of the prostitute."

13. "Then the LORD said to him, 'Know for certain that your descendants will be strangers in a country not their own, and they will be enslaved and mistreated four hundred years.'"

14. "For the day of vengeance was in my heart, and the year of my redemption has come."

15. "As a young man marries a maiden, so will your sons marry you; as a bridegroom rejoices over his bride, so will your God rejoice over you."

16. "So that your days and the days of your children may be many in the land that the LORD swore to give your forefathers, as many as the days that the heavens are above the earth."

17. "To me this is like the days of Noah, when I swore that the waters of Noah would never again cover the earth. So now I have sworn not to be angry with you, never to rebuke you again."

18. *4 Ezra* 7.26–31.

who are considered righteous will begin a life of eternal bliss in the world to come, whereas the unrighteous will be condemned to eternal damnation.[19]

Although Jewish interpretations on the length of days for the messianic kingdom differ extensively, the literature presents a scenario where the hardships and tribulations of earthly life immediately precede the messianic age. Unlike the pretribulational Christian belief that the faithful will be taken from the earth for a period of time before the thousand-year reign of Christ, Judaism presents life in this earthly realm, with its troubles and sorrows, and the messianic age as two consecutive events, without a time gap between them. Consequently, most Jewish interpretations related to the messianic age present a view that parallels more closely that of the Christian posttribulational premillennial view than any of the other Christian views mentioned in this essay.

Old Testament Evidence of an Afterlife and a Resurrection of the Dead

The primary message of the Old Testament—the Hebrew Bible—is not intended to inform the reader on issues related to life after death for the Israelites. On the contrary, it is meant to elaborate on issues of life *before* death, especially for a community of people that is engaged in a covenant relationship with the living God. For this reason, in the Old Testament, emphasis is placed on the behavior of individuals and communities toward their spiritual, moral, and legal responsibilities as covenant people.

When studying the Old Testament, one must remember that its literature spans more than a thousand years, thus revealing traditions that evolved, developed, and mutated over time. It is therefore not surprising that concepts presented from a certain perspective in preexilic Old Testament literature underwent some level of transformation over the centuries and resulted in a redefined or altered picture in postexilic literature. This type of transformation is evident in the theme of life after death.

In some Old Testament books, the concept of an explicit afterlife is absent, and its possibility is considered remote at best, whereas in other books there seems to be evidence of a world beyond this one, a world where communication occurs between its inhabitants, where individuals hold to their earthly identities, and where justice has been rendered for righteous and unrighteous behavior.

In early Old Testament literature—that is, the preexilic texts—information regarding the concept of life after death is sparse. The main emphasis is

---

19. See also *2 Baruch (Syriac Apocalypse)* 29; *1 Enoch* 51; *Testament of Judah* 24–25.

placed on the historical origin of the Jewish people and on its covenantal relationship with the God of Abraham, Isaac, and Jacob, focusing first and foremost on this relationship's legal and moral stipulations for the here and now. Consequently, issues of life after death are almost completely ignored in the Pentateuch and are scantily intimated in historical books. The concept of man having a soul—a *nefesh*—that would leave the body at the moment of death and go to a netherworld developed in greater detail in biblical literature several centuries later.

Afterlife in the Pentateuch

As already stated, the theme of afterlife is barely present in the Pentateuch, and there is very little evidence for it except in a few passages that seem to indicate the presence of another realm. One of the few pentateuchal accounts to provide a glimpse into the existence of a world beyond this one appears in Genesis 5:23–24, where Enoch, after living on earth 365 years, is taken by God to another realm. This event is included in the genealogy of Adam, where each family member is said to "have died"[20] except for Enoch, who was taken by God himself from one location to another without experiencing physical death.[21] Although the passage presents Enoch's transition in a positive light, his ultimate fate remains a mystery.[22] Common Jewish and Christian interpretations of the account imply that Enoch went directly to heaven in bodily form, as did Elijah in 2 Kings 2. Enoch, to whom many apocryphal writings have been attributed, eventually becomes a very important figure in Jewish literature for the development of the apocalyptic tradition of the Second Temple period.[23]

A second pentateuchal account that reveals a location where the dead enjoy a postmortem existence is found in the Joseph narrative. In Genesis 37, Jacob, who is experiencing profound sorrow after the loss of his son Joseph, refuses to be comforted by his family and expresses the wish to die and join him in Sheol.[24] In Genesis 42, threatened by the loss of a second son—this time Benjamin, his youngest—Jacob expresses once again the possibility of finding himself in Sheol should any harm happen to Benjamin during his trip to

---

20. וַיָּמֹת—Gen. 5:5, 8, 11, 14, 17, 20, 27, 31.

21. כִּי־לָקַח אֹתוֹ אֱלֹהִים—Gen. 5:24.

22. Heb. 11:5 provides additional information intimating that Enoch was taken away because he had received favor from God for his faith and his faithfulness to God: "By faith Enoch was taken from this life, so that he did not experience death; he could not be found, because God had taken him away. For before he was taken, he was commended as one who pleased God."

23. See *1 Enoch* and the *Messianic Apocalypse* (4 QMessAp).

24. וַיֹּאמֶר כִּי־אֵרֵד אֶל־בְּנִי אָבֵל שְׁאֹלָה—Gen. 37:35.

Egypt.[25] Although Jacob refers to Sheol as a holding place for the dead, he does not provide a description of the locale, nor does he identify its inhabitants or speak of their activities.[26]

In the patriarchal narratives, the text does not associate Sheol with divine retribution. It simply identifies the site as a place where the dead relocate after their departure from this earthly realm. Only after the Israelites settled in the land of Canaan did Yahwistic monotheism take root in their religious tradition and the place of the dead become a place of divine retribution for the unrighteous. Until then little was known about the physical description of Sheol, and few were the details regarding its goings-on. It is only in the literature of later centuries that we are presented with the notion of an existence in the presence of God for the righteous and a tormented postmortem existence for the unrighteous in Sheol.

Afterlife in Wisdom Literature

Unlike the literature of the Pentateuch with its emphasis on the early history of the Israelite community, Wisdom literature addresses the purposes and conditions of human existence through proverbs, poems, riddles, love stories, and other such literary devices. Two major works of Wisdom literature are Job and Ecclesiastes, whose fatalistic tone and cynicism emphasize the futility of earthly existence and provide very little hope for any form of life after death.

Job's direct approach and honest opinion toward the human condition can be summarized in these words: the righteous suffer while the wicked prosper. From his state of grief and suffering, Job addresses matters of life and death and makes a fascinating comparison between the futility of the human experience, in which humans are denied the prospect of an afterlife, and hope for the rest of creation:

> At least there is hope for a tree: If it is cut down, it will sprout again, and its new shoots will not fail. Its roots may grow old in the ground and its stump die in the soil, yet at the scent of water it will bud and put forth shoots like a plant. But man dies and is laid low; he breathes his last and is no more. As water disappears from the sea or a riverbed becomes parched and dry, so man lies down and does not rise; till the heavens are no more, men will not awake or be roused from their sleep. (Job 14:7–12)

25. וְהוֹרַדְתֶּם אֶת־שֵׂיבָתִי בְּיָגוֹן שְׁאוֹלָה—Gen. 42:38.

26. In early biblical literature, Sheol or the grave is addressed in generic terms as a place where young and old, rich and poor, king and commoner, and master and slave abide after physical death. This abode makes neither social nor moral distinctions. See David S. Russell, *The Method and Message of Jewish Apocalyptic* (Philadelphia: Westminster, 1964), 355.

This passage not only presents Job's denial of any human existence after death; it also denies the possibility of a future resurrection. But as Walter Kaiser points out, Job's pessimistic outlook on life, as expressed in verse 7, is quickly revisited a few verses later in verse 14 with hints of hope that he will live again.[27]

Although seemingly convinced of his belief in total annihilation, as expressed during his interaction with his friends, Job reconsiders his position on life and death, and after emptying himself of his despair and anguish, he comes to the realization that his personal Redeemer will one day welcome him into his presence. Thus far God had been his adversary, one who had caused him deep sorrow, but finally Job expresses with deep conviction his belief in a future encounter with the living God. From despair to triumph and from darkness to radiance, Job's assessment of human existence has been completely transformed.

> I know that my Redeemer lives, and that in the end he will stand upon the earth. And after my skin has been destroyed, yet in my flesh I will see God; I myself will see him with my own eyes—I, and not another. How my heart yearns within me![28]

Ecclesiastes (or Qoheleth), whose notion of pleasure reflects a dark shadow at best, paints a grim picture of the ultimate fate of wretched humanity. In the teacher's view, humans should expect no more than animals and should anticipate the same reward—that is, nothing.

> Man's fate is like that of the animals; the same fate awaits them both: As one dies, so dies the other. All have the same breath; man has no advantage over

---

27. W. Kaiser (*Toward an Old Testament Theology* [Grand Rapids: Zondervan, 1978], 181) points out that few scholars link verses 7 and 14, although a close reading of the Hebrew text reveals that the verb used for the resprouting of the tree (v. 7—יַחֲלִיף) appears a second time in the resprouting of Job (v. 14—חֲלִיפָתִי).

28. Job 19:25–27. Throughout his speeches, Job declares what he firmly believes about God's doings in his life (יָדַעְתִּי—9:28; 10:13; 30:23; 42:2). In great measure, Job portrays God as an enemy whose judgment is harsh and who will eventually usher him into death (30:23). In 19:25–27 Job's despair seems to have lifted as he expresses hope that a *go'el* (traditionally translated "redeemer") will intervene on his behalf and rescue him from inevitable destruction. Scholars have long debated the identity of the *go'el* and have proposed a number of options. Some identify the *go'el* as the "witness" or "advocate" mentioned in 16:18–21; others propose that Job's cry before God is personified as his personal advocate; a common interpretation identifies the *go'el* with God, since God is mentioned elsewhere in Scripture as the *go'el* of the afflicted (e.g., Ps. 78:35; Isa. 49:7, 26); others have linked the *go'el* with a kinsman redeemer, as depicted in the book of Ruth; and yet others identify the *go'el* with an unnamed heavenly being who would play a mediating role before God on Job's behalf. For a full discussion of these views, see David J. A. Clines, *Job 1–20* (Dallas: Word, 1989), 457–66.

the animal. Everything is meaningless. All go to the same place; all come from dust, and to dust all return. Who knows if the spirit of man rises upward and if the spirit of the animal goes down into the earth? So I saw that there is nothing better for a man than to enjoy his work, because that is his lot. For who can bring him to see what will happen after him? (Eccles. 3:19–22)

The Hebrew sage further adds,

This is the evil in everything that happens under the sun: the same destiny overtakes all. The hearts of men, moreover, are full of evil and there is madness in their hearts while they live, and afterward they join the dead. Anyone who is among the living has hope—even a live dog is better off than a dead lion! For the living know that they will die, but the dead know nothing; they have no further reward, and even the memory of them is forgotten. Their love, their hate and their jealousy have long since vanished; never again will they have a part in anything that happens under the sun. Go, eat your food with gladness, and drink your wine with a joyful heart, for it is now that God favors what you do. Always be clothed in white, and always anoint your head with oil. Enjoy life with your wife, whom you love, all the days of this meaningless life that God has given you under the sun—all your meaningless days. For this is your lot in life and in your toilsome labor under the sun. Whatever your hand finds to do, do it with all your might, for in the grave, where you are going, there is neither working nor planning nor knowledge nor wisdom. (Eccles. 9:3–10)[29]

In contrast to the despondent message of Ecclesiastes, the book of Psalms frequently refers to the realities of afterlife in vivid terms and describes Sheol as an undesired and dreadful place reserved for the unrighteous and sinners. Since Psalms is a composite work that represents a broad range of perspectives, the depiction of Sheol is varied and flexible. In some cases, Psalms portrays Sheol as a place where individuals who are experiencing extreme distress in this life are trapped before being rescued by God and set on a hopeful and brighter path. The hyperbolic and evocative language used by these psalmists refers to existential realities lived in the here and now. In other words, Sheol is depicted as a dark and profound state that invades human lives in the form of misery, unhappiness, depression, disease, or often imminent danger.[30] For these psalmists, Sheol is experienced here on earth rather than in the *au-delà*.

29. Michael Eaton (*Ecclesiastes: An Introduction and Commentary*, Tyndale Old Testament Commentaries [Downers Grove, IL: InterVarsity, 1983], 126) points out that concealed within the pessimistic tone of these two passages is a glimpse of hope that the spirit of man may one day live again (3:21). Faint as this hope may be, its mention contributes to mitigation of the gloomy final destiny pronounced by the teacher.
    30. Ps. 18:4–7; 49:14–15; 86:13; 116:3–4.

In other passages, it is the dead who experience Sheol. Its inhabitants are doomed to its confines with no hope of ever returning to the realm of the living. In such cases, references to Sheol are made by a third party, one who is desperately attempting to avoid going down into it and is still able to call on God for deliverance.[31]

Afterlife in the Historical Books

It is mainly during times of oppression and persecution that a discussion on life after death flourishes in Jewish literature. During the Old Testament period, the Israelites were confronted by prophets for their grave transgressions against the Mosaic covenant and for their syncretistic practices. As a result of their refusal to repent and turn from their heinous crimes, God raised up foreign nations who oppressed, threatened, invaded, and conquered the territory the Israelites were given centuries earlier. Such oppression and persecution provided opportunities for prophets to address issues of divine retribution, eschatology, the afterlife, and messianism.

The historical books provide a limited number of details that intimate a possibility of life after death where humans continue their existence in a world beyond this earthly realm. One such account is found in 1 Samuel 28, where King Saul seeks to communicate with the prophet Samuel through the intervention of the witch of Endor, an event that contributes to his eventual downfall. Centuries before Saul's reign, Moses had firmly instructed the Israelites to place their trust in the Lord and to seek his will through divinely appointed leaders—judges and prophets. Strictly forbidden by the Torah was necromancy—communication with the spirits of the dead.[32] Such a practice was performed by pagan priests of the ancient Near East and was associated with idolatry and paganism. The Israelites were therefore forbidden to adopt such a practice in their belief system and religious customs.

Saul was undoubtedly aware of this fact, since, at the beginning of 1 Samuel 28, he expels the mediums and magicians from the land. Nevertheless, when faced with the possibility of losing the battle to the Philistines and after receiving no specific guidance from God through prayer, Saul surrenders to fear and seeks to communicate with the deceased prophet through forbidden means—via a necromancer. Through this event, Saul reveals his belief in a postmortem realm where the dead preserved their identity and where they made themselves available to communicate with the living.

31. Ps. 6:3–10; 9:17–18; 31:16–19; 88:2–18.
32. Deut. 18:9–14.

Although the biblical text does not reveal a detailed picture of the location inhabited by the dead, the information provided in Scripture indicates that both adults and children enjoy a postmortem existence. The story of David and Bathsheba is well known with its fascinating details of deception, manipulation, sexual sin, and murder. Bathsheba's pregnancy by King David leads to a series of unfortunate events that result in the death of Uriah—a husband and faithful military man—and in the death of a child. After Bathsheba gives birth to David's son, the prophet Nathan confronts the king with his evil deed, and shortly thereafter the child born to Bathsheba becomes sick and dies. David's response to this tragic event is both unexpected and revealing. After receiving the sad news, David spruces himself up and wines and dines, baffling with this strange behavior all who are in his household. David's response to his servants' inquiry into his strange reaction reveals his belief in a postmortem existence for the child who has just left him.

> His servants asked him, "Why are you acting this way? While the child was alive, you fasted and wept, but now that the child is dead, you get up and eat!" He answered, "While the child was still alive, I fasted and wept. I thought, 'Who knows? The LORD may be gracious to me and let the child live.' But now that he is dead, why should I fast? Can I bring him back again? I will go to him, but he will not return to me." (2 Sam. 12:21–23)

Through his answer, David reveals two important beliefs: he expresses with confidence, first, that one day he will join his son in a realm beyond this one and, second, that once humans have left this world, they do not return to this earthly realm.

A third significant event in the historical books occurs in 2 Kings 2, where Elijah experiences a dramatic transfer from earth to heaven, an event that resembles Enoch's sudden departure from the earth. After completing his earthly assignment, Elijah is swept up into heaven in a whirlwind.

> When they had crossed, Elijah said to Elisha, "Tell me, what can I do for you before I am taken from you?" "Let me inherit a double portion of your spirit," Elisha replied. "You have asked a difficult thing," Elijah said, "yet if you see me when I am taken from you, it will be yours—otherwise not." As they were walking along and talking together, suddenly a chariot of fire and horses of fire appeared and separated the two of them, and Elijah went up to heaven in a whirlwind. Elisha saw this and cried out, "My father! My father! The chariots and horsemen of Israel!" And Elisha saw him no more. (2 Kings 2:9–12)

Before his departure, Elijah expressed a strong awareness of his upcoming transition to another realm. The event is quite dramatic and vivid as the text describes Elijah being taken into heaven in a whirlwind by a chariot and horses of fire. Again, as in the Enoch account in the book of Genesis, the text withholds any significant information related to Elijah's destination, his whereabouts, and his activities after leaving the earth. The biblical text makes it clear that Elijah does not die. He is lifted from the earth to join the heavenly hosts.[33]

The fact that Elijah departed this earth without experiencing physical death allows for his possible return to earth in "that great and dreadful day of the LORD," as declared by the prophet Malachi (Mal. 4:5). Even until this day, in the modern Jewish Passover seder, a door is left open in anticipation of the return of Elijah as the forerunner of the Messiah. The presence of Elijah is also acknowledged in a circumcision service by the presence of an ornate chair where the child is placed before the act of circumcision is performed. In some traditions, "the chair is left in position for three days, not, as said by some, to give Elijah, the wanderer, time for rest, but because the first three days after circumcision are a period of danger for the child."[34] These customs reveal an active belief that Elijah is still alive and will one day return to fulfill his divine purpose on earth.

Afterlife in the Prophets

Over several centuries, the prophets announced impending judgment on the Israelites for their defiance of the Mosaic covenant and for their participation in forbidden syncretistic practices. To everyone's surprise, divine retribution came through foreign-enemy nations, orchestrated by God, in fulfillment of the curse promised to the Israelites in the Mosaic covenant. As a consequence of disobedience to divine instruction, the Assyrians invaded Canaan and conquered a substantial portion of the territory allotted to the tribes of Israel. Over a century later, the Babylonians, who succeeded the Assyrians as the new rulers of the Fertile Crescent, conquered the remainder of the territory given to the Israelites centuries earlier and destroyed Jerusalem and its temple.

These centuries of hardships, persecution, suffering, and cruelty inflicted by the oppressing nations led to a rise in concerns regarding life after death, and consequently, additional details depicting Sheol and its activities begin

33. וַיַּעַל אֵלִיָּהוּ בַּסְעָרָה הַשָּׁמָיִם—2 Kings 2:11.

34. *Jewish Encyclopedia*, s.v. "Elijah's Chair," www.jewishencyclopedia.com/view.jsp?artid=247&letter=E (accessed February 7, 2007).

to appear in prophetic literature. From this point on, God is depicted as one who has control over the activities of Sheol and also as one who has the power to condemn individuals to its torments and redeem souls from its grasp.[35] During this period, the postmortem world evolves into a place of chastisement and punishment for those who transgress the covenant and reject God's statutes.

The prophet Isaiah provides details of the underworld and describes Sheol as a dreary and gloomy place replete with clouded activity. According to the prophet, Sheol hungers for newcomers, and the dead who enter are greeted by those who have preceded them:

> The grave below is all astir to meet you at your coming; it rouses the spirits of the departed to greet you—all those who were leaders in the world; it makes them rise from their thrones—all those who were kings over the nations. They will all respond, they will say to you, "You also have become weak, as we are; you have become like us." All your pomp has been brought down to the grave, along with the noise of your harps; maggots are spread out beneath you and worms cover you. (Isa. 14:9–11)

In addition to his description of the underworld, Isaiah provides a glimpse into the possibility that one day the dead will rise and that, at God's appointed time, the departed will experience a bodily resurrection:

> But your dead will live; their bodies will rise. You who dwell in the dust, wake up and shout for joy. Your dew is like the dew of the morning; the earth will give birth to her dead. Go, my people, enter your rooms and shut the doors behind you; hide yourselves for a little while until his wrath has passed by. See, the LORD is coming out of his dwelling to punish the people of the earth for their sins. The earth will disclose the blood shed upon her; she will conceal her slain no longer. (Isa. 26:19–21)

Isaiah adds that after the resurrection of God's people, the nation would enjoy a period of political peace and stability under a messianic ruler of the line of David, when

> the cow will feed with the bear, their young will lie down together, and the lion will eat straw like the ox. The infant will play near the hole of the cobra, and the young child put his hand into the viper's nest. They will neither harm nor destroy [each other] on all my holy mountain, for the earth will be full of the knowledge of the LORD as the waters cover the sea. (Isa. 11:7–9)

35. Ps. 49:15; 116:3–8.

Hosea, an eighth-century prophet, informs his readers that a bodily resurrection awaits the departed. He declares that the grave is vulnerable before the redeeming power of God: "I will ransom them from the power of the grave; I will redeem them from death. Where, O death, are your plagues? Where, O grave, is your destruction?" (Hos. 13:14).

Until the sixth century BCE, divine judgment and retribution were connected to nationalism and to the behavior of the community as a whole. The Israelites were promised collective rewards for adhering to the law and collective punishments for breaking the covenant. Deuteronomistic historians focused on the doctrine of corporate responsibility until the prophets Jeremiah and Ezekiel introduced a new concept, that of individual responsibility for sin, a notion heretofore quite unfamiliar to the Israelites. The idea of divine retribution for individual sins introduced a significant shift in the Israelites' understanding of rewards and punishment and formed a basis for further discourse on the topic of life after death for individual Israelites.

Until this time, the Torah held the community responsible for the sins of its forefathers up to the fourth generation (Exod. 20:5; Deut. 5:9). The concept of individual responsibility for sin was still barely acknowledged. The proclamations of Jeremiah and Ezekiel not only placed the responsibility of behavior on each individual but also challenged and even contradicted the dictates of Torah. Jeremiah declares, "In those days people will no longer say, 'The fathers have eaten sour grapes, and the children's teeth are set on edge.' Instead, everyone will die for his own sin; whoever eats sour grapes—his own teeth will be set on edge" (Jer. 31:29–30). Likewise Ezekiel declares,

> What do you people mean by quoting this proverb about the land of Israel: "The fathers eat sour grapes, and the children's teeth are set on edge"? As surely as I live, declares the Sovereign LORD, you will no longer quote this proverb in Israel. For every living soul belongs to me, the father as well as the son—both alike belong to me. The soul who sins is the one who will die. . . . If a righteous man turns from his righteousness and commits sin, he will die for it; because of the sin he has committed he will die. But if a wicked man turns away from the wickedness he has committed and does what is just and right, he will save his life. Because he considers all the offenses he has committed and turns away from them, he will surely live; he will not die. (Ezek. 18:2–4, 26–28)

The Lord explains:

> Therefore, O house of Israel, I will judge you, each one according to his ways, declares the Sovereign LORD. Repent! Turn away from all your offenses; then sin will not be your downfall. Rid yourselves of all the offenses you have committed,

and get a new heart and a new spirit. Why will you die, O house of Israel? For I take no pleasure in the death of anyone, declares the Sovereign LORD. Repent and live! (Ezek. 18:30–32)

After the announcement of this new system of accountability, discussions on judgment, rewards, punishment, the afterlife, and personal resurrection begin to take a new shape in Jewish literature. For example, in the book of Daniel, literature written during the flourishing of noncanonical apocalyptic Jewish literature, the prophet alludes to an individual resurrection of the righteous to eternal life and a resurrection of the wicked to everlasting shame, a topic barely addressed in earlier Jewish texts:

At that time Michael, the great prince who protects your people, will arise. There will be a time of distress such as has not happened from the beginning of nations until then. But at that time your people—everyone whose name is found written in the book—will be delivered. Multitudes who sleep in the dust of the earth will awake: some to everlasting life, others to shame and everlasting contempt. (Dan. 12:1–2)

According to Daniel's writings, after a temporary existence in Sheol, some of the righteous will rise to enjoy life in the messianic kingdom until God's final judgment comes at the end of days. In addition, multitudes will also awake to experience life in a state of everlasting condemnation. According to Daniel, at the end of times, rewards and punishments will be dispensed to each individual based on merit, a concept not previously developed in Jewish literature: "As for you, go your way till the end. You will rest, and then at the end of the days. you will rise to receive your allotted inheritance" (Dan. 12:13).

Afterlife in Intertestamental Literature

During the intertestamental and early rabbinic periods, writers from various Jewish sects composed many texts of an apocalyptic nature that were not incorporated into the official Jewish and Protestant canons. These apocryphal and pseudepigraphic documents were written, for the most part, between 200 BCE and 200 CE. During this politically turbulent period in Palestine, the notion of divine retribution, the concept of an afterlife, and bodily resurrection for Jews increased in complexity.

During the intertestamental period, Jews suffered heavy persecution at the hands of Greek and Roman rulers. As mentioned above, it was during such times of heavy persecution that the Jewish community engaged in discussion on issues of life after death. Such challenging times were eventually described

in the literature as the "birth pangs of the Messiah" or the "Messianic tra-
vail" and prompted the rabbis to ask and answer the question "What must a
man do to be spared the pangs of the Messiah [חבלי המשיח]?" (*Soṭah* 49b,
Sanhedrin 98a, *Šabbat* 118a).[36]

In the second century BCE, under Antiochus IV (Antiochus Epiphanes),
Jews were forbidden to observe Torah and to practice their religious traditions. Whoever was found disobeying the ruler's orders was punished severely
or condemned to death. Women who had their sons circumcised were killed
along with them; religious Jews "were forced to eat pork, which, of course, was
forbidden by the law (cf. Lev. 11:7; Deut. 14:8). In Jerusalem itself the temple
was transformed into a pagan cult center with the altar now dedicated to Zeus.
On the fifteenth of Chislev (December) 167 BC, a pig was offered up on the
great altar in front of the Jerusalem temple."[37] This major event provoked the
Maccabean revolt, which resulted in the Jewish community entering Jerusalem
triumphant over the Seleucids, cleansing the temple that had been desecrated
by Antiochus IV, and reestablishing the sacrificial system at the temple.

Second Maccabees reveals important information regarding a belief in divine
rewards for those who were martyred for the faith and a belief in resurrection
at the end of times. Second Maccabees 7 describes horrifying events in which
Antiochus Epiphanes and his officers attempted to force every member of a
Jewish family to deny their faith, to break the law of their ancestors, and to
worship foreign gods. Whoever was found refusing was tortured with whips,
was scourged, had his tongue and limbs cut out, was scalped, and was fried
alive in a pan. One by one, the family members suffered the same cruel torture
and died standing strong in their faith. Their last words to the king reveal their
hope of divine justice and eventual bodily resurrection:

> With his last breath he [one of the sons] exclaimed, "Cruel brute, you may
> discharge us from this present life, but the King of the world will raise us up,
> since we die for his laws, to live again for ever." After him, they tortured the
> third, who on being asked for his tongue promptly thrust it out and boldly held
> out his hands, courageously saying, "Heaven gave me these limbs; for the sake
> of his laws I have no concern for them; from him I hope to receive them again."
> The king and his attendants were astounded at the young man's courage and
> his utter indifference to suffering. When this one was dead they subjected the
> fourth to the same torments and tortures. When he neared his end he cried,

36. J. Klausner, *The Messianic Idea in Israel: From Its Beginning to the Completion of the
Mishnah* (London: Allen & Unwin, 1956), 440–50.

37. Helyer, *Exploring Jewish Literature*, 116. This outrageous act is mentioned in 1 Macc.
1:54–55.

"Ours is the better choice, to meet death at men's hands, yet relying on God's promise that we shall be raised up by him; whereas for you there can be no resurrection to new life." . . .

But the mother was especially admirable and worthy of honorable remembrance, for she watched the death of seven sons in the course of a single day, and bravely endured it because of her hopes in the Lord. Indeed she encouraged each of them in their ancestral tongue; filled with noble conviction, she reinforced her womanly argument with manly courage, saying to them, "I do not know how you appeared in my womb; it was not I who endowed you with breath and life, I had not the shaping of your every part. And hence, the Creator of the world, who made everyone and ordained the origin of all things, will in his mercy give you back breath and life, since for the sake of his laws you have no concern for yourselves." (2 Macc. 7:9–14, 20–23 NJB)

It was during such turbulent periods that the concept of heaven and hell developed to a high degree of complexity in Jewish literature. Texts about heaven include new and detailed information on topics such as heaven's entrance gates, heaven's dimensions, the journey one follows to reach the throne of God, the presence of angelic bodies, ascension to heaven's location, the presence of houses and palaces, a law court with God as the ultimate judge, passwords to progress from one level of heaven to another, observance of the Sabbath in heaven, and an academy where Torah is studied. A parallel development of the concept of hell likewise takes place during this period, with details on its intermediate purgatorial function for a sinner who will ascend to heaven after atonement (contrasted to the righteous, who go directly to heaven, and the wicked, who are condemned to hell forever), its temperature extremes from burning hot to icy cold, and its gruesome depiction as a fiery pit where the bodies of the wicked burn eternally, rotting away with maggots and worms.[38]

The concept of Sheol went through various transformations in the Jewish literature of this period. Some authors describe it as a place where the dead go immediately after death; others reserve it as a place where the dead go after a bodily resurrection. Apocryphal and pseudepigraphic literature increasingly uses the term "gehenna" to refer to a place of judgment for the dead. Gehenna—meaning "valley of Hinnom"—is located in Jerusalem, west of the city of David, and is mentioned during the monarchy as a place where the Israelites offered sacrifices to the Canaanite god Moloch, a practice strictly

38. See James H. Charlesworth, ed., *The Old Testament Pseudepigrapha*, 2 vols. (Garden City, NY: Doubleday, 1983). See esp. *4 Ezra* 7.36; *1 Enoch* 27.2; 48.9; 54.1; 90.26–27; 103.8; *Assumption of Moses* 10.19; *2 Baruch (Syriac Apocalypse)* 85.12–13.

forbidden by Mosaic law.[39] In later Jewish literature, gehenna appears not only as a place of punishment but also as a type of purgatory where the sins of the righteous would be cleansed during a period of twelve months before they would be permitted to enter paradise (*Gan Eden*) or during a period of twelve months before being annihilated and consequently relieved from all suffering (*Pesaḥim* 94a; *Eduyyot* 10).

The belief that the soul survived death and that the body would one day be resurrected and reunited with the soul became the traditional Jewish view during this period and for many subsequent centuries. The following examples reveal that the notion of a resurrection was well established in Jewish literature:[40]

- "In those days, Sheol will return all the deposits which she had received and hell will give back all that which it owes" (*1 Enoch* 51.1).
- "God himself will again fashion the bones and ashes of men and he will raise up mortals again as they were before" (*Sibylline Oracles* 4.181–82).
- "We hope that the remains of the departed will soon come to light again out of the earth. And afterward, they will become gods" (*Pseudo-Phocylides* 103–4).
- "And the earth shall give up those who are asleep in it; and the chambers shall give up the souls which have been committed to them. And the Most High shall be revealed upon the seat of judgment, and compassion shall pass away and patience shall be withdrawn" (*4 Ezra* 7.32–33).
- "For the earth will surely give back the dead at that time; it receives them now in order to keep them, not changing anything in their form" (*2 Baruch* 50.2).

Afterlife in Rabbinic Literature

The world of rabbinic Judaism with its profoundly extensive body of literature covers close to a thousand years of legal (halakic) and midrashic (haggadic) literature. Until the rabbinic period (AD 70–500), the Jewish community had centered its traditions on the sacrificial system and the Levitical priesthood, but during the first century CE, and especially after the destruction of the temple in Jerusalem (70 CE), every aspect of religious life was threatened.

39. 2 Kings 23:10; 2 Chron. 28:3; 33:6; Jer. 7:31–32.
40. The following translations are taken from Charlesworth, *Old Testament Pseudepigrapha*.

As mentioned above, during times of persecution, rabbis were faced with the need to reassure the righteous that a reward was awaiting them after death, a concept that would energize the righteous who faced persecution.

As a result of the destruction of the temple and its sacrificial system, it became necessary for Jewish scholars of the first century CE to develop a new system of laws and traditions. Consequently, the spiritual leaders—the rabbis—spearheaded efforts to preserve the theological, liturgical, and legalistic customs centered on the observance of Torah. The rabbis' attempts to establish guidelines to preserve the Jewish tradition prompted them to develop a detailed system of moral, religious, and ethical behavior based on their interpretation of the Mosaic law.

During the first centuries CE, the rabbis established centers of learning where issues related to every aspect of Jewish life were discussed, disputed, expounded, and recorded into official legal and nonlegal documents preserved and revered until this day. The most important Jewish texts include the Mishnah, the Talmud (Babylonian and Jerusalem), and midrashic texts. Within these major texts are found collections of teachings on the afterlife, on the postmortem journey of the soul, and on the resurrection of the dead. As is typical of Jewish literature, a variety of opinions, inconsistent with each other, appear on each of these topics. First, the literature offers a variety of Hebrew terms that reveal a clouded understanding of the postmortem experience. The expressions most commonly used to refer to the afterlife include *olam ha-ba'* ("the world to come"), *olam ha-emet* ("the world of truth"), *olam ha-menuchah* ("the world of rest"), *olam ha-nephasho* ("the world of souls"), and *olam she-kulo tov* ("the world of complete goodness").[41] The earliest occurrence, in Jewish literature, of the phrase *olam ha-ba'*, the most common of these terms, is found in *1 Enoch* (71.15), a text dated to the first century BCE.[42] The expression, often juxtaposed to the phrase *olam ha-zeh*, which means "this (earthly) realm," finds its synonym in the phrase *atid lavo*, "what is to come" ('*Arakin* 2.7). The rabbis interpreted the concept of *olam ha-ba'* in a number of ways, sometimes referring to the period of human existence after the termination of one's earthly life, at other times referring to a period of time at the end of history when individuals would experience resurrection and enjoy existence in the messianic kingdom.

41. Alfred J. Kolatch, *Inside Judaism: The Concepts, Customs, and Celebrations of the Jewish People* (Middle Village, NY: Jonathan David, 2006), 5.

42. Samuel Rosenblatt, "Olam Ha-Ba," in *Encyclopaedia Judaica*, ed. Skolnik and Berenbaum, 15:399.

Rabbinic literature is often ambiguous, reflecting the dichotomy we saw in the biblical period between individual and collective conceptions of the afterlife.... Collective and individual eschatological themes are fused and often confused in rabbinic literature. In certain sources, *Olam Ha-Ba* is uniquely associated with teachings about collective redemption and resurrection, but in other places *Olam Ha-Ba* is conceived of as an afterlife realm for the individual.[43]

Such conflicting interpretations are not uncommon in rabbinic literature. For example, in *Pirqe 'Abot*, a section of *Neziqin* in the Mishnah, a prominent rabbi states the following two seemingly contradicting ideas: "Better is one hour of bliss in the world to come than the whole of life in this world; and better is one hour of repentance and good works in this world than the whole life of the world to come" (*'Abot* 4.17). These conflicting statements in the same text seem to indicate that no absolute resolution was necessary on issues of the afterlife, yet it was understood that one must remain alert and conscious of the possibility of reward and punishment both in this world and in the world to come for moral and ethical decisions made during one's earthly existence. Also in *Pirqe 'Abot*, Rabbi Jacob intimates that eternal consequences are determined by one's behavior on earth: "This world is like a vestibule before the world to come; prepare yourself in the vestibule that you may enter into the banqueting hall" (*'Abot* 4.16).[44]

In *Sanhedrin* 10, another section of *Neziqin*, the rabbis introduce the reader to those who will and who will not be permitted to enter the world to come:

All Israelites have a share in the world to come, for it is written [prooftext—Isa. 60:21]; And these are they that have no share in the world to come: he that says that there is no resurrection of the dead prescribed in the Law, and he that says that the Law is not from Heaven, and an Epicurean. Rabbi Akiva says: Also he that reads the heretical books [books excluded from the canon of the Hebrew Scriptures], or that utters charms over a wound and says [prooftext—Exod. 15:26]. Abba Saul says: Also he that pronounces the Name with its proper letters. ... Three kings [Jeroboam and Ahab and Manasseh] and four commoners have no share in the world to come. ... The generations of the Flood have no share in the world to come, nor shall they stand in the judgment, for it is written [prooftext—Gen. 6:3]. ... The men of Sodom have no share in the world to come, for it is written [prooftext—Gen. 13:13]. ... The generation of

43. Raphael, *Jewish Views of the Afterlife*, 124.
44. *The Mishnah; Translated from the Hebrew*, with introduction and brief explanatory notes by Herbert Danby (London: Oxford University Press, 1967), 454.

the wilderness have no share in the world to come nor shall they stand in the judgment, for it is written [prooftext—Num. 14:35].[45]

These statements from *Sanhedrin* indicate that the rabbis were more interested in judging and assessing the behavior of the Israelites during their earthly existence than in describing the conditions of those who would enjoy a postmortem existence in the world to come. Modern Judaism echoes this view, as demonstrated by the words of the rabbis quoted in the introduction to this essay.

The Babylonian Talmud introduces its readers to a scholar of the third century who advocated that before a person would be allowed to enter the world to come, he or she would be asked a series of legalistic questions in order to determine whether the individual met the requirements for heaven. The questions include the following:

- Did you act honorably and honestly in your business dealings?
- Did you set aside time each day to engage in study [of Torah]?
- Did you marry and have children?
- Did you have faith in your salvation?
- Did you engage in examining opinions and ideas logically?
- Did you use your knowledge to arrive at proper conclusions?[46]

Afterlife in Later Jewish Texts

Jewish philosophers of the medieval and later periods continued to address issues of life after death and bodily resurrection. Moses Maimonides (twelfth century), Moses ben Naḥman (Naḥmanides, thirteenth century), Leon of Modena (sixteenth century), Baruch Spinoza (seventeenth century), and numerous other Jewish scholars continued the discussion and provided both similar and contradictory views, as the rabbis of the rabbinic period had so faithfully done. Maimonides underscores the importance of a messianic hope by including the concept in his thirteen principles of Jewish faith. In the Zohar, the Messiah is personal and human, yet endowed with supernatural powers. He ushers in a period of one thousand years "in which the passage of time would be slower than in the pre-messianic era and in which the very nature of the universe would undergo basic change."[47]

45. *Sanhedrin* 10.1–3, from ibid., 397.
46. *Šabbat* 31a.
47. "Messiah," in *The New Encyclopedia of Judaism,* ed. G. Wigoder (New York: New York University Press, 2002), 523.

Modern Orthodox Jewish tradition advocates a messianic era when Jews will be gathered from exile in their homeland and will fulfill all religious obligations, particularly those related to the land of Israel. The Conservative community adheres to the concept of a messianic period characterized by universal peace, social justice, and solutions for all forms of evil. In their understanding, nothing supernatural will be involved in the betterment of society. The world will be redeemed by the good works and efforts of all good people. Today's most liberal branches of Judaism, the Reform and Reconstructionist Jewish communities, have rejected the concepts of a personal Messiah and a messianic age. Instead they advocate for a progressive transformation toward a state of intellectual and moral human perfection. They do not believe in physical resurrection of the dead. They have affirmed in its place the concept of the immortality of the soul.

> The traditional expectation of the sudden "coming of Messiah" was transformed into belief in a gradual process, tending to be identified with the general belief in the progress of humankind. In this garb, messianism was hailed as a central profoundly Jewish concept, especially since one of its expressions was the ongoing process of the Jews' emancipation in modern society.[48]

Although the notion that God will one day establish a messianic kingdom on earth is in flux in Jewish communities around the world, to this day most Jewish prayer books have retained a reference to the resurrection of the dead in the second of the Eighteen Benedictions—the Shemoneh Esre—a prayer that is traditionally recited three times a day, in the morning (*shacharit*), in the afternoon (*minchah*), and in the evening (*ma'ariv*):

> You, O Lord, are mighty forever; *you revive the dead*; you are powerful in saving. You sustain the living with loving kindness. *You give life to the dead* with great mercy. You support the falling, heal the sick, free the captive, and keep faith with those who sleep in the dust. Who compares with you, Master of power, and who is like you, King over life and death, causing salvation to flourish? *You are faithful in bringing life to the dead.* Blessed are you, O Lord, *who revives the dead*.[49]

48. Yehoshua Amir, "Messianism and Zionism," in *Eschatology in the Bible and in Jewish and Christian Tradition*, ed. Henning G. Reventlow, Journal for the Study of the Old Testament: Supplement Series 243 (Sheffield: Sheffield Academic, 1997), 14.
49. *HaNefesh Community*, s.v. "The Shema Prayer & The Amidah Prayer," www.hanefesh.com/edu/amidah.htm (accessed June 10, 2008), emphasis added.

This blessing, attested in Jewish texts since the Second Temple period, continues to make a strong statement regarding God's power over bondage, sickness, and death, pointing toward a day when God will exercise full control over life and death.

Conclusion

In conclusion, centuries of canonical and noncanonical texts reveal that numerous scholars over an extended period of time addressed discussions related to a Jewish afterlife, a bodily resurrection, and a messianic age but that, according to Raphael, "nowhere in rabbinic literature do we find a single, systematized statement on the Jewish understanding of life after death."[50] Such is also the case in the biblical literature. Views differ from author to author and from century to century.

Although preexilic biblical literature provides clear evidence that the Israelites believed in an *au-delà* and interacted with God, angels, and spirits, it is only in later periods that their belief in an afterlife is described in greater detail. As Jewish history progressed, authors of canonical and noncanonical texts revealed an increasingly complex picture of a messianic age and afterlife. As mentioned above, periods of intense persecution became catalysts for the development of Jewish views on the postmortem fate of the righteous and the unrighteous. The fertile imagination and eagerness of the sages of the rabbinic period provide us with conflicting views that are left unresolved to this day.

A clear portrait of the terms, time frame, and dynamics of the messianic age, as they are presented by Jewish scholars of the last three millennia, can never be obtained. For some, no such era is possible, whereas for others, the messianic age will last from forty to seven thousand years. The literature provides neither agreement nor consensus, and the Jewish sages who have left us with an extensive body of literature show no effort to reconcile the differences. Readers are thus often left to their own interpretations.

50. Raphael, *Jewish Views of the Afterlife*, 120.

4

The Posttribulationism of the New Testament

Leaving "Left Behind" Behind

CRAIG L. BLOMBERG

Prevalent Problems

Massive, simultaneous traffic accidents all over the world kill millions as cars with Christians at the steering wheel are suddenly left driverless. Airplanes plummet from the sky and wreak more havoc on the ground as Christian pilots and controllers mysteriously disappear. God forbid that there are any Christians in important political or military offices in our country at this time who are on the verge of making sensitive decisions, giving orders, or pushing or not pushing buttons that might make the difference between war and peace, between a nuclear holocaust or diplomacy, for they too will instantaneously vanish. Is this the New Testament picture of what the end times hold in store for this world?

Countless conservative Christians of recent vintage have believed in some version of this kind of mayhem.[1] These scenarios are an outgrowth of the

1. For a fascinating analysis by a sociologist of religion, see Amy J. Frykholm, *Rapture Culture: Left Behind in Evangelical America* (Oxford and New York: Oxford University Press, 2004).

doctrine known as the pretribulational rapture. The "rapture" refers to the picture, painted in 1 Thessalonians 4:17, of the time of the resurrection of the righteous dead, when living believers will join God's people of all eras of human history and be "caught up" (in Latin *raptus*; thus the English "rapture") to meet the Lord in the air as he descends from heaven on the clouds. The "tribulation" refers to a period of intense suffering on earth before the coming of the Messiah. In first-century Judaism, particularly in apocalyptic literature, the belief often arose that part of the purpose for the precise time of the Messiah's coming would be to intervene and save his people from unprecedented distress in this world (see esp. *1 Enoch*, *4 Ezra*, *2 Baruch* [*Syriac Apocalypse*], and the *War Scroll* from Qumran).[2] Old Testament and intertestamental texts frequently likened this tribulation to the labor pains of a mother about to give birth, and the deliverance that the Messiah would bring to the mother's relief from pain after the birth of the baby.[3]

Jesus himself appropriated this imagery but saw it as something still in the future, just as he envisioned a second part to his messianic ministry, not fulfilled in his earthly life, death, resurrection, and ascension. He spoke indeed of "great tribulation," worse than anything the world had ever experienced or would ever again encounter, and John, penning Revelation, added the definite article and prophesied about "the great tribulation" that would precede Christ's visible, public second coming in glory from heaven. Belief in a "pretribulational rapture," then, means that the picture of 1 Thessalonians 4:17 should be understood as a separate event from the parousia—Christ's public second coming—and altogether prior to the period of intense suffering that is believed to immediately precede the parousia.[4]

Although some have tried to show precedent for this doctrine in the church of the second through fourth centuries,[5] most scholars have remained unconvinced.[6] The first unambiguous articulation of this belief came in 1830 with the founder of the Plymouth Brethren denomination in Scotland, J. Nelson Darby. Debates swirl to this day about the accuracy of the report that he first

2. See further Geert W. Lorein, *The Antichrist Theme in the Intertestamental Period* (London and New York: T&T Clark, 2003).

3. See the lists of references in Andreas Köstenberger, *John* (Grand Rapids: Baker Academic, 2004), 476nn65–66.

4. For a representative, contemporary defense of this perspective, see Paul D. Feinberg, "The Case for the Pretribulation Rapture Position," in *Three Views on the Rapture: Pre-, Mid-, or Post-tribulation*, by Gleason L. Archer et al. (Grand Rapids: Zondervan, 1996), 45–86.

5. E.g., James F. Stitzinger, "The Rapture in Twenty Centuries of Biblical Interpretation," *Master's Seminary Journal* 13 (2002): 149–71, esp. 153–56.

6. Including certain dispensationalists. See, e.g., Charles C. Ryrie, *Dispensationalism Today* (Chicago: Moody, 1965), 77–78.

heard it from a self-styled fifteen-year-old prophetess by the name of Marga-ret MacDonald.[7] The entire theological system of which the pretribulational rapture formed a small part came to be called dispensationalism. This system eventually became far better known in the United States than in any other part of the English-speaking world through the famous Bible reference notes of C. I. Scofield, which were printed with millions of copies of the King James Bible, beginning in 1909, and the writings and ministry of Lewis Sperry Chafer, founder of Dallas Theological Seminary in 1924 and president until 1952.[8] Dallas Seminary, along with the Moody Bible Institute, founded in 1886, in turn spawned countless smaller seminaries and colleges eventually all around the world through a very successful missionary movement that continued to promote their distinctive eschatology.

All of these developments pale, however, in comparison to the effect of the writings of Hal Lindsey in the 1970s and 1980s, particularly through his popular *Late Great Planet Earth*,[9] the best-selling work of nonfiction (or so it was classified) throughout this country in the entire decade of the 1970s (and I am not referring just to sales of Christian works).[10] During the 1990s and the present decade, Lindsey's successors are Tim LaHaye and Jerry Jenkins with their phenomenally successful Left Behind series of sixteen books and three feature-length movies to date.[11] So influential have these works been that more than once I have had occasion to speak in evangelical Presbyterian or Reformed churches, which historically have repudiated dispensationalism, only to find that its members know little or nothing of their tradition's historic eschatology but only Lindsey, LaHaye, and Jenkins. Thus many conservative Christians remain convinced that believers will *not* have to live through the worst era of human history, which will soon be upon us. Only unbelievers alive at the time of the rapture will have to suffer these awful horrors.

Actually, this is an oversimplified description because commentators of all theological persuasions recognize that there are a group of "servants of God" who appear throughout the book of Revelation, protected from God's wrath though not from the persecution and even martyrdom unleashed by Satan and

7. The most vigorous exponent of this theory, though one-sided, has been Dave MacPherson in a series of five books published between 1973 and 1995, none of them with either academic or even well-known popular-level publishers. See Stitzinger ("Rapture," 166–67, with 166n97 for the bibliographic references), who is equally one-sided in his dismissal of this theory.

8. For his own convictions and lines of argumentation, see Lewis S. Chafer, *Systematic Theology* (Dallas: Dallas Seminary Press, 1947), 4:364–73.

9. Hal Lindsey, *The Late Great Planet Earth* (Grand Rapids: Zondervan, 1970).

10. Thus Adela Yarbro Collins, "Reading the Book of Revelation in the Twentieth Century," *Interpretation* 40 (1986): 232.

11. Tim LaHaye and Jerry B. Jenkins, Left Behind (Wheaton: Tyndale, 1995–2007).

unbelieving humans (Rev. 7:1–8; cf. 9:4; 12:17; 16:2; 18:4). Nevertheless, these believers testify boldly on God's behalf, causing some to repent (11:1–13), while many others will likely come to faith because they see the fulfillment of what Christians, before they were raptured, had predicted would occur. Certain versions of the doctrine of the pretribulational rapture add into the mix the conviction that God's people, protected by his seal at the beginning of the tribulation, that is, immediately after the rapture, are Jewish Christians or 144,000 select Jewish Christians, or 144,000 select Christians irrespective of ethnicity.[12] In no version of the pretribulational rapture, therefore, is it quite true that all believers will escape the end-time horrors, but with more than two billion professing Christians in the world today, the odds are certainly good that any given Christian will escape the great tribulation.

One can immediately appreciate the attractiveness of such a doctrine. Who in their right mind would want to experience the worst times in all of world history? It is beyond doubt that many people in our contemporary world, including many Christians, believe a variety of things primarily because they want them to be true, not because there is much (or sometimes any) supporting evidence. When I am thinking just about myself or my Christian friends, I can easily concede that if I must live until the time of the rapture, I would certainly hope that the pretribulational-rapture doctrine is true. It would allow me to watch the deteriorating moral and spiritual standards around me, the growth of non-Christian religions and worldviews, and the proliferation of violence, poverty, and natural disasters and console myself that at least believers will be removed from this dreadful combination of circumstances before the worst arrives. But individuals for whom the Bible is the final authority in all matters that it addresses dare not base anything on what they most want to be true but must ask the question "What does Scripture teach?"

Before turning directly to that question, we must set our topic in additional contexts. Throughout the centuries, what alternatives have Christians held to a pretribulational rapture? Historically, the most common belief by far has been that of a posttribulational rapture: Christ returns *after* the tribulation to gather his people together, and indeed, this return is one and the same as his parousia, ushering in judgment day. A few have argued for a midtribulational rapture, based on their interpretation of the resurrection and ascension of the two witnesses in Revelation 11.[13] In the last two decades, a variation of this view has become popular in some circles—the prewrath rapture. At

---

12. For a full range of the major interpretive options and representative exponents of each, see David E. Aune, *Revelation 6–16* (Nashville: Nelson, 1998), 440–45.

13. See esp. Gleason L. Archer, "The Case for the Mid-Seventieth-Week Rapture Position," in Archer et al., *Three Views on the Rapture*, 113–45.

some point during the tribulation, whether at the midpoint or not, God's wrath is so unleashed on the earth that it would be impossible to protect his people from its consequences, so that God takes them out of harm's way at that point.[14] And with the rise of modern (and now postmodern) liberalism, many authors have simply dismissed biblical apocalyptic as the outmoded husk or shell into which the ancients placed their eschatological beliefs. One need not even debate the timing of the rapture, so the argument goes, because we cannot expect a literal rapture ever to occur, or a literal second coming of Christ for that matter. At best, biblical apocalyptic represents, according to this view, theological encouragement, in primitive garb, for beleaguered Christians that God can and will work through the events of this world and through his people to create a better world and that God's people need not fear that the world will become as bad as it could possibly be.[15]

In other words, the debate over the timing of the rapture is largely limited to *evangelical* Christian circles. It is limited even more because it is predominantly an intramural debate among those who subscribe to premillennialism. Premillennialism is the conviction that the second coming, or parousia, will occur before the millennium—the thousand years, depicted in Revelation 20, during which believers from all eras reign with Christ, a golden age of peace and happiness in human history that foreshadows the perfection of the new heavens and new earth of Revelation 21–22, even if stopping a little short of it. Premillennialism also has three main competitors, one of which takes two forms. Postmillennialism reverses the sequence of end-times events and believes that Christians yielded to the power of the Holy Spirit will usher in this golden age of Christian influence in the world before Christ's literal return. Amillennialists typically have not looked for a literal millennium but have seen believers reigning spiritually with Christ right now during the so-called church age.[16] In recent years, especially under the influence of Anthony Hoekema, a variation has commanded the allegiance of some, in which the millennium is viewed as just another way of depicting the new heavens and new earth.[17] And again, for those inclined to dismiss biblical apocalyptic as mythological or legendary literature, the idea of a millennium is viewed at best as a way of

14. Marvin J. Rosenthal, *The Pre-wrath Rapture of the Church* (Nashville: Nelson, 1990).

15. See the numerous variations on this theme in the helpful survey by Scott M. Lewis, *What Are They Saying about New Testament Apocalyptic?* (Mahwah, NJ: Paulist, 2004).

16. For excellent overviews of the various perspectives by proponents of each, with interaction among the contributors, see Robert G. Clouse, ed., *The Meaning of the Millennium* (Downers Grove, IL: InterVarsity, 1977); and Darrell L. Bock, ed., *Three Views on the Millennium and Beyond* (Grand Rapids: Zondervan, 1999).

17. See esp. Anthony A. Hoekema, *The Bible and the Future* (Grand Rapids: Eerdmans, 1994).

affirming that God's original good purposes for this earth will not be thwarted and God's people should continue to witness to and work for them, and at worst as a fanciful, ancient pipe dream that has often been disproved, can no longer be believed, and distracts or even hinders people from the necessary improvements that they should be making to life in this world.[18]

Premillennialism and amillennialism vied for adherents during the earliest centuries of church history. From the fifth-century writings of Augustine onward, however, amillennialism dominated Christian thinking, especially in Roman Catholicism, and neither Luther nor Calvin broke from this thinking at the time of the Protestant Reformation. Occasional chiliasts (as premillennialists were often called, from the Greek word *chilias*, "a thousand") would emerge, but their influence was short-lived. Postmillennialism has captured Christian allegiance to a significant degree only in times of great missionary expansion, most notably in the nineteenth century and with a bit of resurgence at the end of the twentieth century, when some people have allowed themselves to imagine a fuller Christianization of the earth than the world has heretofore seen.[19] Premillennialism in evangelical Protestant thinking has come to be classified under two main headings, dispensational premillennialism and classic or historic premillennialism (i.e., returning to the beliefs of chiliasts in the early church but without adding modern innovations, most notably the pretribulational rapture).[20]

A moment's thought will disclose why only premillennialists typically debate the temporal relationship between the tribulation and the rapture. For amillennialism, just as there is no discrete millennial period separate from the rest of history, so no unique period of tribulation occurs. Depending on one's perspective and particular experiences, there is great physical tribulation and/or great spiritual victory for God's people in every age of human history. It makes no sense within amillennialism to take any perspective other than post-tribulationism, because there is no period prior to the parousia when one may

18. See, e.g., respectively, Brian K. Blount, *Can I Get a Witness? Reading Revelation through African American Culture* (Louisville: Westminster John Knox, 2005); and Tina Pippin, *The Rhetoric of Gender: Death and Desire in the Apocalypse of John* (Louisville: Westminster John Knox, 1992).

19. For an excellent historical overview, see Arthur W. Wainwright, *Mysterious Apocalypse: Interpreting the Book of Revelation* (Nashville: Abingdon, 1993), 21–103.

20. Dispensationalism itself has gone through several definable phases, the most recent of which has brought it closest to mainstream evangelicalism. But the "pretrib" rapture remains firmly entrenched. Cf. Craig A. Blaising and Darrell L. Bock, *Progressive Dispensationalism: An Up-to-Date Handbook of Contemporary Dispensational Thought* (Wheaton: BridgePoint Books, 1993); and Robert L. Saucy, *The Case for Progressive Dispensationalism: The Interface between Dispensational and Non-dispensational Theology* (Grand Rapids: Zondervan, 1993).

speak of the absence of great tribulation, even if there is an intensification of it just before Christ's return.[21] For the same reason, postmillennialists likewise would have no need to separate the rapture from Christ's public return. For them also, the only tribulation that occurs is throughout the entirety of the church age, particularly in AD 70, and up to but not including the millennium with which that age culminates.[22] For those who see apocalyptic as a genre that in no way refers, however symbolically, to actual future events, there is no literal rapture to worry about at all.

Before turning to the question of what kind of tribulationism appears in the Bible, we must thus consider why premillennialism appears as the best option for our broader eschatological understanding. Fortunately, the remarks here may be brief for three reasons. First, it is widely agreed that the vast majority of the differences between the various millennial views involve Old Testament texts and themes, whereas my purview in this essay is the New Testament. Second, and this is really just the reverse side of the first point, for *evangelical* New Testament interpreters, the millennial debate reduces ultimately to an understanding of Revelation 20. George Eldon Ladd, who died in 1983 after an illustrious career at Fuller Seminary, was without doubt the most famous and most vocal recent exponent of historic or classic premillennialism; he liked to say in class that he could have been an amillennialist if it were not for Revelation 20.[23] Finally, the other contributors to this collection of essays all come back to the millennial question from various angles, whereas I alone have chosen to tackle the tribulational issue more directly.

Why, then, am I a premillennialist from a New Testament point of view? Because, no matter how many flashbacks or disruptions of chronological sequence one might want to argue for elsewhere in Revelation, it makes absolutely no sense to put one in between Revelation 19 and 20 as both amillennialists and postmillennialists must do. For the tribulation to refer solely to the church age or to a large portion of it, Revelation 20 must begin afresh (as Revelation 12 almost certainly does) at Christ's first coming, so that the binding of Satan in 20:1–2 refers to Christ's defeat of the devil on the cross at his first coming (and perhaps, proleptically, in the exorcisms that occurred during his ministry; see esp. Luke 10:18). The reign of Christians with Christ in Revelation 20:4,

21. Cf. Stanley J. Grenz, *The Millennial Maze: Sorting Out Evangelical Options* (Downers Grove, IL: InterVarsity, 1992), 152.

22. Cf. John J. Davis, *Christ's Victorious Kingdom: Postmillennialism Reconsidered* (Grand Rapids: Baker Academic, 1986), 133.

23. His most important work on eschatology was George E. Ladd, *The Presence of the Future: The Eschatology of Biblical Realism* (Grand Rapids: Eerdmans, 1974). Cf. esp. idem, *The Gospel of the Kingdom: Scriptural Studies in the Kingdom of God* (Grand Rapids: Eerdmans, 1959).

then, similarly begins with Christ's first coming—with his resurrection.[24] But the end of chapter 19 depicts how the great battle of Armageddon, with the armies of the earth gathered to fight just before Christ's return, never gets off the ground. Christ intervenes by coming back, bringing his heavenly battalions with him and utterly destroying his opponents. In the process, we are told about the fate of two of the three members of the so-called satanic trinity, introduced in 12:1–13:18. The beast and the false prophet, parodies of Jesus and the Holy Spirit, are captured and thrown alive into the lake of fire (19:20). Readers expect to hear next about the fate of the ringleader of the three, Satan himself, the one who wanted to usurp the place of God the Father, and they are not disappointed. Revelation 20:1 continues seamlessly, describing Satan's confinement to the abyss until the very end of the millennium. The rest of the chapter follows equally inexorably from there on.[25]

It is not quite the case, however, that it all reduces to Revelation 20. Second Temple Judaism frequently articulated hope for what could be called a temporary millennial kingdom. *Fourth Ezra* 3–14 and *2 Baruch* 27–40, 53–72, most likely written between AD 70 and 90 and thus providing immediately relevant background to Revelation, both unambiguously attest to such a belief. *First Enoch* 91 and 93, indisputably pre-Christian, and *2 Enoch* 32, 33, and 65, possibly as late as the second century, both seem to have such a period in view with their imagery. In varying ways, each of these five works anticipates a period of hundreds of years when Jews will live in the land in unprecedented peace and prosperity, sometimes with the Messiah explicitly reigning over them, before giving way to a more permanent, eternal state.[26] With this background, it becomes natural to read various New Testament texts, and not just Revelation 20, in similar fashion even if other interpretations of them remain possible. First Corinthians 15:22–28 appears to set up stages of eschatology with the use of the fairly rare temporal adverbs *epeita* and *eita* for "then," which commonly (though not universally) imply a distinct interval between

24. See, e.g., Dennis E. Johnson, *Triumph of the Lamb: A Commentary on Revelation* (Phillipsburg, NJ: Presbyterian & Reformed, 2001), 283–88; cf. Gregory K. Beale, *The Book of Revelation* (Grand Rapids: Eerdmans, 1999), 984.

25. See esp. Craig S. Keener, *Revelation* (Grand Rapids: Zondervan, 2000), 463–65, with additional arguments why Rev. 20 presupposes what has already happened throughout the book. Cf. Joseph L. Trafton, *Reading Revelation: A Literary and Theological Commentary*, rev. ed. (Macon, GA: Smyth & Helwys, 2005), 185; Frederick J. Murphy, *Fallen Is Babylon: The Revelation to John* (Harrisburg, PA: Trinity, 1998), 395.

26. See esp. Larry R. Helyer, "The Necessity, Problems, and Promise of Second Temple Judaism for Discussions of New Testament Eschatology," *Journal of the Evangelical Theological Society* 47 (2004): 597–615. Cf. Heikki Räisänen, "Towards an Alternative to New Testament Theology: 'Individual Eschatology' as an Example," in *The Nature of New Testament Theology*, ed. Christopher Rowland and Christopher Tuckett (Oxford and Malden, MA: Blackwell, 2006), 176.

events. First Jesus is raised; then those who are in Christ (15:23). Clearly an interval is implied here. It is thus natural, even if not necessary, to envision another gap when Paul continues, "Then the end will come."[27] Pictures of the twelve apostles judging the twelve tribes of Israel and reigning with Jesus upon his return to earth or of the establishment of his kingdom (Matt. 19:28; Luke 13:29–30; 22:28–30) arguably fit most naturally with such a millennial kingdom. Paul even expands the picture to all Christians judging even the angels (1 Cor. 6:2–3).

But does it really matter? The old joke among theological students was to tell the uninitiated that you were a pantribulational panmillennialist. Most had no clue what you meant; a few might recognize *pan-* as the prefix meaning "all" and wonder if somehow you were trying to affirm the best of all views at once. But then you dispelled their perplexity by declaring, "I just believe that it will all pan out in the end." Should we settle for that? I think the answer is "yes and no." In my ideal theological world, there would be no church or parachurch organization, including seminaries, that would make a certain belief about the millennium or the tribulation a requirement of anything, such as membership, employment, or the like. If we believe in the literal, visible, public return of Christ to usher in the judgment of the living and the dead, if we believe in the bodily resurrection of all people, some to eternal life and others to eternal destruction, surely we can agree to disagree in love over the particulars on which intelligent, godly, Bible-believing Christians have never achieved consensus and yet fellowship and work together at every level of Christian service and activity. The classic orthodox creeds of the patristic period, like the major confessions of faith from the Protestant Reformation, never required more than this.[28]

On the other hand, it seems to me that premillennialism does best justice to God's determination to vindicate his purposes in creating *this* universe as originally perfectly good, despite the corruption that sin introduced, yet without introducing the unrealistic expectation that Christians can produce this millennium apart from God's supernatural intervention. But I actually think the doctrine of the tribulation is more important than the doctrine of the millennium. What might happen if millions of Christians in the twenty-first

27. F. F. Bruce, *1 and 2 Corinthians* (London: Oliphants, 1971; repr., Grand Rapids: Eerdmans, 1980), 147, contra most commentators.

28. As recently as the mid-twentieth century, Louis Berkhof (*The History of Christian Doctrines*, 2 vols. [Grand Rapids: Eerdmans, 1937–53; repr., London: Banner of Truth, 1969; Grand Rapids: Baker Books, 1975], 264) could write, "Up to the present time, however, the doctrine of the millennium has never yet been embodied in a single Confession, and therefore cannot be regarded as a dogma of the Church."

century count on pretribulationism being true, only to have to live through this awful period? Our Christian counselors and therapists tell us that contemporary Americans may be the least theologically equipped generation in church history when it comes to dealing with personal and collective suffering and evil.[29] Look at the sensationalized quasi-hysteria that preceded the now infamous Y2K nonevent at the end of 1999. Six of the ten best-selling Christian books that year confidently predicted that this was the beginning of the end, just preceding a pretribulational rapture.[30] Every time things take a turn for the worse in the Middle East, some enterprising Christian publishes the latest unabashed analysis of how end-times prophecies are being fulfilled and believers will soon be escaping from this world. And a frightening percentage of the evangelical Christian public seems always to suffer a collective amnesia, forgetting how the same kinds of publications just a decade or two earlier turned out to include a considerable amount of false prophecy. The one statistic that remains unvarying is that to date, 100 percent of all such scenarios have proved wrong.[31] This alone should inspire a certain amount of reluctance to pin our hopes on the next round of speculation. Perhaps we ought actively to look in a different direction altogether. This is the advice that the rest of this essay seeks to buttress.

Suggested Solutions

The Greek word *thlipsis* ("tribulation") occurs forty-five times in the New Testament.[32] In perhaps the oldest New Testament writing, the Letter of

29. Outstanding resources include C. S. Lewis, *The Problem of Pain* (London and New York: Macmillan, 1944; repr., San Francisco: HarperSanFrancisco, 2001); Philip Yancey and Paul Brand, *Pain: The Gift Nobody Wants* (New York and London: HarperCollins, 1993); and D. A. Carson, *How Long O Lord? Reflections on Suffering and Evil*, rev. ed. (Grand Rapids: Baker Academic; Nottingham: InterVarsity, 2006). Cf. also N. T. Wright, *Evil and the Justice of God* (London: SPCK; Downers Grove, IL: InterVarsity, 2006).

30. For the spectrum of Christian fears and predictions leading up to 2000, set in a historical context and with sane antidotes, see Robert G. Clouse, Robert N. Hosack, and Richard V. Pierard, *The New Millennium Manual: A Once and Future Guide* (Grand Rapids: Baker Academic, 1999).

31. See esp. the thorough history in Bernard McGinn, *Antichrist: Two Thousand Years of the Human Fascination with Evil* (San Francisco: HarperSanFrancisco, 1994).

32. W. Bauer, F. W. Danker, W. F. Arndt, and W. F. Gingrich, *Greek-English Lexicon of the New Testament and Other Early Christian Literature*, 3rd ed. (Chicago: University of Chicago Press, 1999), 457, gives as the main cluster of meanings "trouble that inflicts distress, *oppression, affliction, tribulation*," with a secondary, much less frequent cluster of "inward experience of distress, *affliction, trouble*." H. Balz and G. Schneider, eds., *Exegetical Dictionary of the New Testament* (Grand Rapids: Eerdmans, 1990–93), 1:151, reduces the meanings to "affliction, hardship"; C. Brown, ed., *New International Dictionary of New Testament Theology* (Grand

James, believers must care for orphans and widows in their tribulation (James 1:27)—paradigms of the dispossessed of the ancient Mediterranean world. In Paul's letters, *thlipsis* refers once to a feature of married life that singles can be spared (1 Cor. 7:28); once to his emotional pain in dealing with the man in Corinth who had to be excommunicated (2 Cor. 2:4);[33] once to what Paul does not want the Corinthians to experience, which they would if the rich merely traded places with the poor (2 Cor. 8:13); and once to what the rival but orthodox Christian leaders in Philippi wanted to cause for him as their ministries thrived while he languished in prison (Phil. 1:17). Twice *thlipsis* depicts what the wicked will receive on judgment day (Rom. 2:9; 2 Thess. 1:6).

The other eighteen occurrences in Paul all refer to the common feature of hardships and suffering in first-century Christian life, due either to religious persecution of some kind or just to the travails of life in a fallen world.[34] Yet Paul stresses the joy that is possible in the midst of such hardships, because of their character-forming nature (Rom. 5:3 [2x]; 2 Cor. 7:4; 8:2; 1 Thess. 1:6); their inability to separate us from Christ's love (Rom. 8:35); God's abundant comfort, which we in turn should pass on to others who are similarly suffering (2 Cor. 1:4 [2x], 8); the eternal perspective that will one day make them seem as if they had been "light" and "momentary" (2 Cor. 4:17); and thus the need to endure them (Rom. 12:12; 2 Cor. 6:4; Eph. 3:13; 1 Thess. 3:3, 7; 2 Thess. 1:4). He commends the Philippians for sharing in his *thlipsis*, by which he apparently means their financial donation to help him while he is imprisoned (Phil. 4:14). In his most cryptic reference of all, Paul speaks of his filling up what was lacking in Christ's *thlipsis* (Col. 1:24), probably alluding to the Jewish notion of a fixed amount of suffering that God's people would have to endure in the days leading up to the Messiah's ultimate vanquishing of his enemies—the messianic woes, as they were sometimes called.[35] Thus the more Paul suffered, the less would be left for other believers to endure.[36]

Rapids: Zondervan, 1975–85), 2:807, reduces them to "oppression, affliction, tribulation" and treats the word as a series of Greek terms under the English entry "Persecution."

33. This is on the assumption, which I think most likely, that 2 Cor. 2:5–11 refers to the same individual disciplined in 1 Cor. 5:1–5.

34. Cf. further Colin G. Kruse, "The Offender and the Offense in 2 Corinthians 2:5 and 7:12," *Evangelical Quarterly* 60 (1988): 129–39. This is the "traditional" interpretation, very widely (and in my opinion too quickly) rejected by many modern commentators.

35. The fullest study of this theme is now C. Marvin Pate and Douglas W. Kennard, *Deliverance Now and Not Yet: The New Testament and the Great Tribulation* (New York: Peter Lang, 2003).

36. See, e.g., F. F. Bruce, *The Epistles to the Colossians, to Philemon, and to the Ephesians* (Grand Rapids: Eerdmans, 1984), 83–84. Cf. Marianne M. Thompson, *Colossians and Philemon* (Grand Rapids: Eerdmans, 2005), 45–46.

In Hebrews, *thlipsis* appears once, in the context of the tribulation the letter's readership endured at some earlier time when they "joyfully accepted the confiscation" of their property (Heb. 10:33–34). If Hebrews was written to primarily Jewish-Christian house churches in Rome in the early 60s, as seems likely, then this allusion probably harks back to Claudius's edict in 49 expelling all Jews from Rome, including Christian Jews, at which time the state seized vacant properties.[37] The remaining General Epistles do not employ any forms of the word *thlipsis* or its cognates.

In the Gospels and Acts, Jesus tells the parable of the sower and includes *thlipsis* as one of the reasons that the seed that falls in rocky places does not produce a plant that grows big enough to yield actual fruit (Matt. 13:21; Mark 4:17). He predicts that his followers will have tribulation as a characteristic feature of life in this fallen world, especially in light of hostility to the gospel (John 16:33), but promises joy after sorrow just as a mother rejoices, despite her intense labor pains, after a successful delivery of a baby (John 16:21). Stephen, in the address he delivers just before he is stoned to death, twice alludes to the tribulation in Egypt in Joseph's day (Acts 7:10–11), on the second occasion using the expression *thlipsis megalē* (great tribulation). Luke refers to the persecution and scattering of Christians after Stephen's martyrdom as *thlipsis* (Acts 11:19); his summary of Paul's teaching in his follow-up ministry to the cities of southern Galatia after initial hostilities there states that Paul and Barnabas were "strengthening the disciples and encouraging them to remain true to the faith." For, they explained, "we must go through many hardships (*thlipseōn*) to enter the kingdom of God" (14:22). Paul takes it for granted that this is a natural and expected part of the Christian life. He applies this generalization to himself in Acts after the Holy Spirit has revealed to him his coming suffering and imprisonment in Jerusalem (20:23). Not for a moment does he let it deter him from his course (cf. esp. 21:10–14).[38]

Of the remaining six references to *thlipsis*, five occur in Christ's eschatological Olivet Discourse (actually only three are distinct, as two are simply duplicate references to the same teaching in Matthew and Mark). In Matthew 24:9 tribulation, in the context of persecution, forms one of the elements of life in this world that the disciples must experience after Christ's death and

---

37. Thus, e.g., William L. Lane, *Hebrews 1–8* (Dallas: Word Books, 1991), li–lxvi. George H. Guthrie (*Hebrews* [Grand Rapids: Zondervan, 1998], 17–18) offers a wonderful excerpt of historical fiction, presenting these and related circumstances from the perspective of a young Jewish-Christian member of one of the Roman house churches.

38. On tribulations in Luke-Acts, see esp. Scott Cunningham, *"Through Many Tribulations": The Theology of Persecution in Luke-Acts*, Journal for the Study of the New Testament: Supplement Series 142 (Sheffield: Sheffield Academic, 1997).

resurrection, even though the end is *not* yet (24:6).[39] In Mark 13:19 Jesus predicts days of tribulation "unequaled from the beginning, when God created the world, until now—and never to be equaled again." Not surprisingly, the parallel passage in Matthew adds the word "great" as a modifier of "tribulation" (Matt. 24:21; NIV "distress"). A few verses later, both evangelists record Jesus as declaring that *after* that tribulation the cosmic upheavals ushering in the return of Christ would unfold (Mark 13:24; Matt. 24:29). Matthew complicates matters by adding the adverb "immediately" to modify the phrase "after the tribulation of those days."

One can understand why many premillennialists conclude that this tribulation must refer to a short but intense and unprecedented period of suffering during the days just before the parousia. On the other hand, the context of "those days" in Jesus's larger discourse is the destruction of the temple. Jesus has piqued the disciples' curiosity by predicting that no stone of the eighth wonder of the ancient world, which they looked down on from the Mount of Olives, would be left on top of another (Mark 13:2 and parallels). In amazement, the disciples have asked when this would happen and what signs would point to its occurrence (13:3–4). When Jesus speaks of the abomination of desolation standing where it should not (13:14), he is alluding to the prophecy of Daniel 9:27, which refers explicitly to the Jewish temple. Indeed, Jews in the days of the Maccabees thought they had seen the fulfillment of that prophecy in the desecration of the temple by Antiochus Epiphanes (1 Macc. 1:54). So it makes no sense in Jesus's context to take the abomination of desolation as some desecration of a rebuilt temple hundreds or thousands of years later; in this interpretation, Jesus would never have answered the disciples' question, nor could they ever have been expected to understand that he was referring to any temple other than the one before their very eyes at that moment.[40]

For Jesus, then, "great tribulation" refers neither to the events of the second century BC nor to a period of time only just preceding his return but, at least in part, to the distress at the time of the destruction of Jerusalem, the burning of the city, and the razing of the temple by the Romans in AD 70.[41] But can

39. Indeed, a key purpose of Christ's Olivet Discourse is to *dampen* eschatological enthusiasm. See Timothy J. Geddert, *Watchwords: Mark 13 in Markan Eschatology* (Sheffield: JSOT Press, 1989). Cf. Ben Witherington III, *The Gospel of Mark: A Socio-rhetorical Commentary* (Grand Rapids: Eerdmans, 2001), 340–41.

40. Similarly, R. T. France, *The Gospel of Mark* (Carlisle, UK: Paternoster; Grand Rapids: Eerdmans, 2002), 519–20; Ben Witherington III, *Matthew* (Macon, GA: Smyth & Helwys, 2006), 446–47; and John Nolland, *The Gospel of Matthew* (Bletchley, UK: Paternoster; Grand Rapids: Eerdmans, 2005), 972.

41. Arguably, this great tribulation had begun already with the hostility that led to his crucifixion. See esp. Brant Pitre, *Jesus, the Tribulation, and the End of the Exile: Restoration*

those days qualify for times of "unequaled distress," either before or after? From one perspective, it makes little sense to intone solemnly that tribulation at the *end* of human history, just before Christ's return, the millennium, and new heavens and new earth will "never be equaled again." Of course it will not, by definition, since it ushers in the end of such horrors. When my daughters were smaller, they would have replied to such a pronouncement by exclaiming, "Well, duh!"[42] But if this great tribulation occurs in the *middle* of human history, then it is greatly comforting to be told that nothing as bad as this will ever again afflict the world. Yet after the Holocaust, various attempted genocides, and the decimation produced by atomic bombs—all this just in the last seventy years—it is hard to imagine the destruction of Jerusalem qualifying as the fulfillment of Jesus's prediction of unprecedented tribulation, even though D. A. Carson observes that there was "never so high a percentage of a great city so thoroughly and painfully exterminated and enslaved" as in Jerusalem in AD 70.[43]

The problem is solved, however, if we understand Jesus to mean that this great tribulation beginning at AD 70 would in some way continue until his second coming. Then it makes sense for Matthew to add that the parousia and its accompanying cosmic signs would occur "immediately" after the tribulation.[44] One is reminded of cases of prophetic foreshortening in the Old Testament, where the New Testament would later, with easy hindsight, see both a near fulfillment in the time of the prophet and a more distant fulfillment in Jesus.[45] Here Christ, particularly in Matthew's version of the Olivet Discourse, is trying to help the disciples separate in their minds what they initially must have thought were inseparable—the total destruction of the temple and the end of the age (see Matt. 24:3).[46] To describe most of what we popularly call the church age as a time of great tribulation does not rule out

---

Eschatology and the Origin of the Atonement (Tübingen: Mohr Siebeck; Grand Rapids: Baker Academic, 2005).

42. D. A. Carson (*Matthew*, Expositor's Bible Commentary 8 [Grand Rapids: Zondervan, 1984], 501) remarks, "That Jesus in v. 21 promises that such 'great distress' is never to be equaled implies that it cannot refer to the Tribulation at the end of the age, for if what happens next is the Millennium or the new heaven and the new earth, it seems inane to say that such 'great distress' will not take place again."

43. Ibid.

44. W. D. Davies and Dale C. Allison Jr., *A Critical and Exegetical Commentary on the Gospel according to Saint Matthew* (Edinburgh: T&T Clark, 1997), 3:331.

45. See esp. the discussion of this phenomenon in Craig L. Blomberg, "Interpreting Old Testament Prophetic Literature in Matthew: Double Fulfillment," *Trinity Journal* 23 (2002): 17–33.

46. R. T. France, *The Gospel according to Matthew: An Introduction and Commentary* (Leicester, UK: Inter-Varsity; Grand Rapids: Eerdmans, 1985), 337. Cf. Craig S. Keener, *A Commentary on the Gospel of Matthew* (Grand Rapids: Eerdmans, 1999), 562.

other quite different features from characterizing this era as well. Many periods of church history have experienced great joy and sorrow simultaneously, great persecution and great growth of the church at the same time.[47] And to borrow a page from the dispensationalist's book for a moment by thinking of all world history as a series of eras of God's distinctive dealings with humanity, if Jesus is teaching that the church age, as opposed to the ages that preceded it *and* the millennium and eternal state to follow, is the age characterized by unprecedented tribulation, then we have a period of time that is *not* the last one under consideration, and it does make sense to rank its wickedness against the others. It also becomes clear that only a posttribulational rapture would make any sense to Jesus, since a pretribulational rapture would have had to occur before AD 70.

But we have one final reference to tribulation left, perhaps the most famous of all. Revelation 7:14 portrays the numberless white-robed multitude of people of every ethnicity praising God and Christ in heaven as "they who have come out of the great tribulation" and who "have washed their robes and made them white in the blood of the Lamb." Because Revelation 8 proceeds immediately to depict the trumpet judgments and because the trumpet judgments and the bowl judgments that follow together constitute what appears to be an unprecedented unleashing of God's wrath on earth, it is understandable why many interpreters view the period of time represented by these judgments as the "great tribulation" (some would include the earlier seal judgments as well). It is equally plain why at least some of these same interpreters would then understand the latter part of Revelation 7 as portraying the worldwide church of all people groups raptured before that tribulation unfolds or "tribulation saints"—people who come to faith only during the tribulation and thus did not have the chance to escape it when the church was raptured.[48]

The first of these two suppositions is probably true. Just as Jesus could employ Daniel's imagery and anticipate a fuller fulfillment than that which occurred at the time of the Maccabees, John, writing most likely in the middle of the final decade of the first century, can speak of *the* great tribulation and focus solely on the end of the period of suffering that Jesus had described.[49] Whether the second supposition is true depends mainly on the relationship

47. Recall Tertullian's famous epigram "The blood of the martyrs is the seed of the church" (*Apology* 1).

48. E.g., Robert L. Thomas, *Revelation 1–7* (Chicago: Moody, 1992), 486–87; 497n119; and John F. Walvoord, *The Revelation of Jesus Christ* (Chicago: Moody, 1966), 145–46, respectively.

49. Grant R. Osborne, *Revelation* (Grand Rapids: Baker Academic, 2002), 324–25; following Richard Bauckham, *The Climax of Prophecy: Studies on the Book of Revelation* (Edinburgh: T&T Clark, 1993), 226; and Aune, *Revelation 6–16*, 473–74.

evelation 7 between the 144,000 sealed from every tribe of Israel in verses 8 and the numberless multiethnic multitude in verses 9–17. The expression "they who have come out of the great tribulation" reads far more naturally as referring to people who had been in some place or had some experience that they are now said to have left. I do not normally say that I have come out of my house, for example, unless I have first been in it.[50]

A comparison of the two groups that make up Revelation 7, however, clarifies matters. Despite John's portrayal of the groups in about as stark a series of contrasts as possible, many commentators today recognize that both descriptions most probably refer to the same entity. In verses 1–8 John does not see in his vision 144,000 people sealed so that they are protected from God's wrath while living through the tribulation—12,000 from each of the twelve tribes of Israel. Instead he hears their number. This reminds us of what has already happened to John once before, as described in Revelation 5. There, just as in Revelation 7, an angelic elder describes to him in symbolic language a figure that, when John turns to look, appears strikingly different from the description just offered. The elder tells John to look and see "the Lion of the tribe of Judah, the Root of David," who has triumphed and is able to open the scroll containing the seven seals (5:5). But when John turns to look at this "Lion," he sees no king of beasts but a fragile sheep—"a Lamb, looking as if it had been slain" (5:6). The Lamb is Jesus, neither literal lion nor literal sheep but both substitutionary sacrifice and conquering king, despite the apparent oxymoron created by the juxtaposition of the two opposing images.[51]

The identical phenomenon recurs in Revelation 7. John *hears* the number of those God protects on earth during the tribulation, and it sounds very Jewish (the number of the twelve tribes times itself times a big round number), but when he looks to *see* the throng, he recognizes people from every ethnic group on earth. This is the church of Jesus Christ, the ultimate fulfillment of many

50. None of the thirty-five other uses of *erchomai* ("come") in Revelation is modified by a prepositional phrase beginning with *ek*, nor does this construction appear in the Johannine Epistles. In the Gospel of John, however, it appears eight times. Jesus comes out of heaven (John 3:31), as does a heavenly voice (12:28); people travel and thus come from Judea (4:54) and Tiberias (6:23); many come from the Jews (11:19, 45); it is believed that the Christ is not to be born in Galilee and hence not to come from there (7:41); and a woman comes from Samaria even while remaining in Samaria (4:7). In five instances, then, something comes out of a place it once was but no longer is; twice the *ek* functions partitively (some of the Jews), though perhaps suggesting coming out of Jerusalem to Bethany in the context of the resurrection of Lazarus; and in one instance a person comes from a place even though she has not left it. In no instances, however, do persons or things come out of a place that they have not previously been.

51. See, e.g., Donald Guthrie, *The Relevance of John's Apocalypse* (Exeter, UK: Paternoster; Grand Rapids: Eerdmans, 1987), 46–51; Richard Bauckham, *The Theology of the Book of Revelation* (Cambridge: Cambridge University Press, 1993), 73–76.

promises to Israel, symbolically depicted *as* Israel, though with an unparalleled list of twelve names, given the omission of Dan and the inclusion of one (but only one) of Joseph's two sons, along with Joseph himself. Whatever else this means, the church has not entirely replaced Israel.[52] Moreover, in reality, the church is a much larger and more diverse community than just believing Jews. Finally, since they have been protected by God's seal so that they were not harmed by his judgments (7:3), they must have lived through the tribulation before coming out of it.[53]

The New Testament's teaching on any topic is seldom exhausted simply by looking up each occurrence of one key word that summarizes that topic. We need to consider the verbal cognate to *thlipsis*—*thlibō* ("to press hard," "to crush," or, in the passive voice, "to experience trouble or difficulty")— along with verbal and nominal synonyms of "tribulation," such as "trial" (the *peira-* word group), "persecution" (the *diōk-* word group), "suffering" (the *pasch-* word group), and "distress" (the *stenochōr-* word group).[54] We also need to look at passages that appear to teach about our topic even if none of the key words that elsewhere trigger the concept appear in them. And since all parties in the debate admit that no text of Scripture speaks of both rapture and tribulation at the same time, we have to consider also texts that are believed to depict the rapture all by itself. Fortunately, there are only a handful of passages in these additional categories that require surveying here.

A perusal of the other terms for tribulation and related concepts confirms what we saw already in abundance with Paul's use of *thlipsis*. The New Testament writers uniformly expected suffering and hardship to be the common lot of believers throughout their earthly existence. Two additional illustrations suffice. First, in Matthew 7:14 Jesus warns his listeners that the road that leads to life is "narrow." This word is an adjectival participle in the Greek, the perfect passive form of the verb *thlibō*; the way is narrow because it squeezes one

52. For a detailed survey of interpretations of the list, see Richard Bauckham, "The List of the Tribes in Revelation 7 Again," *Journal for the Study of the New Testament* 42 (1991): 99–115. Cf. also Christopher R. Smith, "The Portrayal of the Church as the New Israel in the Names and Order of the Tribes in Revelation 7.5–8," *Journal for the Study of the New Testament* 39 (1990): 111–18.

53. Jürgen Roloff, *The Revelation of John: A Continental Commentary* (Minneapolis: Augsburg, 1993), 98.

54. *Greek-English Lexicon of the New Testament: Based on Semantic Domains*, ed. J. P. Louw and E. A. Nida, 2nd ed. (New York: United Bible Societies, 1989), 1:242–44, groups *thlipsis* with *ananke, asthenēs, baros, kakia, loimos, kopos, oknēros, ouai, stenochōria, talaipōria* and *-ōros, plēgē*, and *proskopē* to create the subdomain "Trouble, Hardship, Distress" under the larger semantic domain of "Trouble, Hardship, Relief, Favorable Circumstances."

with hardships and sorrows.[55] Second, in 2 Timothy 3:12 Paul declares flatly, "everyone who wants to live a godly life in Christ Jesus will be persecuted." Again, neither of these texts insists that this is all there is to the Christian life, but they do affirm one important way of characterizing it.[56] Should we then expect a God who so emphasizes our living through tribulation and trials in this life suddenly to exempt us from "the great tribulation"?

What, then, of the various proof texts most commonly cited on behalf of a pretribulational rapture? In the Gospels, Matthew 24:40–41, paralleled in Luke 17:34–35, prophesies that "two men will be in the field; one will be taken and the other left. Two women will be grinding with a hand mill; one will be taken and the other left." Proponents of a pretribulational rapture regularly appeal to this picture as an illustration of how believers will suddenly be taken away to heaven, leaving their unbelieving companions behind on earth. But Matthew's larger context suggests that this interpretation has it backward. The two immediately preceding verses (Matt. 24:38–39) predict that the time just before Christ's return will resemble the days before Noah's flood—with most people oblivious to the imminent catastrophe: "they knew nothing about what would happen until the flood came and *took* them all away." Although Matthew uses two different words for "take" with slightly different semantic ranges (*airō* and *paralambanō*), their use in back-to-back verses on eschatological judgment suggests that they appear here as synonyms. The "all" who were "taken away" in the flood were the wicked who were judged by it. The man in the field and the woman grinding at the mill who are "taken," then, must likewise be those taken away for *final* judgment, so that we have here a picture of part of the parousia, not a portrait of some secret rapture at an earlier date. In this context, *Christians* will be the ones left behind—on earth to enjoy the glory and grandeur of reigning with Christ during the millennium.[57]

John 14:3 is sometimes cited in defense of a pretribulational rapture ("If I go and prepare a place for you, I will come back and take you to be with me that you also may be where I am") because it parallels the concept of Jesus coming at least partway to earth, gathering his followers, and returning to heaven. But in this context, the place to which Christ is going is his "Father's house [where there] are many rooms" (14:2), a probable allusion to the temple.

---

55. Cf. A. H. McNeile, *The Gospel according to Matthew* (London and New York: Macmillan, 1915), 94. Cf. Hans D. Betz, *The Sermon on the Mount* (Minneapolis: Fortress, 1995), 526.

56. William D. Mounce (*Pastoral Epistles* [Nashville: Nelson, 2000], 560) observes that "v 12 hammers the final nail into the coffin of any aberrant gospel that preaches an abundant life devoid of persecutions."

57. Robert H. Gundry, *Matthew: A Commentary on His Handbook for a Mixed Church under Persecution*, rev. ed. (Grand Rapids: Eerdmans, 1994), 494; Robert H. Mounce, *Matthew* (Peabody, MA: Hendrickson, 1991; Carlisle, UK: Paternoster, 1995), 229.

Not that heaven (or, more correctly put, the new heavens and new earth) will have a literal temple but that, just as in Revelation 21–22, the new Jerusalem, shaped like the perfect cube that characterized the holy of holies (Rev. 21:16), with God's eternal presence dwelling there, will replace the need for a literal temple (21:22).[58] Jesus, however, will not take us there until after the millennium, so this verse proves irrelevant to the rapture debate.

In the Pauline Epistles, 1 and 2 Thessalonians take pride of place in this conversation. First Thessalonians 4:17 has already been mentioned—the sole text in Scripture referring to the "catching up" of believers to meet the Lord in the air. There the term *apantēsis* is used for the meeting with Christ, a term regularly used in Hellenistic Greek to refer to a welcoming party leaving a city or a house in order to go down the road to meet an honored guest, visiting dignitary, or triumphant military leader and form an escort party to accompany the person back to his home or town.[59] This is exactly how the term is used in its two other New Testament occurrences—when the wise bridesmaids meet the bridegroom and escort him back to his home for the continuation of the wedding party and the new couple's first night there (Matt. 25:6) and when believers from Rome travel south on the Appian Way to meet up with Paul and escort him back to the capital (Acts 28:15). Given all the other imperial language in Thessalonians that Paul applies to Christ—most notably *sōtēr* (Savior), *epiphaneia* (epiphany), *parousia* ([royal] presence or coming), and *euangelion* (good news, especially about peace and safety, precisely what 1 Thess. 5:3 heralds)—it would be amazing if Paul was not also thinking of an imperial *apantēsis* when he used that word—the large entourages that formed welcoming parties for the emperors as they traveled from one city to the next.[60] This imagery, then, virtually requires that the rapture be the catching up of believers from earth into the air to meet the Lord descending in the clouds

58. See esp. James McCaffrey, *The House with Many Rooms: The Temple Theme of Jn. 14, 2–3* (Rome: Pontifical Biblical Institute, 1988).

59. So John Chrysostom, *Homilies on 1 Thessalonians* 8. Cf. Robert H. Gundry, "A Brief Note on 'Hellenistic Formal Receptions and Paul's Use of ΑΠΑΝΤΗΣΙΣ,'" *Bulletin for Biblical Research* 6 (1996): 39–41; F. F. Bruce, *1 and 2 Thessalonians* (Waco: Word Books, 1982), 101–3; Gene L. Green, *The Letters to the Thessalonians* (Grand Rapids: Eerdmans; Leicester, UK: Apollos, 2002), 226–28; I. Howard Marshall, *1 and 2 Thessalonians* (London: Marshall, Morgan & Scott; Grand Rapids: Eerdmans, 1983), 141; John Stott, *The Gospel and the End of Time: The Message of 1 and 2 Thessalonians* (Downers Grove, IL: InterVarsity, 1991), 104; Michael W. Holmes, *1 and 2 Thessalonians* (Grand Rapids: Zondervan, 1998), 151; D. Michael Martin, *1, 2 Thessalonians* (Nashville: Broadman & Holman, 1995), 155.

60. Ben Witherington III, *1 and 2 Thessalonians: A Socio-rhetorical Commentary* (Grand Rapids: Eerdmans, 2006), 138–41; following esp. Karl P. Donfried, "The Imperial Cults and Political Conflict in 1 Thessalonians," in *Paul and Empire*, ed. Richard A. Horsley (Harrisburg, PA: Trinity, 1997), 215–23.

and to escort him *back to earth* in triumph—imagery that is consistent only with a posttribulational rapture.

The trumpet call of God in 1 Thessalonians 4:16 calls to mind similar imagery in 1 Corinthians 15:52. The two trumpets need not be the same, but if they are, then we have further support for posttribulationism, since the Corinthian trumpet is called the "last" one and coincides with the final, general resurrection (cf. 1 Cor. 15:53–57).[61] It is sometimes argued that 1 Thessalonians 5:2, echoing Jesus's little parable of Matthew 24:43 and parallel, cannot be harmonized with this view. In these passages Christ comes "like a thief in the night," catching people by surprise, whereas 2 Thessalonians proceeds to explain that certain signs must precede and portend the parousia. Surely 1 Thessalonians must thus be talking about a secret rapture. But all one has to do is read on to 1 Thessalonians 5:4 to see that only those who pay no heed to Paul's teaching need be surprised: "you, brothers and sisters, are not in darkness so that this day should surprise you like a thief."[62]

Second Thessalonians reinforces this perspective. We need not delve here into the disputed nature of the particular signs that Paul insists must come first (2 Thess. 2:3–12), namely, who or what is the restrainer that is currently keeping the man of lawlessness from appearing or what his subsequently being revealed and setting himself up in God's temple entails.[63] There is virtually no lexical support for equating the *apostasia* of 2:3 with the rapture. Metaphorically, apostasy means a falling away, not a catching up, and in this context the New International Version is almost certainly correct to render it as "rebellion."[64] What is crucial to the present discussion is that Paul is announcing these coming events to reassure the Thessalonians that they have not missed the parousia (2:2), as some were falsely claiming, perhaps believing that Christ's

---

61. Cf. Abraham J. Malherbe, *The Letters to the Thessalonians* (New York and London: Doubleday, 2000), 274–75.

62. G. K. Beale (*1–2 Thessalonians* [Downers Grove, IL: InterVarsity, 2003], 137) provides a helpful chart of the numerous parallels between Matt. 24 and 1 Thess. 4:16–5:7, a majority of them in the same sequence, to demonstrate that 1 Thess. 4:15–17 and 5:1–11 most likely refer to "the same end-time scenario." See David Wenham, "Paul and the Synoptic Apocalypse," in *Gospel Perspectives: Studies of History and Tradition in the Four Gospels*, ed. R. T. France and David Wenham (Sheffield: JSOT Press, 1981), 2:245–75.

63. For the various options, see Colin Nicoll, "Michael, the Restrainer Removed (2 Thess. 2:6–7)," *Journal of Theological Studies* 51 (2000): 27–53. Cf. Paul Metzger, *Katechon: II Thess 2,1–12 im Horizont apokalyptischen Denkens* (Berlin: de Gruyter, 2005), 1–47.

64. Bob Gundry, *First the Antichrist* (Grand Rapids: Baker Academic, 1997), 21. Bauer, Danker, Arndt, and Gingrich, *Greek-English Lexicon*, 120, s.v. *apostasia*, lists as definitions only "defiance of established system or authority, *rebellion, abandonment, breach of faith*." *New International Dictionary of New Testament Theology*, 1:606, s.v. *apostasia*, offers "rebellion, abandonment, state of apostasy, defection."

second coming was entirely invisible and spiritual in some fashion. Had Paul believed in, and previously taught the Thessalonians about, a pretribulational rapture, all he would have had to do was remind them that they had not yet been caught up to meet the Lord in the air. And if they somehow feared that not a single member of their fledgling church was a true Christian, he could have simply stressed that no one anywhere had yet been raptured.[65]

Revelation 3:10 is often played as the final trump card to demonstrate that believers will ultimately be exempt from the great tribulation. Could any text be clearer than Christ's promise to the church in Philadelphia ("Since you have kept my command to endure patiently, I will also keep you from the hour of trial that is going to come upon the whole world to test those who live on the earth")? In fact, quite a few texts are much clearer. The Greek verb for "keep" in this verse is *tēreō*; the preposition for "from" is *ek*. The only other passage in the New Testament that combines these two terms appears in another Johannine composition, in John 17:15. There, the night before his crucifixion, Jesus clarifies his petition to his heavenly Father: "My prayer is not that you take them out of the world but that you protect them from the evil one." This text could hardly be more explicit in what it requests: protection from something harmful while Jesus's disciples remain on earth. Revelation 3:10, if it is referring to the great tribulation, thus more likely supports posttribulationism than pretribulationism.[66]

But are we perhaps overinterpreting this verse by assuming that it is teaching about the distant end in the first place? Revelation 3:10 appears in the midst of the letters to the seven churches, the two chapters of the entire book that are clearly anchored in the first-century circumstances of the Christian congregations to which they are addressed. The rest of John's encouragement and warnings to the various churches are seldom if ever taken as referring to the time of the great tribulation; it would be surprising if this verse alone broke the pattern. The trial that is about to come on the whole world may well just refer to the increasingly empirewide persecution and hostility against Christians begun under Domitian in the mid-90s and intensified under various later emperors.[67] The word translated "whole world" (*oikoumenē*) was often applied

65. Yet "our being gathered to him" in 2 Thess. 2:1 suggests the same event as that described in 1 Thess. 4:17. Green (*Thessalonians*, 301n4) concludes that "the present verse brings to grief the popular notion that the rapture of the church will somehow take place before the tribulation."

66. Robert H. Mounce, *The Book of Revelation*, rev. ed. (Grand Rapids: Eerdmans, 1998), 103; Ian Boxall, *The Revelation of Saint John* (London: Continuum; Peabody, MA: Hendrickson, 2006), 73.

67. Cf. David E. Aune, *Revelation 1–5* (Dallas: Word Books, 1997), 240; Keener, *Revelation*, 154.

in Roman circles, with a bit of pompous hyperbole, to the empire—the only part of the world that really counted, as we might put it today—and the word for "earth" (*gē*) can just as easily be translated "land."[68] But this question can be left open because nothing in the larger argument here hinges on it.

Other texts and issues in Revelation may be dispensed with more rapidly. The reason the word "church" does not appear after Revelation 3 has nothing to do with the timing of the rapture. The only way in which Revelation 1–3 uses the word "church" is in reference to one of the seven local churches to which this book is addressed. Since the rest of the document turns to visions of heaven and of earth's more distant destiny, the churches do not reappear.[69] But as noted already, *believers*—God's servants on earth protected from his wrath during the outpouring of the twenty-one judgments that form the backbone of this document—reemerge throughout the book. Revelation 4:1 hardly refers to a rapture of the church; it is only John who is caught up to heaven to see things that he can then report to the rest of his fellow Christians who still remain on earth.[70] One can understand why the resurrection and ascension of the two witnesses in 11:11–12 could be seen as supporting a midtribulational rapture. But if chapter 12 begins with a flashback to the *first* coming of Christ, then chapter 11 may well bring us up to the threshold of the *end* of the tribulation and thus, in fact, support a posttribulational rapture.[71] As for a prewrath rapture, this is unnecessary once opponents of posttribulationism recognize what they often do not: that no competent posttribulationist argues for God's people having to experience *his* wrath, for they are protected from the plagues and judgments God unleashes, just not from satanic attack or state-endorsed persecution.[72] Indeed, a number of the trumpet and bowl judgments—hail, boils, blood, darkness—closely parallel the plagues God inflicted on the Egyptians and Pharaoh. And it is significant that the Israelites were never removed from the land during the plagues, just protected from them.

---

68. As the second of its four main definitions of *oikoumenē*, Bauer, Danker, Arndt, and Gingrich, *Greek-English Lexicon*, lists, "the world as administrative unit, *the Roman Empire*" (699). As the third of six options for *gē*, it supplies, "portions or regions of the earth, *region, country*" (196).

69. Gundry (*First the Antichrist*, 83–84) observes that the word "church" also appears nowhere in the heavenly scenes in Rev. 4–22. If its absence from the earthly scenes of these chapters means the church's absence from earth, then, by the same logic, it should be absent from heaven as well.

70. George E. Ladd, *A Commentary on the Revelation of John* (Grand Rapids: Eerdmans, 1972), 71–72.

71. Ben Witherington III, *Revelation* (Cambridge: Cambridge University Press, 2003), 159–60.

72. Cf., e.g., Murphy, *Fallen Is Babylon*, 260.

The upshot of our survey, then, is that without exception every relevant Scripture supports posttribulationism over pretribulationism. A key objection, however, must be addressed. How could Christians throughout the centuries have believed in the doctrine of the imminence of Christ's return—that he could come back at any moment—unless pretribulationism (or at least midtribulationism) were true? After all, so the argument goes, as long as the final signs of the parousia have not yet occurred—the appearance of the antichrist and the worst of the tribulation—Christ cannot come back publicly at any time. The return of Christ that has always been imminent must therefore be a separate, secret return and thus the rapture of the church.

Historically, posttribulationists have offered at least three main replies. First, because Revelation provides no indication of the speed with which the final events of the tribulation will unfold, perhaps they will occur so quickly that they are seen as virtually part and parcel of the return of Christ itself and not separate events[73] that allow believers the leisure time, for instance, to write books warning others about the impending parousia. This view proves particularly appealing if one does not look for a literal rebuilt temple in Jerusalem.[74] Second, the judgments depicted in Revelation during the tribulation period may all be sufficiently symbolic so as to prevent anyone from knowing how far into the tribulation we might already be at any period of human history. Satan has had his potential antichrists in virtually every generation.[75] For example, Revelation 6:8 is often misread to say that one-fourth of the inhabitants of the earth would be killed, when it in fact says that the power to kill by sword, famine, or plague was given to the fourth horseman over (or within) one-fourth of the earth, however many or few the number of actual individuals killed.[76] Or again, in 9:15, where the text does refer to the death of one-third of humanity, it is crucial to observe that the attackers are symbolized by locusts from the home of demons—the abyss. This may well refer to

73. Cf. Beale, *1–2 Thessalonians*, 204–5n.

74. The biggest obstacle to rejecting a literal "third" temple is the exquisite and seemingly superfluous detail of Ezek. 40–48 if all this is fulfilled fully in the new-Jerusalem community of the redeemed in the new heavens and earth. But with Ezek. 38–39 supplying the background for the imagery of the rebellion of Gog and Magog, paralleled at the *end* of the millennium in Rev. 20, it is hard to see how Ezek. 40–48 could be referring to anything before, rather than after, the end of the millennium.

75. Keener (*Revelation*, 342–43) perceptively observes that because Satan is not omniscient and no one but God himself knows the time of Christ's return, the devil must have people ready in every age to play the role of the antichrist if necessary.

76. Ladd, *Revelation*, 101. Cf. J. Ramsey Michaels, *Revelation* (Downers Grove IL: InterVarsity, 1997), 103–4.

demonic and therefore spiritual warfare, not literal human warfare.[77] And the percentage of non-Christians in the world today, though at an all-time low, still remains more than two-thirds, not just one-third of humanity.[78] Indeed, it is interesting to see the recurring use of the fraction one-third throughout the trumpet judgments to indicate how much of the earth is affected by various plagues. Yet today we speak of the *two*-thirds world as experiencing terrible suffering. Little wonder that most indigenous Christians in these portions of the globe, unless brought to faith by Western dispensational missionaries or their legacies, usually find the notion of a pretribulational rapture offensive and counterproductive to social action and justice for the oppressed now in this world.[79] If God is so concerned to protect his people from awful, prolonged suffering, why has he not done anything to alleviate the suffering, starvation, and butchery of hundreds of millions of Christians in the two-thirds world that has already occurred?[80]

The third, final, and most convincing reply to the question about imminence distinguishes it from immediacy. The book of Revelation speaks of the parousia as something that will happen *tachu*, both soon and/or, once it begins to unfold, quickly (Rev. 2:16; 3:11; 22:7, 12, 20).[81] But no text of Scripture ever claims that it must be possible for the parousia to occur at any given second, minute, hour, day (or any other precise measurement of time) within some fixed interval from some earlier sign.[82] Indeed, this point was one often emphasized

77. Aune, *Revelation 6–16*, 527. Cf. Stephen S. Smalley, *The Revelation to John: A Commentary on the Greek Text of the Apocalypse* (London: SPCK; Downers Grove, IL: InterVarsity, 2005), 240.

78. For full details, see throughout David B. Barrett, George T. Kurian, and Todd M. Johnson, *World Christian Encyclopedia: A Comparative Survey of Churches and Religions in the Modern World*, rev. ed. (Oxford and New York: Oxford University Press, 2001).

79. See, e.g., throughout Pablo Richard, *Apocalypse: A People's Commentary on the Book of Revelation* (Maryknoll, NY: Orbis Books, 1995). Cf. Allan A. Boesak, *Comfort and Protest: Reflections on the Apocalypse of John of Patmos* (Philadelphia: Westminster, 1987).

80. Cf. the comments in Witherington, *Mark*, 357.

81. Both of these concepts find Old Testament conceptual parallels but reach their apogee in Christianity and early Judaism. The latter clearly allows for an interval between prophecy and fulfillment, not a literal, "any moment" imminence. See Moshe Weinfeld, "Expectations of the Divine Kingdom in Biblical and Postbiblical Literature," in *Eschatology in the Bible and in Jewish and Christian Tradition*, ed. Henning G. Reventlow (Sheffield: Sheffield Academic, 1997), 218–32.

82. Similarly, Douglas J. Moo, "The Case for the Posttribulation Rapture Position," in Archer et al., *Three Views on the Rapture*, 207–11. It is interesting to see how Wayne A. Brindle ("Biblical Evidence for the Imminence of the Rapture," *Bibliotheca Sacra* 158 [2001]: 138–51) tries to find such texts. His four criteria for passages that teach imminence are that they speak of Christ's return (1) at any moment, (2) as "near" without stating any signs that must first intervene, (3) as giving believers encouragement with no indication that they will suffer tribulation, and (4) as giving hope with no reference to the judgment of unbelievers. But Brindle never supplies an

in the late nineteenth and early twentieth centuries, when dispensationalists were not as monolithically pretribulational as they became after about 1910.[83] But in more recent debates, the point has often disappeared from view.

One last objection comes from a quite different direction. If posttribulationism is the dominant view in church history across all the millennial perspectives and if the errors of pretribulationism could emerge only within premillennialism, why not reconsider more seriously the historically dominant millennial perspective, namely, amillennialism? After all, two very pointed challenges to premillennialism have often kept Christians from accepting it, regardless of the most natural narrative flow of Revelation 19 and 20, discussed earlier. First, is not a return to earth to live in a wonderful but still imperfect world a huge anticlimax for those who have already died and gone to heaven? Second, is not the notion of people with glorified, resurrected bodies mixing together with the unbelievers still alive at the parousia, still in their old sin-prone bodies, more the stuff of science fiction than of anything credible?

The first of these questions reflects a faulty premise that afflicts many premillennialists as well—the notion that dying and going to heaven are the best that it will ever be for us. As Tom Wright puts it so memorably and repeatedly in his huge and hugely persuasive book on every question one could ever want to ask about the resurrection, the Christian hope is not about life after death; it is about life *after* life after death.[84] It is about embodied existence for all eternity, a crucial part of our destiny yet missing from the intermediate state between our death and resurrection. Even to live in a slightly less than perfect millennial kingdom *in our resurrection bodies* is an advance on a sinless but disembodied state in heaven.

As for people with resurrected bodies mingling with still mortal, sinful humans, if we believe the gospel message about Jesus, it has already happened once—when the resurrected Jesus mingled with his followers for forty days. What is more, Matthew 27:51–53, raising more questions than it answers, discloses that some other select group of saints was resurrected immediately after Jesus[85] and appeared to many in and around Jerusalem. Whether or not it suits our sensibilities about the way God should do things, it has already occurred, so it makes good sense to believe it could occur again.

---

unambiguous example of the first criterion, and the other three are all arguments from silence, susceptible to equally or more compelling alternative interpretations.

83. Richard R. Reiter, "A History of the Development of the Rapture Positions," in Archer et al., *Three Views on the Rapture*, 11–44.

84. N. T. Wright, *The Resurrection of the Son of God* (London: SPCK; Minneapolis: Fortress, 2003), e.g., 31.

85. See John W. Wenham, "When Were the Saints Raised? A Note on the Punctuation of Matthew xxvii.51–3," *Journal of Theological Studies* 32 (1981): 150–52.

Conclusion

Eugene Peterson has summarized what he calls "one of the unintended and un-happy consequences" of Revelation in about the most pointed words possible:

> It has inflamed the imaginations of the biblically illiterate into consuming end-time fantasies, distracting them from the daily valor of dogged obedience, sacrificial love, and alert endurance. This is exactly what St. John did not intend, as even a cursory reading of his Revelation makes evident. When people are ignorant of the imagery of prophets and gospels, and untutored in the metaphorical language of war in the story of salvation, they are easy prey for entertaining predictions of an end-time holocaust at Mount Megiddo in Israel, conjured up from newspaper clippings on international politics. Jesus told us quite clearly that the people who make these breathless and sensationalist predictions are themselves the false Christs and false prophets that they are pretending to warn us against (Matt. 24:23–26).[86]

Although we might think Peterson's rhetoric a bit hyperbolic, the question of whether we in North America in the early twenty-first century are even remotely prepared for the possibility that we might live through the tribulation is a haunting one. We marvel and lament the tribal genocide that recurs in Africa, but if we were reduced to the levels of poverty and desperation to which many Africans have been, would our tribalisms—in Christian circles as well as in others—prove any less pronounced, especially in a society with an almost pathological aversion to gun control? A rare, popular prophecy paperback from the late 1970s that supported posttribulationism read like a handbook for survivalists, including guidelines for stockpiling food for oneself and one's family and guns to keep one's less-prepared neighbors from storming one's property and stealing one's goods.[87]

   Classic or historic premillennialism (i.e., posttribulational premillennialism) does best justice *both* to the awful suffering that God's people have already had to endure through the ages, by not offering them potentially unrealistic hopes about escaping the worst, *and* to the vindication of God's intentions for this earth and this cosmos (not just a new heavens and earth), which he created perfectly good for humanity's sanctified enjoyment.[88] And God's purposes

86. Eugene H. Peterson, *Reversed Thunder: The Revelation of John and the Praying Imagination* (San Francisco: HarperSanFrancisco, 1988), 165.
87. James M. McKeever, *Christians Will Go through the Tribulation: And How to Prepare for It* (Rock Rapids, IA: Alpha Omega, 1978).
88. Cf. Heikki Räisänen, "Towards an Alternative to New Testament Theology: 'Individual Eschatology' as an Example," in *The Nature of New Testament Theology*, ed. Christopher Rowland and Christopher Tuckett (Oxford and Malden, MA: Blackwell, 2006), 176.

are never ultimately thwarted. The suffering will not prove pointless, for it will lead to God many who may not come any other way than by seeing that Christians can suffer and even die differently than all other people—a form of evangelism already well documented in the history of Christian missions.[89] The redemption of this earth alone does full justice to the doctrine of the incarnation, which John in his Gospel likewise stresses. Only posttribulational premillennialism

> da suficiente peso a la gracia de Dios que *opera en la tierra*, es decir a la victoria de Jesucristo gracias a su *encarnación*. Como puede un autor como Juan postergar el triunfo visible de Jesús hasta un momento posthistórico, en el que la presente creación habrá desaparecido? Dónde está la eficacia de la obra "consumada" por aquel "Verbo hecho carne" que vino a "echar su tabernáculo entre la humanidad"? . . . Para Juan de Patmos, el Dios Creador y Redentor tiene un plan no solo para individuos humanos aislados, sino para su creación entera. Este plan, realizado paulatinamente en la historia, tiene que buscar su vindicación tambien en la historia.[90]

This vision, most consistent with inaugurated eschatology more generally, likewise allows God the greatest freedom to create as much good and allow as much evil as he may choose to on this earth, without dictating to God where his limits are. In a secular culture that retains a fascination with apocalyptic that its conscious worldviews cannot justify, this is a vision worth articulating and commending widely not just among Christians but in every part of the world.[91] It is well past time to leave "Left Behind" behind.

89. Cf. Keener, *Revelation*, 327.

90. "gives sufficient weight to the grace of God that *operates on earth*, that is to say, toward the victory of Jesus Christ thanks to his *incarnation*. How can an author such as John defer the visible triumph of Jesus to a time after history, in which the present creation will have disappeared? Where is the efficacy of the 'completed' work by that 'Word made flesh' who came to 'pitch his tent among humanity'? . . . For John of Patmos, the Creator and Redeemer God has a plan not just for isolated human individuals but also for his entire creation. This plan, realized slowly in history, has to find its vindication also in history" (Ricardo Foulkes, *El Apocalipsis de San Juan: Una lectura desde América Latina* [Buenos Aires: Nueva Creación; Grand Rapids: Eerdmans, 1989], 214; translation mine).

91. Cf. esp. L. Boeve, "God Interrupts History: Apocalypticism as an Indispensable Theological Conceptual Strategy," *Louvain Studies* 26 (2001): 195–216.

5

The Theological Method
of Premillennialism

DON J. PAYNE

As we progress through life, it is not uncommon to stop and ponder where we are with respect to our relationships, our vocations, our health, and other domains of significance to us. This can often lead to reflection on the paths we took, whether these paths were intentional, by default, forced on us, or some combination of these. As with other areas of life, when it comes to our systems of belief, the path we took to these beliefs is vital to the way these beliefs are shaped and expressed. A destination is always the result of the path taken; we cannot fully understand where we are in life, including our theology, without understanding at least a bit of how and why we arrived there. Though understanding the paths toward a particular belief does not necessarily invalidate that belief, it can be healthy for diagnosis, correction, and maturity.

The path toward a theological belief, as well as the way in which that theology operates and is sustained, is often referred to as "theological method." In addition to commitment to biblical inspiration and authority, every theology and theologian has a method, whether this method functions at a level of self-awareness or more tacitly. A theological method is the way in which a theology was developed and operates. Understanding theological method allows adherents of a theology to better recognize that system's limitations and strengths within the life of faith. This, after all, is a central function of belief systems. If they do not help us live well before God, with others, and in God's world, we should question either their intrinsic validity or the health of our engagement with them. If we know how and why a belief works the way it does, we can more easily identify the negotiable and the essential elements in that system.

The purpose of this chapter is to move toward a better understanding of the well-known and widespread eschatological system known as premillennialism by exploring its theological method or, to borrow one of T. F. Torrance's favorite phrases, its "inner logic."[1] This exploration will reveal some of the reasons premillennialism has maintained a considerable following even in the shadow of views that were sometimes more widely held. Additionally, we will gain a diagnostic lens through which to identify and draw from the wisdom of premillennialism. By using premillennialism as a case study in theological method, we can refine our skills for interacting with other areas of theology as well.

My general thesis is that premillennialism depends upon a distinct theological method that involves factors and influences beyond its overt commitment to certain hermeneutical and exegetical procedures. These factors and influences are vital to premillennialism even if they are unrecognized, unstated, or understated by adherents (including this author). More specifically, I will first attempt to define what is meant by the phrase "theological method." Second, I will survey some features of the theological method that drives premillennialism. Third, I will suggest a few ways in which premillennialists can learn from criticisms of this doctrine while maintaining their core values.

Theological Method

What does the phrase "theological method" mean? J. I. Packer uses the phrase to describe both the procedures by which theology is done and the justification for those procedures.[2] He identifies two basic types of theological method. One gives priority to the Bible as God's Word, providing authoritative guidance as it is progressively understood through research and the illumination of the Spirit. The other type gives priority to the institutional church as the authoritative interpreter of Scripture.[3] These are certainly two models of

---

1. T. F. Torrance, *God and Rationality* (London: Oxford University Press, 1971), 202–3.
2. J. I. Packer, "Method, Theological," in *New Dictionary of Theology*, ed. S. B. Ferguson, D. F. Wright, and J. I. Packer (Leicester, UK: Inter-Varsity, 1988), 424–25.
3. Ibid., 425.

theological method, but a good bit more is entailed as we try to discern how particular doctrines or theological systems are developed.

"Theological method" refers to the logic and process by which a system of thought is developed and sustained. The expression does not have as much name recognition within more conservative sectors of evangelicalism, possibly due to the high value we place on the written Word of God as inspired, infallible, inerrant, authoritative (the list of adjectives and qualifiers could go on), and perspicuous. That is to say, God gave Scripture so as to be read and understood by all, not just by those with special knowledge or some secret decoder rings. So discussions about method may seem irrelevant or irreverent to some. Is not a commitment to the authority of Scripture and to a straightforward reading of it all the method we need?

At its best, the history of evangelical approaches to Scripture is marked by an insistence on taking the text at face value, letting it speak for itself (exegesis) rather than reading into it (eisegesis). Premillennialists could easily view contemporary discussions about theological method as merely a diversion from the simple hermeneutical commitments and procedures on which *sola scriptura* is based. Charles Ryrie, though equating true premillennialism with its dispensational version, anchors premillennialism in the doctrine of verbal inspiration and the commitment to let the straightforward meaning of the text carry the day theologically.[4] Thus premillennialists have generally believed that these interpretive principles for reading Scripture are both necessary and sufficient conditions for comprehending God's message. Ryrie and others have insisted that we attend to the grammatical, historical, and contextual dimensions of the text; that we allow Scripture to interpret Scripture; that we consider the literary genre of a particular book or passage; that we opt for the most obvious meaning of a text; and that we make a clear distinction between interpretation and application when we engage Scripture. Granted that supporting disciplines such as textual criticism and literary criticism are sometimes necessary in order to follow these principles, it has often been suggested that when these principles are followed, especially in regard to eschatology, our exegesis will most naturally lead us to a premillennial understanding of God's work throughout human history.[5]

In an earlier day, an interesting feature of premillennialism's theological method was the role it sometimes played as a litmus test for the integrity of a

4. Charles C. Ryrie, *The Basis of the Premillennial Faith* (Neptune, NJ: Loizeaux Brothers, 1953), 35.

5. Paul L. Tan, *The Interpretation of Prophecy* (Winona Lake, IN: Assurance, 1974), 26, 29–39. This is also clearly assumed in J. Dwight Pentecost, *Things to Come: A Study in Biblical Eschatology* (Grand Rapids: Zondervan, 1958).

theological system. Timothy P. Weber quotes the famous William Bell Riley's claim in 1913 that premillennialism is "the sufficient if not solitary antidote to the present apostasy."[6] Weber goes on to observe, "To arrive at a premillennialism position, one had to correctly and literally interpret the Bible, thus ensuring that one grasped the other essential doctrines of the faith as well."[7] Although it would not be accurate to suggest that all premillennialists see this doctrine in such a telling theological role, the amount of weight that some earlier adherents asked premillennialism to bear suggests a distinct methodological commitment. The commitment seems to have derived not so much from a particular interest in eschatology as from a particular set of assumptions: (1) faithfulness to God depends on properly understanding and following the teachings of Scripture, (2) properly understanding and following the teachings of Scripture depend on a particular set of hermeneutical commitments, and (3) these hermeneutical commitments are reflected most clearly and directly in eschatology.

Not all premillennialists, certainly in the present day, would identify with such strict and exclusive claims. Yet these hermeneutical and exegetical claims are the methodological history that still shapes the identity of premillennialism to a considerable extent. Rival eschatologies were assessed and rejected on the basis of these canons of interpretation. Nonpremillennial eschatologies were themselves seen as evidence of a deficient commitment or approach to Scripture. Still, many other premillennialists who have wrestled with other eschatological systems come away convinced that those other systems take the text just as seriously and are just as committed to letting it speak for itself. Apparently, something else important is taking place underneath our common commitments to Scripture, our exegetical methods, and our stated hermeneutical principles. That is where theological method enters the picture. This is not to suggest that theological method is "the theory behind everything," to borrow a popular phrase. Still, it does help us recognize otherwise hidden factors in the way we interpret as we do.

Albert Outler, a Methodist theologian who identifies what he calls the Wesleyan quadrilateral, presents one of the better-known frameworks for theological method. The quadrilateral is composed of four components that he observes in John Wesley's approach to biblical interpretation: Scripture, tradition, reason, and experience.[8] According to Outler, Wesley understood

6. William B. Riley, *The Evolution of the Kingdom* (New York: Charles C. Cook, 1913), 5; cited in Timothy P. Weber, *Living in the Shadow of the Second Coming: American Premillennialism, 1875–1982* (Chicago: University of Chicago Press, 1987), 29.

7. Weber, *Living in the Shadow*, 29.

8. Albert C. Outler, ed., *The Works of John Wesley*, bicentennial ed., 24 vols. (Nashville: Abingdon, 1984), 1:55–66.

theology as the product of those four sources working in that order, each subservient to the greater authority of the factors preceding it. For Wesley, Scripture was primary.

Even outside the Wesleyan theological tradition, these four sources are often recognized as playing an important role in the construction of theology. Vast differences are found, however, regarding which component carries the greatest weight and, even among those who would agree that first place goes to Scripture, regarding the relative pecking order of the other three and the particular manner in which all four relate to each other in the formation of theology. When we examine the way or ways in which we relate these four factors in developing theological beliefs, we sometimes discover that what we do in practice is not precisely aligned with what we think we are doing. Among scholars, discussions of theological method can encompass a dizzying array of issues—epistemology, the historical development of theology, cultural and anthropological analysis, and on and on. Surely, Qoheleth must have had the subject of theological method in mind when he claimed that "of making many books there is no end" (Eccles. 12:12).

To return to our primary focus, we must ask the following questions: Is there a stated theological method entailed in premillennialism? What seems to be the functional theological method that produced premillennialism? To what extent, if at all, are there differences between premillennialism's stated and functional theological methods? Of what significance are any differences in how we understand and how we might embrace premillennialism both today and in the future?

Theological Method in Premillennialism

Scripture

It is difficult to find a stated theological method in premillennialism beyond its assumption of biblical authority (generally taken to imply inerrancy or infallibility) and its claim to a straightforward and objective reading of Scripture. This is articulated by Charles Ryrie, who cites numerous ante-Nicene church fathers and other sources to demonstrate that they understood Scripture to teach a literal, future, one-thousand-year millennium.[9] Ryrie recognizes that, later on, other factors began to alter this eschatological position. Specifically, he points out that premillennialism began to fade from theological dominance

9. Ryrie, *Premillennial Faith*, 19–23.

when Constantine declared Christianity to be the official religion of the Roman Empire. Ryrie then makes the following claim:

> Immediately the Church found herself confronted by new conditions. No longer poor but now overburdened with wealth and worldly honors, she saw that to maintain the doctrine of pilgrimage and separation and to hope for a coming King and an earthly kingdom would be extremely displeasing to Constantine. Thus patronage of the Church by the world and the resulting prosperity brought the great loss to the Church of the hope of the soon Coming of her Lord.
>
> Hitherto the Scriptures had supported the Church in her separation from the world, but since that course had been changed, the interpretation of the Scriptures also had to be changed in order to justify her position. Consequently, the rise of the Alexandrian school was a major factor in the rejection of chiliastic beliefs. Origen, the theologian of this school, openly attacked chiliasm and introduced the allegorical method of interpretation by which he interpreted spiritually and not literally the passages of Scripture which announced the millennium.[10]

Ryrie goes on to argue that a remnant of theologians and church movements maintained belief in a premillennial system of eschatology throughout the medieval period and the Reformation, although it was obscured by various theological, cultural, and political forces that diminished the type of hermeneutics that would naturally lead to premillennial belief. Initially, Ryrie's claim could indicate that when factors other than a supposedly straightforward reading of Scripture enter the process, theological conclusions are necessarily skewed and that nothing more is involved in the theological method of premillennialism than the exegetical commitments previously mentioned.

The return to a more literal hermeneutic and the consequent popularity of premillennialism can be partially attributed to the battles over the integrity of Scripture that were waged in the late nineteenth and early twentieth centuries. Premillennialism was prominent within fundamentalist circles that were more grassroots in nature, whereas fundamentalists in more established institutional and academic circles (e.g., B. B. Warfield and the Old Princeton theologians) maintained alternative eschatological schemas. It must be noted, however, that the return of premillennialism goes back even further than the battle between modernism and fundamentalism.

Ryrie is a decidedly dispensational premillennialist, and he offers his evidence for premillennialism in much the same way that he later argues for the dispensational version of the doctrine. Historically, the return of premillen-

10. Ibid., 23–24.

nialism in about the last two hundred years did seem to go hand in hand with dispensationalism. Yet,

> although dispensationalism has remained the dominant eschatological viewpoint among the movement as a whole, its unchallenged monopoly on the allegiance of evangelicalism began to wane during the second half of the twentieth century. This development was especially evident within evangelical academic circles. Beginning in the 1950s several influential scholars came to reject the central tenets of the reigning eschatology, claiming they were contrary to sound biblical teaching and out of step with the historic position of the church. . . . To their delight, they discovered that a tradition of nondispensational premillennialism had been present in the church since at least the patristic era.[11]

Adherents of historic premillennialism began to see in Scripture a blurring of the clear distinction—which lay at the heart of the dispensational version—between Israel and the church. George Ladd's well-known emphasis on the present/future nature of God's kingdom expresses this type of premillennial position.[12] The key point here is that both dispensational and nondispensational versions of premillennialism claim a similar hermeneutic and reflect a common heritage in pre-Constantinian Christianity. Despite the claim that premillennialism is upheld by a particular hermeneutic that is unaffected by extrabiblical factors, the differing versions of premillennialism suggest that other factors are indeed operative within premillennialism, even if they are less overt.

Despite the differences between dispensational and nondispensational premillennialism and the intense concern of their respective adherents that they not be confused, I shall treat them as examples of a similar (though not identical) theological method. One methodological distinction not to be overlooked (which Grenz is careful to emphasize) is the theological weight assigned by historic premillennialism to the New Testament as the interpretive lens for the Old Testament, and vice-versa for dispensational premillennialism.[13] This is one example of theological method, that is, the interpretive roles we assign to some doctrines or sections of Scripture in relation to other doctrines or sections and our reasons for making these decisions. It can be quite difficult to defend the claim that our choice of one part of Scripture as definitive for other parts has no other basis than the text itself. Other factors are always

11. Stanley J. Grenz, *The Millennial Maze: Sorting Out Evangelical Options* (Downers Grove, IL: InterVarsity, 1992), 127–28.

12. George E. Ladd, *A Theology of the New Testament* (Grand Rapids: Eerdmans, 1974), 105–19.

13. Grenz, *Millennial Maze,* 137.

and unavoidably at play. As hermeneutical specialists frequently point out, all interpretation is "located" in, and affected by, the multifaceted context of the interpreter. As Kevin J. Vanhoozer has contended, this does not imply that biblical interpretation is a merely human enterprise or that the text is nothing more than whatever a given reader decides. The text does indeed have meaning and significance for our lives even though that meaning and significance are known through the relativities of the human interpretive act.[14] To admit this is merely to realize that inspired Scripture—God's truth—is embedded in, and communicated through, an entirely human medium. Packer helpfully insists that this need not lead to notions of biblical fallibility any more than the full humanity of Christ implies his sinfulness.[15]

The role of culture and history in methodological questions is beyond the scope of this chapter but is worth noting, in part because it suggests that exegesis alone simply cannot supply all that is needed to construct a theological system. Contrary to popular opinion (at least in the bias of this theologian), neither premillennialism nor any other doctrine is the product of a merely unilateral move from exegesis to theology. Other significant questions and assumptions are involved, consciously or unconsciously, both before we deal with the text and as we engage the text through exegesis. These values and assumptions are reflected in our theological method, which, like hermeneutics, incorporates but goes beyond exegetical procedures.

Craig Blaising, who holds to a progressive dispensational version of premillennialism, acknowledges that the difference between interpretations, which avow to recognize Scripture as authoritative yet come to quite different conclusions on eschatology, must be attributed to hermeneutics: "In spite of the fact that most evangelicals expressly affirm literary, grammatical, and historical hermeneutics, we do have preunderstandings, traditional and even confessional precommitments, that affect the way we read and understand Scripture."[16] I would like to explore in more detail the nature of some of these preliminary and even intrahermeneutical factors that have shaped the way Scripture is read in order to sustain premillennialism. Identifying these factors does not invalidate premillennialism. Rather, it should lead to a more accountable version of premillennialism that is ever reforming toward greater apprehension of God's revelation.

14. Kevin J. Vanhoozer, *Is There a Meaning in This Text?* (Grand Rapids: Zondervan, 1998), 367.
15. J. I. Packer, *Truth and Power: The Place of Scripture in the Christian Life* (Wheaton: Harold Shaw, 1996), 121.
16. Craig A. Blaising, "Premillennialism," in *Three Views on the Millennium and Beyond*, ed. Darrell L. Bock (Grand Rapids: Zondervan, 1999), 227.

One feature of the theological method that differentiates historic premillennialism from older dispensational versions of premillennialism is its recognition of, and willingness to live with, tension. Having chosen a basic posture of literal interpretation yet recognizing that in some spiritual sense the church does fulfill the role of Old Testament Israel, historic premillennialists live with tension and are criticized by both dispensationalists and amillennialists for their apparently selective approach.[17]

What are some other methodological distinctives of all versions of premillennialism? Craig Blaising suggests that premillennialism reflects a "new creation model" of eternal life in contrast to the "spiritual vision model" that marked eschatological belief for centuries from about the time of Origen.[18] Essentially, Blaising claims, the spiritual-vision model sees the goal of eternal life in rather Platonic terms as the realization of human teleology in a noncorporeal state of relationship with God. In contrast, the new-creation model envisions the eternal state as in some type of continuity with the current created order. Our eternal communion with God will be anchored in the context of the embodied existence that God blessed in creation.[19] Although he does not wish to suggest an absolute distinction between these two models or the ways in which various eschatological systems may incorporate them, Blaising still insists that a new-creation model of eternal life is most consistent with the hermeneutics of premillennialism.

What can we learn about premillennialism's theological method by using the other three vertices of Outler's quadrilateral as a diagnostic paradigm? The priority of Scripture is unquestioned within premillennialism. But tradition, reason, and experience are involved in significant ways that may be overlooked. As previously stated, this does not compromise the integrity of biblical revelation. It merely points out the fact that theology is an enterprise undertaken by humans in human contexts. God does not circumvent but enters human culture in revelation.

Tradition

What can be observed about the role of tradition in premillennialism? It might seem that tradition plays little or no role in its theological method when one considers the fact that premillennialism has been identified by its commitment to Scripture alone without anchors in the classic creeds or confessions. Furthermore, it has been most prevalent outside denominations that have a

17. Grenz, *Millennial Maze*, 139–41.
18. Blaising, "Premillennialism," 160–76.
19. Ibid.

self-conscious creedal identity. When premillennial apologists appeal to the eschatology of pre-Constantinian theologians, however, an argument from tradition is being made. The Protestant Reformers' appeal to *sola scriptura* has generated a suspicion of, and resistance toward, allowing tradition to dictate theology. Still, premillennialists implicitly value arguments from history.

Furthermore, premillennialism has developed its own tradition of sorts. Premillennialism began to appear in the statements of faith of various free-church denominations such as the Conservative Baptists and the Evangelical Free Church in the middle of the twentieth century. Perhaps this indicates a deeply entrenched creedal instinct in even those who are most resistant to the risks and restrictions of tradition. What we believe to be most important we embed in confessions and then ask for commitment to these confessions in order to preserve not merely the tenet but the integrity of life and faith that we believe the tenet upholds. When a doctrine acquires a diagnostic status within a theological system, the boundaries of a tradition have been drawn and perpetuated, even if it is not institutionally defined.

Reason

Premillennialism's approach to Scripture must also be viewed against the broader intellectual backdrop of a philosophical current known as common-sense realism. The "common sense" philosophy popularized in Scotland by Thomas Reid (1710–96)[20] became an important intellectual resource for evangelical Christians because it provided a methodology that restored hope in the perspicuity of the Bible's message and the reasonableness of faith in that message. Reid contended that David Hume's philosophy posited a false disjunction between objects that are known and the ideas by which knowledge of them resides in the mind.[21] He further argued that ideas or perceptions of objects are perceptions of the objects themselves, not merely a mediating presence of the objects. Reid attempted to eliminate the grounds for scepticism of sense perceptions by arguing that human sense, or "common sense," is in

20. Frederick Copleston, *A History of Philosophy*, vol. 4, *Descartes to Leibniz*, Bellarmine Series (Paramus, NJ: Newman, 1958), 37–38.
21. Thomas Reid, *An Inquiry into the Human Mind: On the Principles of Common Sense*, critical ed. (University Park: Pennsylvania State University Press, 1997), 34. Reid claims that "the triumph of ideas was completed by the *Treatise of human nature*, which discards spirits also, and leaves ideas and impressions as the sole existences in the universe." He goes on to turn Hume's argument back on him by stating, "It seemed very natural to think, that the *Treatise of human nature* required an author, and a very ingenious one too; but now we learn, that it is only a set of ideas which came together, and arranged themselves by certain associations and attractions" (p. 35).

fact innately capable of perceiving reality because the capability of perception corresponds to the reality that may be perceived.[22]

Historians such as David Bebbington,[23] George Marsden,[24] and Mark Noll[25] have thoroughly traced the intellectual influence of common-sense realism on evangelicalism. Common-sense realism made its most overt mark on American evangelicalism through what is known as the Old Princeton theology, which was clearly not premillennial. Yet the overarching impact of common-sense realism was to provide concurrently a basis for pragmatism and for rationalism in the practice of Christian faith. The Princeton theology of the nineteenth and early twentieth centuries was practiced in the manner of Francis Bacon's scientific method, that is, by putting a question to the Bible, collecting the facts, and then building a synthesis.[26] It served to present ultimate, religious truth as accessible to the common person. The ability to understand the rational infrastructure of the Christian faith was no longer seen as the exclusive domain of trained theologians. God's revealed truth and its practical implications could be discerned with confidence and precision in the lives of all reasonable, sincere seekers.[27]

American premillennialists drew strength from an unexpected alliance with scholars of the Old Princeton tradition, luminaries such as J. Gresham Machen, Charles Hodge, and B. B. Warfield, as these premillennialists looked to the Princeton tradition for intellectual resources to combat their common enemy, "modernism," in the late nineteenth and early twentieth centuries. Common-sense realism, through the Old Princeton theology, provided an apologetic

22. S. A. Grave, "Reid, Thomas," in *The Encyclopedia of Philosophy*, ed. Paul Edwards, 8 vols. (New York: Macmillan, 1967), 7:119–21, 261. Reid (*Inquiry into the Human Mind*, 261) states, "This Connexion which Nature hath established betwixt our Sensations and the conception and belief of external Objects, I express two ways: Either by saying that the Sensations suggest the objects by a natural principle of the Mind; or by saying that the Sensations are natural Signs of the Objects. These Expressions signify one and the same thing, and I do not pretend by them to account for this Connexion, but only to affirm it as a fact that by the constitution of our nature there is such a Connexion."

23. David W. Bebbington, *Evangelicalism in Modern Britain: A History from the 1730s to the 1980s* (London: Unwin Hyman, 1989), 59.

24. George M. Marsden, *Fundamentalism and American Culture: The Shaping of Twentieth Century American Evangelicalism, 1870–1925* (Oxford and New York: Oxford University Press, 1980), 110.

25. Mark A. Noll, introduction to *The Princeton Theology, 1812–1921: Scripture, Science, and Theological Method from Archibald Alexander to Benjamin Breckinridge Warfield*, ed. Mark A. Noll (Grand Rapids: Baker Academic, 2001), 30–32.

26. Ibid., 31; Don J. Payne, *The Theology of the Christian Life in J. I. Packer's Thought: Theological Anthropology, Theological Method, and the Doctrine of Sanctification* (Milton Keynes, UK: Paternoster, 2006), 64.

27. Payne, *Theology of the Christian Life*, 41–46, offers a more extensive overview of common-sense realism's influence on American evangelicalism as the backdrop for Packer's theology.

methodology that fit with the existing commitments of millenarians.[28] In this manner the theological method of premillennialism reflects a particular relationship between Scripture and reason. Thus it turns out that premillennialism's apparent reliance upon a rather objective, unencumbered reading of Scripture in fact depends on a particular epistemology, giving reason a much more influential role in its method than is typically recognized.

Experience

Does premillennialism's theological method appeal to, or draw upon, experience in any manner? Certainly, it does not appeal to experience in the rather direct fashion that John Wesley did when he leaned so heavily on the experimentation ethos of the Enlightenment in granting epistemological status to experience.[29] Appealing to experience in that direct fashion would seem to undermine the commitment to the priority of Scripture taken at face value. Apart from this sort of direct role, however, we might ask whether premillennialism's insistence on a more-or-less literal approach to apocalyptic literature has fostered a preoccupation with world events and how they might correspond to biblical prophecy. Watching events in the Middle East unfold on the news is certainly an *experience* that has kept many premillennialists vigorously engaged with their eschatology. Whether their conclusions have been galvanized or modified along the way, this type of experience has actively contributed to shaping premillennial thought.

What we call historic premillennialism, as differentiated from dispensational premillennialism, resurfaced after premillennialism was brought back into popular currency by the dispensational version.[30] Consequently, experience and culture have had a measure of influence on the theological method of premillennialism through those dispensational roots. The type of experience represented in the personal lives and backgrounds of dispensational premillennialism's main proponents is still evident in current versions of premillennialism despite numerous modifications over the decades.

We should note a few of these modifications and their experiential character. Changes within dispensational premillennialism are not limited to the revised and progressive dispensationalism that emerged from the version popularized by C. I. Scofield (1843–1921) and Lewis Sperry Chafer (1871–1952).[31] Although

28. Ibid., 46.
29. Ibid.
30. Grenz, *Millennial Maze*, 127.
31. On Scofield, see below. Chafer was founder, longtime president, and professor of systematic theology at Dallas Theological Seminary. Lewis Sperry Chafer, *Systematic Theology*, 8

progressive dispensationalism has perhaps made a more dramatic shift by softening its insistence on stark contrasts between Israel and the church, dispensationalism underwent numerous developments in the way the dispensations were understood up until the Scofield-Chafer version.

Dispensational emphases in premillennialism are often attributed to the influence and the outline of John Nelson Darby (1800–1882). Darby was an Irish cleric whose dispensationalism was constricted in its influence in his homeland because his ecclesiology ran straight up against the ecclesiastical structure and values of the national Church of Ireland. When Darby came to the United States, where there was no established church, his views spread rapidly and widely throughout the grassroots, revivalistic culture of American evangelicalism. Although Darby may have popularized a dispensational approach to Scripture, the dispensational paradigms that were so influential in this country were developed by C. I. Scofield, a prominent associate of D. L. Moody,[32] in the Bible study notes published in his 1909 *Scofield Reference Bible*. Scofield's dispensational paradigm, which is noticeably different from Darby's paradigm, is an almost exact duplicate of the dispensationalism developed by the English Nonconformist hymn writer Isaac Watts (1674–1748).[33]

Some of the earliest evidence of a dispensational approach to Scripture appears also in the French mystic Pierre Poiret (1646–1719).[34] Poiret was resistant to creedalism and advocated the religion of the heart. Both Watts and Poiret were philosophically oriented, reflecting Enlightenment emphases on the power of reason. Arthur Pollard notes that Watts "never subscribed to those versions of Calvinism which espoused the doctrine of total depravity. The 'remains' of reason after the Fall might be 'ruinous,' but Watts insisted on making the best use of them."[35] In Watts, the element of reason reappears within the influence of experience or culture.

In the theological lineage of dispensationalism, we can observe three features that its major proponents and popularizers held in common. First, on both sides of the Atlantic, it is found along with a decidedly low-church or congregationalist ecclesiology. This stems from dispensationalism's suspicion of institutionalized religion and its focus on the universal church as the true people of God, not bound by human ecclesiastical structures. Second, Enlight-

---

vols. (Dallas: Dallas Seminary Press, 1947–48), was the first multivolume systematic theology written from a clearly dispensational perspective.

32. Marsden, *Fundamentalism and American Culture*, 37.

33. Charles C. Ryrie, *Dispensationalism Today* (Chicago: Moody, 1965), 73–76. See also idem, *Dispensationalism*, rev. ed. (Chicago: Moody, 1995), 68.

34. Ryrie, *Dispensationalism Today*, 71.

35. Arthur Pollard, "Watts, Isaac (1674–1748)," in *The New International Dictionary of the Christian Church*, rev. and ed. J. D. Douglas (Grand Rapids: Zondervan, 1978), 1031.

enment rationalism has had a notable role in the way theology is understood and the way theological systems are developed by key dispensationalists. The particular feature of this rationalism was its love for fine distinctions and tight categories. Third, the two primary developers of dispensationalism in North America, J. N. Darby and C. I. Scofield, were both trained as attorneys before moving into vocational ministry.[36] They approached theology with rigorous legal minds, a trait that their biographers are quick to admire. Though short of constituting proof, these features do raise questions about the role of experience and reason in the theological method of premillennialism.

Implications

Although this essay is devoted to premillennialism, not dispensationalism, we cannot overlook the intellectual and methodological legacy of dispensationalism as the primary carrier of premillennialism until the last sixty or so years. What might this legacy mean? We must ask what methodological differences exist between dispensational and nondispensational forms of premillennialism. Although the same basic commitments regarding Scripture and exegesis uphold both forms, dispensational premillennialism (at least in its older cast) has been shaped by cultural and philosophical forces that thrived on clear, tight categories and distinctions. These fine distinctions so characteristic of older dispensationalism are not derived entirely from a straightforward reading of the text, as is sometimes claimed, but reflect the intellectual culture of the times and, to some extent, the personal background and training of its proponents. Nondispensational forms of premillennialism resurfaced while Enlightenment rationalism was still a powerful intellectual current but more respectfully engaged with the broader field of biblical scholarship. As both dispensational and nondispensational premillennialists have become less suspicious of nonpremillennialists, the basic hermeneutical approaches of premillennialists have been able to flex and to accommodate "both-and" exegetical conclusions.

We must also recognize that even when we are most vigorously committed to taking Scripture at face value and avoiding eisegesis, no theology takes place in a vacuum. Premillennialism, as we find it today, is well suited for less

36. Max S. Weremchuk, *John Nelson Darby* (Neptune, NJ: Loizeaux Brothers, 1992), 32–33; Joseph M. Canfield, *The Incredible Scofield and His Book* (Vallecito, CA: Ross House, 1988), 48–64. See also Marsden, *Fundamentalism and American Culture*, 59–60. Marsden notes, "Dispensationalist leaders [such as Scofield] regarded these methods of dividing and classifying as the only scientific ones" (ibid., 60).

institutionalized, less hierarchical ecclesiastical environments and therefore continues to be found most frequently there. It fits with the culture and history of Pietism, which insists on the primacy of personal faith in, and personal experience of, our Triune God. Despite differences regarding the precise nature of the church's relationship to Israel, premillennialism still insists that history matters in the unfolding of God's redemptive narrative. It would be easier to avoid these tensions by assuming that Israel's role has been entirely fulfilled now and we merely await the culmination, but as premillennialists, we are willing to live with these tensions.

Premillennialism reminds us that we are a sojourning people who should never overidentify with the prevailing culture, however much we may feel called to appreciate it, engage it, and transform it. Premillennialism insists that being the people of God entails something more, even historically, than what we see now. Premillennialists still value hermeneutical commitments (however nuanced they may be) that reflect the conviction that God wants to be understood and intends the Scriptures to be beneficial to all people. These commitments keep me, even if ever so humbly and sometimes haltingly, inside the camp of premillennialism.

Premillennialism does in fact utilize—sometimes tacitly—a theological method that is somewhat different from its stated method but driving its explicit exegetical commitments from behind the scenes. Premillennialism is not thereby invalidated. All theological systems and doctrines are developed this way. Probing into the method of most any system of belief will reveal that it has been shaped by tacit influences that seem inconsistent with stated values and procedures. The danger is that when our theological methods remain unexamined, we are less able to hold our conclusions with appropriate humility and to continue learning. It is also true that we are less able to identify what is enduring in our theological conclusions and thus cling to that with confidence.

The theological method of premillennialism begins with and unapologetically upholds a commitment to the inspiration and authority of Scripture. The fascinating irony is that although its proponents and developers have been clearly suspicious of tradition, reason, and experience (Outler's other categories), it turns out that these factors have been, and continue to be, significant influences in the formation of premillennialism's conclusions. Tradition, reason, and experience have shaped the way Scripture has been read and which parts of Scripture have been granted controlling status. The core values of premillennialism have remained intact even though the expression of these values has changed as particular ecclesiastical issues have faded and the church's philosophical and cultural context has shifted.

What new directions and challenges do we face as we probe the theological method of premillennialism? If we already have a "kinder, gentler" premillennialism, we also need a premillennialism that can recognize and wrestle well with the new issues in hermeneutics and epistemology, remaining tethered to the enduring gospel of Jesus Christ as that against which all will ultimately be assessed (1 Cor. 3:10–15).

Studying theological method involves a relatively new conversation within some sectors of evangelicalism. It represents an attempt to discern how theology is done, why it is done in particular ways, and how all of this allows theological conclusions to function as they do in the life of faith. The range of factors encompassed by the phrase "theological method" can be so diverse as to be perplexing at first. But if theology is a way of expressing our knowledge of God, reflecting on theological method allows us to better understand ourselves as the ones knowing God. It can help us know better what to take seriously and what to hold loosely in our theology, and so it contributes to theological humility. Studying theological method can also help us differentiate between our theology and God himself, a distinction sometimes easy to forget.

Premillennialism utilizes a method that can give us a greater appreciation for the values of this theological system, whether or not we accept all of its conclusions. Probing into its theological method can open the way for the type of theological growth and development that will help us become more faithful as we continue to grapple with what it means to know our God. This God has revealed himself in Jesus Christ, sets up residence with us through the Holy Spirit, speaks to us through Holy Scripture, and yet continues to elude our efforts to reduce his ways to a neat, simple package. May our continued explorations into both premillennialism and theological method stoke our hunger for more of God's truth as we discover how, through his Spirit, it persistently finds its way to us even through our human processes of interpretation and discernment. The path may not be the destination, but the two are more related than we sometimes realize.

6

Contemporary Millennial/Tribulational Debates

Whose Side Was the Early Church On?

DONALD FAIRBAIRN

It is well known that on any given theological issue, biblical interpretation is never simply a matter of exegesis but instead entails an interplay between exegesis, theology, history, and culture. The question is never simply, "What do the relevant biblical passages mean?" Rather, theological, historical, and cultural concerns affect the interpreters' decisions (whether those decisions are arrived at consciously or merely assumed unconsciously) about which biblical passages are relevant to the issue, which of the relevant passages are central and which are peripheral, and how these passages should be understood and applied. When a theological issue is debated, the parties in the dispute often seek to show not only that their exegesis of certain biblical passages is correct but also that, historically, the Christian church has been on their side, has interpreted these passages in the same way. Of all such appeals to historical precedent, perhaps the most common is the appeal to "the early church," to Christians in what we call the patristic period,[1] who were chronologically,

---

1. The period of the church fathers, roughly AD 100–600.

linguistically, and geographically close to the New Testament and who thus (we suppose—rightly or wrongly) should have known best how to interpret the Scriptures. This is certainly true for the issues of this book—the relations between the return of Christ, the great tribulation, and the millennial kingdom. Proponents of one position or another argue that the early church affirmed their own view and thus that their view must be taken seriously. Indeed, the very name for the position this book espouses, historic premillennialism, is itself an appeal to the early church. The name derives from the belief that this position was the consensus of the church during its first few centuries, a belief that is by no means universally accepted, as this chapter will show.

Furthermore, historical, cultural, and theological concerns also affect interpreters' estimates of the relevance and significance of a given theological issue—why the issue matters and how it contributes to the overall picture of Christian faith we seek to paint. This is one area in which eschatology has an advantage over other theological issues, since people are inherently fascinated by the future and by any claims that we might make to know what that future holds. We do not need to convince people that the future is interesting, since virtually everyone already believes this. But we need to remember that the mere idea that the future is fascinating does not mean that it is automatically significant. It is important for us to ask how eschatology functions theologically and how it contributes to our understanding of the Christian faith as a whole and to our living of Christian lives in the here and now. And on this issue as well, a foray into the world of the early church may prove very fruitful, since the writers of the first few Christian centuries had definite ideas about how eschatology functioned and why it was significant, ideas that we might do well to heed today.

Accordingly, this essay seeks to accomplish three things. First, it addresses the question of whether premillennialism was the consensus view of the church during its first few centuries. Second, it seeks to resolve the issue of what kind of premillennialism was found in the early church—something akin to modern dispensational premillennialism (with a pretribulational rapture of the church) or something more like what is today called historic premillennialism (in which, among other differences, the rapture of the church comes at the end of the tribulation and is part of the single return of Christ to earth to begin the millennial kingdom). Third, it more briefly examines the way premillennialism functioned in the theology of the early church, so as to draw some lessons for contemporary Christians. I will focus on the period prior to the conversion of the Roman Empire—in particular, on the second century and the early part of the third.[2]

2. The most readily accessible collection of writings from the early church is the three-series set composed of *The Ante-Nicene Fathers*, ed. Alexander Roberts and James Donaldson, 9 vols.

Was Premillennialism the Consensus of the Early Church?

If one looks at patristic eschatology as a whole, it becomes apparent that there are relatively few references to what we today call millennial questions. The early church placed enormous stress on the return of Christ, the bodily resurrection of believers and unbelievers, the last judgment, and the eternal condition, but in comparison with these emphases, patristic writers expended much less effort to describe the relation between the return of Christ and the thousand-year kingdom of Revelation 20.[3] Among contemporary scholars of patristic eschatology, two major ways of interpreting this evidence prevail. A few examples of these two patterns follow.

The View That Premillennialism Was Not the Consensus

First, some scholars argue that from the beginning of the patristic period, both chiliastic (that is, premillennial)[4] and nonchiliastic understandings of the end times were present, neither of which can be considered the consensus view of the church. For example, George Lyons argues that chiliasm was never a majority opinion in the church but was, rather, primarily a phenomenon of Asia Minor, the region that produced the New Testament book of Revelation and the second-century fathers Papias, Justin Martyr, and Irenaeus: "Central and western Asia Minor was the hotbed of Christian millennial speculation. Some Christian communities in this region expected a 'millennium' following the

(1885–87; repr., 10 vols., Peabody, MA: Hendrickson, 1994); *The Nicene and Post-Nicene Fathers*, Series 1, ed. Philip Schaff, 14 vols. (1886–89, repr., Peabody, MA: Hendrickson, 1994); and *The Nicene and Post-Nicene Fathers*, Series 2, ed. Philip Schaff and Henry Wace, 14 vols. (1890–1900, repr., Peabody, MA: Hendrickson, 1994). Because these series are widely available, they are cited here (as *ANF*, *NPNF*[1], and *NPNF*[2]). But since this corpus represents mid-nineteenth-century scholarship, the translations are in somewhat archaic English, and in many cases the texts from which the translations have been made are precritical texts. Therefore the quotations in this essay will be from more recent translations based on critical texts where they are available. The best collections of these recent translations are in the Fathers of the Church (FC) and Ancient Christian Writers (ACW) series.

3. See Justin Martyr, *Dialogue with Trypho* 31–32, 80–81, 139 (FC 6:192–96, 275–78, 361–62; *ANF* 1:209–10, 239–40, 268–69); Irenaeus of Lyons (late second century), *Against Heresies* 5.23–36 (*ANF* 1:551–67); Tertullian of Carthage (late second/early third century), *Against Marcion* 3.25 (*ANF* 3:342–44), *On Spectacles* 30 (FC 40:104–7; *ANF* 3:91); Hippolytus of Rome (early third century), *On the Antichrist* 5 (*ANF* 5:205); Methodius of Olympus (late third century), *Symposium* 9.5 (ACW 27:139–40; *ANF* 6:347); and Lactantius (early fourth century), *Divine Institutes* 7 (FC 49:470–541; *ANF* 7:194–223).

4. Scholars of the early church generally refer to premillennialism using the words "chiliasm" and "millenarianism," derived from the Greek *chilias* and the Latin *mille*, both of which mean "a thousand." This chapter uses "premillennialism," "chiliasm," and "millenarianism" as synonyms.

second coming of Christ, during which all believers—living and risen—would enjoy an Eden-like earthly paradise of luxury and sensual delights."[5] Here one should notice the phrase "luxury and sensual delights." The opponents of premillennialism (both in the early church and among modern scholars such as Lyons) often base their criticism on the sensuous nature of the millennial kingdom; I will discuss this criticism later. Lyons concludes, "It must be emphasized that the rejection of millenarian interpretation did not begin with Alexandrian allegorists nor with fourth-century triumphalists who imagined that the kingdom of God had dawned with the conversion of the Roman Emperor Constantine. Nonmillenarian interpretations of Revelation were at least as early and geographically more diverse than were the millenarian."[6] Lyons's link between premillennial eschatology and Asia Minor is fascinating for historical reasons, but he does not ultimately succeed in limiting this view to a certain geographical region, since premillennialism is also found in very prominent early fathers who had no connection to Asia Minor. Among these the most significant are the Western fathers Hippolytus and Tertullian, and indeed Lyons himself discusses Tertullian.[7] As further support for his contention that nonchiliastic eschatology was also common in the early church, Lyons argues that Justin Martyr, Irenaeus, and Tertullian are inconsistent in their eschatology, sometimes positing a literal millennium and at other times assigning Revelation 20 to the eternal state of believers.[8]

Everett Ferguson argues that both a chiliastic and a nonchiliastic pattern of Christian hope emerged early in Christianity, although, unlike Lyons, he does not try to limit chiliasm to Asia Minor. Ferguson writes, "Chiliasm was an integral part of the polemic against Marcion and the Gnostics in Justin Martyr, Irenaeus, and Tertullian." At the same time, he asserts, the nonchiliastic current "was widely pervasive in early Christianity and is represented in such writers as Hermas, Polycarp, the authors of the *Epistle to Diognetus*, *Ascension of Isaiah*, *Apocalypse of Peter*, *Martyrdom of Polycarp*, and *Letter of the Churches of Vienne and Lyons*, Clement of Alexandria, Origen, and Cyprian."[9]

5. George Lyons, "Eschatology in the Early Church," in *The Second Coming: A Wesleyan Approach to the Doctrine of the Last Things*, ed. H. Ray Dunning (Kansas City, MO: Beacon Hill, 1995), 110. For a similar appraisal of the link between Asia Minor and chiliasm, see John A. McGuckin, "Chiliasm," in *The Westminster Handbook to Patristic Theology* (Louisville: Westminster John Knox, 2004), 58.

6. Lyons, "Eschatology in the Early Church," 114.

7. Ibid., 112–13.

8. Ibid., 114–15.

9. Everett Ferguson, *Church History*, vol. 1, *From Christ to Pre-Reformation* (Grand Rapids: Zondervan, 2005), 158.

Some scholars argue not only that nonchiliastic eschatologies were common but even that chiliasm itself was rare in the second century and thus nonchiliastic approaches were the majority. See, for example, Thomas Falls, the translator of Justin Martyr's *Dialogue with Trypho*. Commenting on Justin's assertion that chiliasm was the opinion of the orthodox, Falls writes, "The belief in the millennium was not as general as Justin's words imply. The only other early supporters of this doctrine were Papias of Hierapolis and Irenaeus. Many other Christian writers then opposed this belief of a thousand years' *earthly* happiness with Christ at Jerusalem after the resurrection from the dead."[10]

The problem with interpretations such as those of Lyons and Ferguson, or the more extreme one espoused by Falls, is that they equate silence about the millennium with a denial of an earthly kingdom. Lyons, like many scholars before him, finds it surprising that Justin does not mention an earthly millennium in either of his two apologies (he describes such a kingdom only in his *Dialogue with Trypho*) or that Irenaeus mentions the millennium only in book 5 of *Against Heresies*, not in books 1–4. Similarly, Ferguson takes the absence of references to a literal millennium in the writers he cites above as an indication that these writers held to a nonchiliastic eschatology. But silence about the millennium is emphatically not the same thing as stating that Revelation 20 should be interpreted another way. Indeed, both A. J. Visser and Art Marmorstein have offered persuasive explanations for the silence of many early writers about the earthly kingdom. Visser argues correctly that the fathers had to exercise much caution when writing documents intended for the Roman public (such as Justin's two apologies, each of which is addressed to the current Roman emperor). Although Rome would hardly have looked twice at another religion offering the hope of eternal life in heaven (there were many of these in Roman times), a religion that held out to its followers the hope of an *earthly* kingdom following imminent cataclysmic events (including the fall of Rome) would surely have attracted unwanted attention from the empire. It should hardly be surprising, then, that Christians might firmly hold to the hope for an earthly millennium and yet mention this hope in public documents rarely or not at all. From this reasoning, Visser argues that one should not take the silence of most second-century apologists on the millennium to mean that they were not chiliasts.[11] Marmorstein echoes Visser's explanation and offers two others as well. He asserts that Christian writers often seemed to shy away from

10. Thomas Falls, trans., *Justin Martyr*, FC 6 (Washington, DC: Catholic University of America Press, 1948), 277n5, emphasis original.
11. A. J. Visser, "A Bird's-Eye View of Ancient Christian Eschatology," *Numen* 14.1 (1967): 9.

controversy over nonessentials and that when they were writing apologetically, they usually dealt only with eschatological ideas that found some precedent in pagan writers (most notably, the state of the soul after death) whereas when they were writing to Christians, they elaborated in much greater detail on biblical eschatology. As a result, only in these documents did they discuss the earthly millennial kingdom.[12]

Therefore it appears that scholars who argue that chiliastic and nonchiliastic eschatologies were both widespread in the early centuries of Christianity are making too much of a silence that can readily be explained in another way. To demonstrate that amillennialism was common before AD 250, one would need to point to explicit rejections of premillennialism or explicit interpretations of Revelation 20 in nonliteral ways. As we will see, this kind of evidence is abundant in the fourth and fifth centuries, but it appears to be lacking in the second and early third centuries.[13] Instead one finds many writings from the earlier period that focus on the return of Christ, resurrection, judgment, and the eternal state, with no mention one way or another of the millennium. There are a few writings with explicit (and sometimes extensive) descriptions of an earthly kingdom following the return of Christ. Thus the case for a *widespread* nonchiliastic eschatology prior to about AD 250 is not convincing.

The View That Premillennialism Was the Consensus

This brings us to the second major way scholars interpret early patristic eschatology, namely, arguing that premillennialism was the consensus of the church before the middle of the third century and that from this time until the early fifth century, it was gradually replaced by something akin to modern amillennialism. In the late nineteenth century, Philip Schaff commented, "The most striking point in the eschatology of the ante-Nicene age is the prominent chiliasm, or millenarianism, that is the belief of a visible reign of Christ in glory on earth with the risen saints for a thousand years, before the general resurrection and judgment."[14] More recently A. Skevington Wood has argued

12. Art Marmorstein, "Eschatological Inconsistency in the Ante-Nicene Fathers?" *Andrews University Seminary Studies* 39.1 (2001): 129–30.

13. I write "appears to be lacking" because I have not found such evidence and those scholars who argue for the widespread presence of nonchiliastic eschatology do not themselves produce patristic writings that argue against an earthly millennium. As we will see, Justin and Irenaeus both assert that there were some who explicitly rejected the idea of an earthly millennium, but not very many, and we do not seem to have their writings today.

14. Philip Schaff, *History of the Christian Church*, vol. 2, *Ante-Nicene Christianity from the Death of John the Apostle to Constantine the Great, A.D. 100–325*, 5th ed. (New York: Scribner's Sons, 1889; repr., Peabody, MA: Hendrickson, 1996), 614.

that Irenaeus's premillennialism is hardly original and simply develops teaching found in the *Didache*, Ignatius, Polycarp, Barnabas, Hermas, and Justin.[15] Wood concludes, "The very fact that so much of what Irenaeus propounded covers ground which is now familiar to us, bears witness to the antiquity of what is accurately labeled historic premillennialism. Whatever conclusions may be drawn from the testimony of Scripture on this controverted issue, it must be conceded that in the first three centuries the premillennial interpretation predominated. Irenaeus was perhaps its most distinguished and consistent exponent."[16] Similarly, David Dunbar argues that Hippolytus's eschatology (also decidedly premillennial, like that of Irenaeus) is largely traditional and, in fact, Hippolytus adds very little that is new to the various strands of Jewish and early Christian thought he learned from others.[17] Dunbar concludes, "This suggests that in Hippolytus we find a kind of 'main-line' eschatology which may have been quite widespread during the closing decades of the second century."[18] Similarly, Robert Clouse asserts, "During the first three centuries of the Christian era, premillennialism appears to have been the dominant eschatological interpretation."[19]

These modern scholars are in good company because Christian writers from the second and third centuries themselves argue that chiliasm is the most common view (albeit not the only one) in the church. Justin Martyr, in *Dialogue with Trypho* (written ca. AD 135), asserts that Jerusalem will be rebuilt in the last days. Trypho, his imaginary Jewish interlocutor, asks whether Justin really believes this or whether he is just trying to win an argument.[20] Justin's reply (already alluded to above) is that "there are many pure and pious Christians who do not share our opinion," but he goes on to argue that those who deny a future millennial kingdom are not real Christians.[21] He concludes, "But I and every other completely orthodox Christian feel certain that there will be a resurrection of the flesh, followed by a thousand years in the rebuilt, embellished, and enlarged city of Jerusalem, as was announced by the prophets

15. A. Skevington Wood, "The Eschatology of Irenaeus," *Evangelical Quarterly* 40 (1968): 36.

16. Ibid., 41.

17. David G. Dunbar, "Hippolytus of Rome and the Eschatological Exegesis of the Early Church," *Westminster Theological Journal* 45 (1983): 338.

18. Ibid., 339.

19. Robert G. Clouse, introduction to *The Meaning of the Millennium: Four Views*, ed. Robert G. Clouse (Downers Grove, IL: InterVarsity, 1977), 9. Cf. Clouse's similar statement in idem, "Millennium, Views of the," in *Evangelical Dictionary of Theology*, ed. Walter A. Elwell, 2nd ed. (Grand Rapids: Baker Academic, 2001), 771.

20. Justin Martyr, *Dialogue with Trypho* 80 (FC 6:275; ANF 1:239).

21. FC 6:276; ANF 1:239.

Ezechiel, Isaias, and the others."[22] This response is difficult to interpret because Justin first says that true Christians may disagree with him and then asserts that those who disagree with him are not true Christians. Perhaps one may resolve the difficulty by assuming that when he says his opponents are still Christians, he is referring to those who do not believe Jerusalem will be literally rebuilt but when he says his opponents are not Christians, he is referring more generally to those who deny a millennial kingdom at all. Be that as it may, it is clear that Justin regards chiliasm as the dominant and correct view and that there are people who disagree with him.

Similarly, Irenaeus regards premillennialism as the traditional and dominant view of the church. He concludes *Against Heresies* (written ca. AD 180) with an extended discussion of the end times (to which this chapter will return). During this discussion, Irenaeus argues that certain people, although they are orthodox Christians, have nevertheless been influenced by the opinions of heretics (that is, gnostics) and thus these Christians "are both ignorant of God's dispensations, and of the mystery of the resurrection of the just, and of the [earthly] kingdom which is the commencement of incorruption."[23] Irenaeus goes on to make three major arguments in support of his contention that there will be an earthly kingdom after the return of Christ. First, he claims, Christ's statement in the upper room that he will not drink wine again until he does so with his disciples in his Father's kingdom (Matt. 26:29) constitutes an assertion that there will be an earthly, material kingdom, since only bodily beings can drink. Second, Irenaeus argues that John the apostle not only announced the millennial kingdom in Revelation 20:4–6 but also gave oral descriptions of conversations Jesus had with the Twelve in which the Lord described this kingdom in more detail. Third, Irenaeus writes that Papias claims (in a work now lost) that in one such conversation between Jesus and the disciples, Judas expressed incredulity about whether such an earthly kingdom could really come about and that Jesus replied that those who came to these times would see it.[24] This discussion shows that, in Irenaeus's eyes, chiliasm is the teaching of both the Lord and his church and nonchiliastic eschatologies are the product of gnostic influence, even when they are held by genuinely orthodox Christians.

22. FC 6:277; *ANF* 1:239.
23. Irenaeus, *Against Heresies* 5.32 (*ANF* 1:561).
24. Irenaeus, *Against Heresies* 5.33 (*ANF* 1:562–63). Eusebius of Caesarea (writing in the mid-fourth century) argues in his *Ecclesiastical History* 3.39.12–13 (*NPNF*[2] 1:172) that the reason Papias misunderstood what Jesus and John were saying was that he took them too literally, not realizing that they were speaking in figures. Eusebius concludes of Papias, "For he appears to have been of very limited understanding."

I will return to the relation between gnosticism and Christian eschatology. For now, the point is that Justin, the greatest of the second-century apologists, and Irenaeus, the first great theologian of the church, both believed that a physical, earthly kingdom of Christ after his return was the teaching of the Lord, the Scriptures, and the majority of the church. If these two seminal thinkers were correct, then premillennialism was the majority view during this period, although it was not the only view among Christians. A major argument against the conclusion that premillennialism predominated, however, is the fact that by the mid-fifth century it was such a marginal position that many considered it heretical. One might argue that if premillennialism had ever been as dominant as I am claiming, it could not have become so marginal in only about two hundred years (from the mid-third to the mid-fifth century). Because of this potential argument, one cannot confidently conclude that premillennialism predominated in the early patristic period until one has satisfactorily explained the backlash against it in the third through fifth centuries. This is the issue to which I will now turn.

The Decline of Premillennialism in the Patristic Period

After Origen's critique of chiliasm in the mid-third century, it declined very quickly in the Eastern, Greek-speaking church, to the point that by the late fourth century, it was considered such a monstrosity that Epiphanius dared not even accuse a heretic (Apollinarius) of holding to such a view. In the West, however, chiliasm persisted longer and never fully disappeared, but it was doomed to long-term marginalization by the fact that Augustine rejected it in the early fifth century.[25] As we consider whether this was the decline of a view that had been the majority or merely the church's ridding itself of a pesky minority opinion, it will be useful to look in some detail at Origen's and Augustine's critiques.

In *On First Principles* (written before AD 231), Origen addresses the question of an earthly kingdom:

Now some men, who reject the labour of thinking and seek after the outward and literal meaning of the law, or rather give way to their own desires and lusts, disciples of the mere letter, consider that the promises of the future are to be looked for in the form of pleasure and bodily luxury. And chiefly on this account they desire after the resurrection to have flesh of such a sort that they will never lack the power to eat and drink and to do all things that pertain to flesh and

25. Visser, "Bird's-Eye View," 19.

blood, not following the teaching of the apostle Paul about the resurrection of a "spiritual body."[26]

He goes on to describe some of the abhorrent characteristics his adversaries describe when they speak of the kingdom: the continuation of marriage, the rebuilding of Jerusalem and the covering of its walls with precious stones, the giving of unbelievers to the saints as servants, and the saints' receiving the wealth of the nations. Origen concludes, "And, to speak briefly, they desire that all things which they look for in the promises should correspond in every detail with the course of this life, that is, that what exists now should exist again. Such are the thoughts of men who believe indeed in Christ, but because they understand the divine scriptures in a Judaistic sense, extract from them nothing that is worthy of the divine promises."[27] Origen's major qualms about an earthly millennium are that it entails reading Scripture too literally (as the Jews would read it) and that it conceives of the Christian hope too sensuously.

In place of premillennialism, Origen offers a Christian hope that is almost exclusively spiritual and intellectual. He argues that at death the souls of believers go to some sort of paradise on earth, where they learn the operations of this world. Then, when believers meet the Lord in the air at the end of history (1 Thess. 4:17), the souls go to the spheres of the atmosphere/space/heaven, learning the workings of each sphere before passing on to the next one, until finally the souls reach their ultimate dwelling place, in heaven with God.[28] Origen concludes, "I think that the mind, when it has come to perfection, still feeds on appropriate and suitable food in a measure which can neither admit of want nor of superfluity. But in all respects this food must be understood to be the contemplation and understanding of God, and its measures to be those that are appropriate and suitable to this nature which has been made and created."[29]

Two major factors lie behind Origen's critique and his alternative eschatology here. First and most important, he was reading the Bible in light of the Platonic philosophical mind-set, which subtly denigrated the material realm (in a way similar to gnosticism but not to the same degree) and understood salvation as the soul's escape from the body rather than as the redemption of

26. Origen, *On First Principles* 2.11.2. The text of this work is quite problematic, and that used for the translation in *ANF* is not very reliable. The best English edition is Origen, *On First Principles*, trans. G. W. Butterworth (London: SPCK, 1936). In this chapter, I will refer to this edition rather than to *ANF*. The passage quoted here is found in Butterworth, 147–48.

27. Origen, *On First Principles* 2.11.2 (Butterworth, 148).

28. Origen, *On First Principles* 2.11.6 (Butterworth, 151–52).

29. Origen, *On First Principles* 2.11.7 (Butterworth, 154).

the body. Origen's commitment to Scripture prevented him from rejecting the redemption of the body altogether, but his Platonic background led him to seize on Paul's use of the phrase "spiritual body" in 1 Corinthians 15:42–57 to argue for a profound transformation of believers' bodies at the resurrection. Indeed, this transformation is so profound that one could argue that it constitutes a denial of the bodily resurrection.[30] Second, Origen was writing at a time when Christianity was trying to disengage itself from its Jewish roots, and at that time, it was very common to reject any interpretation of Scripture that had Jewish precedent. As other contributions to this collection of essays show, the idea of an earthly kingdom at the end of history was a prominent feature of Jewish apocalyptic thought, and ipso facto this idea was suspect in his eyes.

Origen was very much a man of his time, and on this issue, contemporary theologians are likely to disagree with him substantially. Instead of downplaying Christianity's stress on the material realm by rejecting the idea of an earthly millennium, they properly want to emphasize the importance of the human body and the physical realm in God's purposes, and premillennialism does this. And continuity between a given eschatological view and Jewish antecedents is now seen as an argument in that view's favor, not a reason to reject it. Origen's thought was considered questionable in his own time as well, and much of the subsequent history of Eastern theology can be seen as a series of attempts to correct the problems Origen presents to us. Nevertheless, even though the church rejected his implicit antimaterialism and his virtual denial of the bodily resurrection, Eastern Christendom accepted his critique of premillennialism.[31] Very likely, a major reason for this was that, with the conversion of the empire in the early fourth century, Christians' perception that their earthly condition was temporary and soon to change began to wane dramatically. With the bitterness of persecution past, they felt less need to cling fervently to the scriptural promises that the saints' fate on earth would ultimately change, and so there was more openness to interpreting biblical passages about such hope in a less earthly way.[32]

30. The previous chapter of *On First Principles*, 2.10, contains a discussion of the resurrection and the spiritual body. There are many problems here with the text and the translation, but even by the most charitable reading, Origen's thought here sounds much too Platonic and not nearly scriptural enough.

31. One of the last holdouts was Methodius of Olympus, who in the late third century criticized Origen's views on the resurrection and offered a Christian hope akin to that of Irenaeus. See Methodius, *Symposium* 9.5 (ACW 27:139–40; ANF 6:347).

32. Schaff (*Ante-Nicene Christianity*, 619) makes this case succinctly: "But the crushing blow came from the great change in the social condition and prospects of the church in the Nicene age. . . . The millennial reign, instead of being anxiously waited and prayed for, began to be

Origen's critique of premillennialism was not as highly regarded in the West as in the East, and in neither West nor East did his alternative proposal (a gradual spiritual education of the souls after death, leading ultimately to heaven) find acceptance. Instead the task of providing the alternative that would come to dominate Christian eschatology during the Middle Ages fell to Augustine. In his magnum opus, *The City of God* (written from ca. AD 413 to ca. 426), Augustine argues that many Christians misunderstand Revelation 20:1–6 by thinking that the first resurrection is physical and that the thousand years will be a form of Sabbath rest for God's people: "This notion would be in some degree tolerable if it were believed that in that Sabbath some delights of a spiritual character were to be available for the saints because of the presence of the Lord. I also entertained this notion at one time. But in fact those people assert that those who have risen again will spend their rest in the most unrestrained material feasts."[33] Here again we see a rejection of chiliasm because of the sensuous nature of the delights it offers. As with Origen, so also with Augustine, the fact that an avowed Platonist whose understanding of Christianity is decidedly spiritual in nature criticizes premillennialism may say as much about the critic as it does about the view being criticized. But Augustine's admission that he used to be a chiliast and his use of the phrase "unrestrained material feasts" suggest that the problem, in his mind, is not premillennialism per se but an overly extravagant version of it that turns the kingdom into an occasion for the exercise of gluttony and other lusts.

In place of chiliasm, Augustine offers a view of Revelation 20 in which the thousand years represent the last period of history, the age of the church, during which Satan is prevented from controlling believers. Those who reign with Christ are the ones who do as he commands, and thus believers themselves constitute the kingdom. Furthermore, Augustine argues that the first resurrection is the passing of a person from death to life, or what we would call conversion. Those who partake of the first resurrection are all those who, during the entire course of the church age (the thousand years), are converted to Christ. Those who do not come to life until the end of the thousand years are unbelievers, and because they have not "come to life" (that is, become believers) during the church age, they will be resurrected to judgment at the end of history.[34]

---

dated either from the first appearance of Christ, or from the conversion of Constantine and the downfall of paganism, and to be regarded as realized in the glory of the dominant imperial state-church." Cf. Clouse, "Millennium," 771.

33. Augustine, *City of God* 20.7. The best translation of this work is Augustine, *Concerning the City of God against the Pagans*, trans. Henry Bettenson (London: Penguin Books, 1984); this passage is found on pp. 906–7. The passage is also found at *NPNF*[1] 2:426.

34. Augustine, *City of God* 20.9 (Bettenson, 914–18; *NPNF*[1] 2:427–31).

Augustine's explanation is clearly a much more responsible attempt at a biblical eschatology than what we find in Origen, and it became the basis for amillennialism, which would dominate the Christian church until well into the modern period (albeit with notable exceptions, for premillennialism never died out completely in the Western church). But one should notice that this interpretation emerges only rather late in the patristic period, in a social-political context vastly different from that of the New Testament or the earliest church. By this time, the institutional stability of the church-state structure[35] had replaced the fervent hope of most Christians for a quick end to the world as we know it and a transformation of believers' fortunes through the millennial kingdom. It is fair to say not only that a view such as Augustine's was not common before the conversion of the empire (as far as we can tell from the available evidence) but also that it could scarcely have arisen at all without that dramatic change in the church's social and political condition.

Conclusions about the Prevalence of Premillennialism

From the preceding survey, several things have emerged. First, there is clear evidence of chiliastic expectation in the early part of the patristic period. Second, arguments that nonchiliastic eschatologies were also common during this period are largely based on silence, but the silence of many second-century authors about an earthly kingdom can easily be explained without assuming that these authors held to a view other than premillennialism. Third, because there are few (if any) explicit rejections of chiliasm before the third century, one should regard the later prominence of amillennialism as a shift in patristic eschatology rather than as the ascendance of a view that had already been common. Fourth, the shift away from premillennialism in the third and fourth centuries bears the unmistakable influence of a philosophical framework whose view of the physical world was suspect, as well as of the rise of a church-state structure that dampened eschatological expectation in general. From these points, one can conclude that for more than a century after the close of the apostolic era, when the church was living in a social-political climate basically similar to that of the New Testament period, the church understood the New Testament as holding forth the promise of an earthly kingdom after the return of Christ. Such a hope was evidently never the only view, but there is no compelling reason to dispute that it was the primary view before Origen in the third century.

35. One noteworthy detail is that Augustine, *City of God* 20.9 (Bettenson, 916; *NPNF*[1] 2:430), interprets the thrones of Rev. 20 as "the seats of the authorities by whom the Church is now governed, and those sitting on them are the authorities themselves."

What Kind of Premillennialism Did the Early Church Advocate?

If one accepts this assessment that the church before Origen was predominantly premillennial, then it is important to ask whether the early church's
eschatological expectation was akin to what we today call dispensational or
historic premillennialism. Unquestionably, elements of early Christian eschatology were akin to modern dispensationalism, and three such elements are
especially noteworthy. First, many early Christians understood the history of
the world as comprising a symbolic week, in which each day stands for one
thousand years. (This understanding is much less common among current
dispensationalists than it was among earlier dispensationalists.) Just as God
finished his creative work in six days and rested on the seventh, so also God is
completing his historic work in six days (i.e., six thousand years, since for the
Lord a day is like a thousand years) and will provide a rest for his people on the
seventh (i.e., a thousand-year period to follow the return of Christ).[36] Second,
as we saw above, many Christians held out hope that the city of Jerusalem
would be literally rebuilt.[37] Third, in the interpretation of the "seventy weeks"
of Daniel 9:24–27, Irenaeus and Hippolytus posited a gap between the sixty-
ninth and seventieth weeks, such that the final week (i.e., the final seven-year
period) would take place at the end of history, just before the return of Christ.[38]
On the basis of this interpretation, Louis Knowles argues that Irenaeus and
Hippolytus "are undoubtedly the forerunners of the modern dispensational
interpreters of the Seventy Weeks"[39] and that "we must regard them as the
founders of a school of interpretation, and in this lies their significance for
the history of exegesis."[40]

But as Knowles no doubt recognized but did not state (since his subject
in the article cited is exclusively the interpretation of the seventy weeks, not
eschatology as a whole), a similarity on this point, or even on several points,

36. See Irenaeus, *Against Heresies* 5.23 (ANF 1:551), 5.28 (ANF 1:557); Methodius, *Symposium* 9.1 (ACW 27:132; ANF 6:344); and Lactantius, *Divine Institutes* 7.14 (FC 49:510; ANF
7:210). Lactantius writes in *Divine Institutes* 7.25 (FC 49:535; ANF 7:220) that there was dis-
agreement about how far into the six thousand years of human history people were at the time
he was writing (the early fourth century). But he confidently predicts that the consummation
would occur in less than two hundred years. Thus Lactantius places the creation in ca. 5500 BC,
a bit earlier than the date some modern dispensationalists give.

37. See Justin Martyr, *Dialogue with Trypho* 80 (FC 6:275; ANF 1:239); Tertullian, *Against
Marcion* 3.25 (ANF 3:342–43).

38. See Irenaeus, *Against Heresies* 5.25 (ANF 1:553–54); Hippolytus, *On the Antichrist* 43
(ANF 5:213).

39. Louis E. Knowles, "The Interpretation of the Seventy Weeks of Daniel in the Early Fathers," *Westminster Theological Journal* 7.2 (1945): 136.

40. Ibid., 139.

does not mean that Irenaeus and Hippolytus were similar to modern dispensationalism overall. In fact, the early church's eschatology differed substantially from contemporary dispensational premillennialism in several major ways. First, the dispensational hermeneutic would have been foreign to the early church. Second, the dispensational attitude toward suffering and tribulation would have been unthinkable to the early church. And third, patristic writers do not show any awareness of a two-part return of Christ, and they give the definite impression that they believe the church will be present on earth during the final tribulation that precedes Christ's return.

Dispensationalism and Patristic Hermeneutics

One of dispensationalism's major hallmarks is its insistence on a literal hermeneutic. Dispensationalists pride themselves on interpreting each passage of Scripture at face value, in the way it would—they contend—have been understood by its original audience. This is something, however, that all serious biblical interpreters seek to do, and the question is how one integrates various passages of Scripture that appear to be saying different things. In particular, how does one integrate God's promises made to Israel in the Old Testament and the hope held out to (mostly gentile) Christians in the New Testament? Dispensationalism handles this integrative challenge by distinguishing sharply between the Old Testament people of God and the New Testament church and thus by arguing that the Old Testament promises and the New Testament promises, for the most part, fall into different categories. They are addressed to different groups, and thus, once God has completed his purposes for the church, he will send his Son to remove that church from earth (through the rapture, the first phase of Christ's return) and then turn his attention (back) to Israel during the tribulation.

One cannot emphasize strongly enough that this hermeneutic is utterly foreign to the early church. The overwhelming concern of all patristic writers was to read the entire Bible as a Christian book, and they did so by understanding a given passage of the Old Testament in terms of either its relation to Christ, its relation to the church, or its relation to the individual believer. This desire to read the Old Testament in reference to one of these three often led the church fathers into what we call allegorical exegesis, and modern interpreters usually reproach them for their allegorical tendencies. But such modern criticism of patristic exegesis is at least overdone, and perhaps even unwarranted, because our criticism fails to grasp the fundamental conviction that binds patristic interpretation together—the Bible is a unified book whose theme is Jesus Christ. We may well disagree with the way the church fathers related specific Old Testament texts to Christ and the church, and we may be uncomfortable with their allegorism, but we should be willing to acknowledge that their fundamental belief is correct. The Bible *is* a unified book, and the single story it tells *is* the story of God's action on behalf of his people, culminating in his action through his incarnate Son and applied to us by his Spirit.[41]

For our purposes here, the most significant thing about patristic and dispensational exegesis is that the interpretive arrows of the two systems are pointing in the opposite directions. When confronted with an apparent tension between the way Old Testament promises and prophecies seem to apply in their original contexts and the promises God makes to the New Testament church, dispensationalists favor the plain-sense interpretation of the Old Testament above the applicability of these promises/prophecies to the church. But the church fathers, when faced with the same apparent tension, favor the direct applicability of the promises/prophecies to the church over interpreting them in their plainest possible sense. In other words, dispensationalists tend to take such passages scrupulously literally, but argue that they do not apply to the church, whereas the fathers insist that they apply to the church, but do not always take them as literally. As a result, when patristic writers do insist on the literal fulfillment of Old Testament promises, they also insist that the church takes part in this fulfillment, and so they make utterly no distinction between the Old Testament people of God and the New Testament people of God. Thus the hermeneutical differences between the fathers and modern dispensationalists on this point are related to theological differences in how the two groups conceive the relation between Israel and the church.

Irenaeus provides the clearest example of this as he refutes gnosticism in *Against Heresies*. One of gnosticism's chief flaws was that it postulated two different gods, a lesser god who created the material world and authored the Old Testament, and the supreme God, who created the spiritual realm and authored the New Testament. Irenaeus's refutation of gnosticism included proving the utter unity of Scripture. He argues that the faith of the patriarchs is the same as the church's faith and that the church is prefigured in the history of God's people in Genesis.[42] Irenaeus insists further that Christ came

---

41. For a fuller discussion of this point, see Donald Fairbairn, "Patristic Exegesis and Theology: The Cart and the Horse," *Westminster Theological Journal* 69.1 (2007): 1–19. For further information about patristic exegesis as a whole, see the works cited in that article, esp. John J. O'Keefe and R. R. Reno, *Sanctified Vision: An Introduction to Early Christian Interpretation of the Bible* (Baltimore: Johns Hopkins University Press, 2005).

42. Irenaeus, *Against Heresies* 4.21 (ANF 1:493).

for all people, both those before and those after him and, in the context of this argument, he discusses the second advent:

> Wherefore He shall, at His second coming, first rouse from their sleep all persons of this description [i.e., believers from before the time of Christ's first coming], and shall raise them up, as well as the rest who shall be judged, and give them a place in His kingdom. For it is truly "one God who" directed the patriarchs towards His dispensations, and "has justified the circumcision by faith, and the uncircumcision through faith." For as in the first we were prefigured, so, on the other hand, are they represented in us, that is, in the church, and receive the recompense for the things which they accomplished.[43]

Here Irenaeus sees the church as the fulfillment of the Old Testament hopes, and it is through the church that faithful men and women of the Old Testament receive the promises.

Later in the work, Irenaeus comments on God's promise of the land to Abraham (Gen. 13:14–17): "If, then, God promised him the inheritance of the land, yet he did not receive it during all the time of his sojourn there, it must be, that together with his seed, that is, those who fear God and believe in Him, he shall receive it at the resurrection of the just. For his seed is the church, which receives the adoption to God through the Lord."[44] This passage is especially germane to our purposes because it deals directly with an earthly promise. Irenaeus does not say that the Jews forfeited the promise of the land through disobedience (as some amillennialists would say today), nor does he "spiritualize" the promise of the land in order to argue that believers receive it in a nonphysical way, nor does he try to dissociate the promise of the land from the New Testament church (as many dispensationalists would do). Rather, he insists that the promise of an earthly, material land will be fulfilled on earth. The fact that this promise has not yet been fulfilled must mean that it will be fulfilled in the events surrounding the second coming of Christ. Abraham will receive this promise through his seed, which Irenaeus identifies with the church, not with the literal nation of the Jews.

Justin Martyr makes exactly the same argument as Irenaeus. Speaking of the promised land, Justin asserts,

> Christ has come in His power from the Almighty Father, and, calling all men to friendship, benediction, repentance, and community life, which should take place in the same land of all the saints, of which He has pledged that there shall

43. Irenaeus, *Against Heresies* 4.22 (ANF 1:494).
44. Irenaeus, *Against Heresies* 5.32 (ANF 1:561).

be an allotted portion for all the faithful, as has been shown before. Where-
fore, men from every land, whether slaves or free men, who believe in Christ
and recognize the truths of His words and those of the Prophets, fully realize
that they will one day be united with Him in that land, to inherit imperishable
blessings for all eternity.[45]

Here again, the literal fulfillment of the promise is presented, and believers
from all lands will take part in this fulfillment. The land promised to Israel
was, in effect, promised to all the people of God, and all believers will enjoy
it during the millennial kingdom.

Thus, because of the differences in hermeneutic between the early church
and modern dispensationalism, patristic writers (even those such as Irenaeus,
who in some respects seem similar to dispensationalists) make no distinction
between Israel and the church. Promises made to believing Israel and not yet
fulfilled are to be fulfilled for the entire church (including both Jewish and
gentile believers) in the events surrounding the second coming. This identification of the Old Testament and New Testament people of God obviates
any theological need to postulate that God might finish his purposes for the
church and then return to his purposes for Israel. As a result, the impetus that
might lead one to interpret the Thessalonian correspondence as teaching a
pretribulational rapture of the church is simply not present in the minds of
patristic writers.

The Early Church's Attitude toward Suffering

A second major way patristic eschatology differs from dispensationalist
teaching is in the attitude toward suffering and trial. Modern dispensationalism shies away from asserting that God would allow his people to suffer
severely, and this attitude is part of the reason for affirming a pretribulational
rapture of the church. Granted, this attitude is by no means universal, and
some dispensational theologians point out that God can and does allow suffering to befall his people, but God does not allow us to suffer his own wrath.
Therefore, if the tribulation is the time when God will pour out his wrath on
the unbelieving world, it follows that God ought to remove his church from
the world before that period.[46] But regardless of whether one distinguishes

45. Justin Martyr, *Dialogue with Trypho* 139 (FC 6:361–62; ANF 1:269). Cf. Tertullian, *On
the Resurrection of the Dead* 25 (ANF 3:563).
46. Some theologians argue that only part of the tribulation will constitute the outpouring
of God's wrath, and thus they allow for a rapture in the middle of the tribulation rather than
at the beginning. Cf. the arguments in Gleason L. Archer et al., *The Rapture: Pre-, Mid-, or
Post-tribulational* (Grand Rapids: Academie Books, 1984).

between suffering in general and suffering God's wrath, it is fair to argue that dispensationalism as a whole is undergirded by the assumption that God will protect his people from excessive suffering.

If this is correct, then one must acknowledge that such an assumption is diametrically opposed to the early church's attitude toward suffering (and especially the second-century church's attitude). Christians before the conversion of the empire not only accepted suffering as something inevitable; they in fact courted it. Suffering for the faith was a badge of honor, a link between oneself and one's Lord. (John 21:18–19 formed part of the biblical basis for this attitude.) When Irenaeus, Tertullian, and Hippolytus wrote, the memory of the apostles' martyrdom was still fresh in the people's collective mind, and more recent martyrs such as Ignatius of Antioch (executed in Rome ca. 110), Polycarp (martyred in Smyrna ca. 155), and Perpetua and Felicitas (martyred in Carthage in 203) were celebrated as well. Especially significant was the attitude of Ignatius, who wrote letters to churches in Asia Minor as he was escorted to Rome to be executed during the reign of the emperor Trajan. Ignatius feared that his loyal supporters in the various churches would petition the emperor for his release and thus prevent him from being martyred. He therefore implores them not to interfere but to allow his execution to go forward.[47]

The second-century church's embrace of suffering and martyrdom affected its interpretation of the tribulation. Instead of seeing this as a time when God would pour out his wrath on unbelievers, patristic writers viewed the tribulation as the final persecution of the saints by unbelievers (especially by the Antichrist) and thus as the final opportunity for believers to glorify God through suffering. This way of looking at the tribulation set up the fathers to assert that the church will be present on earth during that time, and so predisposed them against the idea of a pretribulation rapture. This point leads directly to the next issue, the patristic understanding of the relation between the church and the tribulation.

The Church and the Tribulation

The dispensational pretribulational understanding of the Thessalonian correspondence offers three major reasons that the rapture of 1 Thessalonians 4:17 will occur at the beginning of the tribulation. First, there would be no point in believers' meeting Christ in the clouds if we were not going to continue

47. See Ignatius, *To the Romans* 1–4 (*ANF* 1:73–75). See also Ignatius, *To the Ephesians* 10 (*ANF* 1:54), in which he links imitation of Christ to suffering.

on from there to heaven. Second, the "apostasy"[48] of 2 Thessalonians 2:3 is a reference to the rapture of the church. Since the Greek word *apostasia* can mean any sort of departure or dissolution, in this passage it means an exit from the world, not a departure from the faith. Third, the "restrainer"[49] of 2:7 is the Christian church; that is, the church is presently the primary force through which God restrains evil, and when the church is removed (raptured), the power of lawlessness will increase. On these three points, the eschatological thought of the early church once again differs markedly from that of dispensational pretribulationism. I will now consider each of these points in turn.

Irenaeus and other early patristic writers do not address the question why we would be caught up into the air to meet Christ if he were going to continue down to earth, but an indication of how they might have answered this question comes later, in John Chrysostom's homily on 1 Thessalonians 4 (preached in Constantinople, probably in the spring of AD 402):

> If He is about to descend, on what account shall we be caught up? For the sake of honor. For when a king drives into a city, those who are in honor go out to meet him; but the condemned await the judge within. And upon the coming of an affectionate father, his children indeed and those who are worthy to be his children, are taken out in a chariot, that they may see and kiss him; but those of the domestics who have offended remain within. We are carried upon the chariot of our Father. For He received Him up in the clouds, and "we shall be caught up in the clouds." Seest thou how great is the honor? and as He descends, we go forth to meet Him, and, what is more blessed than all, so we shall be with Him.[50]

This passage is noteworthy as much for what it assumes as for what it declares. The possibility that Christ might come down partway to retrieve the church and return with her to heaven does not seem to have entered Chrysostom's mind. Thus, when he asks why the church would go up to meet Christ and then return to earth with him, his point (unlike that of contemporary pretribulationists) is not to suggest that there could be no purpose for such an action and therefore that such an action would not happen. Instead his point is to remind his hearers of the purpose for going to meet Christ in the air and then returning with him to earth: believers will be honored to be a welcoming party as Christ comes down. Furthermore, the fact that Chrysostom does

48. The word "apostasy" in this sentence is the reading of the NAS. The KJV has "a falling away," and the NIV reads "the rebellion."
49. The word "restrainer" in this sentence comes from the NAS reading "he who restrains." The KJV has "he who letteth," and the NIV reads "the one who now holds it back."
50. John Chrysostom, *Homilies on 1 Thessalonians* 8 (NPNF[1] 13:356).

not even feel compelled to state directly that the rapture will be a welcoming party implies that this view has been traditional and accepted for quite some time before him. This, coupled with the lack of references in earlier patristic writings to any hypothetical division between the rapture and the return of Christ to earth,[51] suggests that the patristic church has long (or perhaps always) understood the rapture the way Chrysostom does here.

In addition to apparently understanding the purpose of the rapture differently from contemporary pretribulationists, the early church also understood the apostasy and the restrainer of 2 Thessalonians 2 quite differently. In *On the Resurrection of the Dead*, Tertullian gives the clearest explanation of a pattern that is common to others as well. During a long discussion in which he quotes 1 Thessalonians 4:13–5:3 and 2 Thessalonians 2:1–7, Tertullian interprets the *apostasia* as the dissolution of the Roman Empire. Speaking of the "restrainer," he writes, "What obstacle [to the proliferation of unrighteousness] is there but the Roman state, the falling away of which, by being scattered into ten kingdoms, shall introduce Antichrist upon its own ruins?"[52] The fact that this is what Tertullian and others believed makes it all the more obvious why they often discussed eschatology without mentioning the millennial kingdom after the return of Christ. If word got out among the Roman elite that the Christians specifically believed that Rome must fall before history's climactic events would be set in motion, this would surely have created trouble for the church. So they mentioned this aspect of their belief rarely; nevertheless, this was what they thought.

Furthermore, writers from the pre-Constantinian church also give the distinct impression that they believe the church will be present on earth during the tribulation. Irenaeus has by far the fullest treatment. During his long discussion of the antichrist's reign during the tribulation, Irenaeus explains that Daniel's "time, times, and half a time" are an indication that the tyranny

51. Justin, Irenaeus, Tertullian, and Hippolytus, as well as later writers such as Lactantius, have extensive descriptions of the events of the tribulation and the millennial kingdom; these descriptions are generally in chronological order. In such lengthy treatments of these events, in which the writers frequently quote and comment on the Thessalonian correspondence, one would expect some mention of the rapture as a separate event from the return of Christ to earth if the writers believed there would be such a separation. But in fact, there is no hint at all of any separation between a return of Christ to the air to retrieve the church and a return of Christ all the way to earth to rule over the millennial kingdom.

52. Tertullian, *On the Resurrection of the Dead* 24 (*ANF* 3:562–63). Irenaeus and Hippolytus also identify the dissolution of the Roman Empire as the precursor to the antichrist's reign, although their discussions deal with the interpretation of Daniel, not 1 and 2 Thessalonians. See Irenaeus, *Against Heresies* 5.26 (*ANF* 1:554); Hippolytus, *On the Antichrist* 25 (*ANF* 5:209). Lactantius has a similar discussion in *Divine Institutes* 7.15 (*FC* 49:513; *ANF* 7:212). See also Dunbar, "Hippolytus of Rome," 329.

will last three and a half years. He says that during this time, "the saints will be put to flight, they who offer a pure sacrifice unto God."[53] One could take the "saints" of this sentence as a reference to people who have become believers during the tribulation, after the church has been removed. Indeed, the reference to the saints as offering pure sacrifices could be read as an indication that during the tribulation, the new (Jewish) believers will worship in Old Testament ways. The whole point of Irenaeus's discussion, however, is that the Old and New Testaments are a unity, and as we have seen, he makes no distinctions between Israel and the church. It is better therefore to take "saints" as a reference to believers in general, not to Jews who have become Christians after the removal of the (largely gentile) church from the earth.

Not long after this statement, Irenaeus relates his understanding of the antichrist's reign to his six-thousand-year scheme for understanding human history. He continues,

> And therefore throughout all time, man, having been moulded at the beginning by the hands of God, that is, of the Son and of the Spirit, is made after the image and likeness of God: the chaff, indeed, which is the apostasy, being cast away; but the wheat, that is, those who bring forth fruit to God in faith, being gathered into the barn. And for this cause tribulation is necessary for those who are saved, that having been after a manner broken up, and rendered fine, and sprinkled over by the patience of the Word of God, and set on fire [for purification], they may be fitted for the royal banquet.[54]

Here Irenaeus identifies the great tribulation (about which he has been writing) as a particular instance of a general pattern that God has followed in his work to sanctify believers throughout Christian history. The wheat must be separated from the chaff before it can be gathered in. Persecution and tribulation are what God uses to perform this separation. If this is true throughout Christian history, then it is especially true at the end of history. The final tribulation will complete the process that God has been carrying out all along, and thus it (like all the lesser trials and sufferings that Christians undergo) will serve to make believers fit for the marriage supper of the Lamb. This is a crucial passage because dispensationalism forces one to argue that the tribulation constitutes a drastic departure from the way God has operated previously. But Irenaeus argues that throughout history, and especially at the end of history, God works through the persecutions that unbelievers inflict upon the saints, to purify us and to prepare us for his presence. Indeed, only if there is

53. Irenaeus, *Against Heresies* 5.25 (ANF 1:554).
54. Irenaeus, *Against Heresies* 5.28 (ANF 1:557).

continuity between the way God will use the great tribulation and the way he uses trials and suffering now will apocalyptic prophecy be of direct relevance to God's people today.

Almost immediately after this passage, Irenaeus asserts,

> I have set forth the causes for which God permitted these things [the atrocities of the antichrist, which he has just discussed] to be made, and have pointed out that all such have been created for the benefit of that human nature which is saved, ripening for immortality that which is [possessed] of its own free will and its own power, and preparing and rendering it more adapted for eternal subjection to God.[55]

Here again there is no hint of a distinction between Jewish believers and the church, nor is there any sense that the tribulation and the antichrist's reign are a radically different way for God to operate than he has used previously. Irenaeus speaks of "that human nature which is saved." Speaking of all saved people in this kind of language is a reflection of the Platonic notion that the human race is a collective entity, and this collective way of speaking underscores the fact that in Irenaeus's mind there are no distinctions between Jews and gentiles or between the way God operates with the two groups. Furthermore, it is clear that God's purpose in the tribulation is not to bring wrath on unbelievers (that will come later) but, rather, to finish purifying his people in preparation for them to be his eternal servants.[56]

In the same chapter, Irenaeus describes the unbelieving nations as stubble that helps wheat to grow, as straw that enables one to make gold. "And therefore, when in the end the church shall suddenly be caught up from this, it is said, 'There shall be tribulation such as has not been since the beginning, neither shall be.' For this is the last contest of the righteous, in which, when they overcome, they are crowned with incorruption."[57] One could read this passage as a reference to a pretribulational rapture, since the phrase "caught up" precedes the quotation from Matthew 24:21 about the great tribulation. Taking the sentence in this way, however, would do violence to the entire

---

55. Irenaeus, *Against Heresies* 5.29 (ANF 1:558).

56. Thomas D. Lea ("A Survey of the Doctrine of the Return of Christ in the Ante-Nicene Fathers," *Journal of the Evangelical Theological Society* 29.2 [1986]: 177) makes this point: "The return of Christ as taught by the ante-Nicene fathers was an event that occurred after tribulation and persecution for God's people. Christians were urged to expect to pass through a period of great tribulation and persecution for their faith. They were urged to be faithful. They were encouraged to feel that they must endure in their faithfulness in order to reap blessing from the Lord."

57. Irenaeus, *Against Heresies* 5.29 (ANF 1:558).

thrust of Irenaeus's argument. His point is that God will use the tribulation as the "last contest of the righteous," the final preparation of believers for the eternal kingdom. As terrible as the reign of the antichrist will be, God will work through it, and indeed the antichrist and the unbelieving nations that follow him will be like straw that God uses to transform his people into gold. In such a view of the tribulation, the church's absence from earth would be unthinkable. So, although Irenaeus does not say it explicitly, the "catching up" of the church must come at the end of the tribulation, as Christ returns to earth, not earlier.[58]

Conclusions regarding the Tribulation and the Rapture

From this discussion it has become clear that among early patristic writers who deal with the great tribulation, there is no evidence of a belief that the rapture of the church would come before the tribulation. The patristic identification of the Old Testament and New Testament people of God, coupled with the early church's attitude toward suffering, predisposes the fathers against such a view. More important, the early church saw the tribulation as the final proving ground for the saints and thus indicated that the church would be present on earth during that time. Lea aptly concludes: "It is impossible to see how the ante-Nicene fathers can be described as giving teaching that supports the view of a pretribulational return of Christ. Every reference that betrays any idea of a relationship between the tribulation and the return of Christ suggests that the return follows the tribulation."[59] The premillennialism of the early church was posttribulational, and in substance it was very different from dispensational premillennialism even though there were some noteworthy points of contact.

The Theological Function of Chiliasm in Early Patristic Theology

Thus far this essay has considered questions of direct interest to contemporary readers (the questions that this book as a whole seeks to address) and has summarized the way the early church dealt with these questions. Because of such an organizational scheme, this essay has so far only hinted at the way

---

58. Hippolytus's discussion of the antichrist and the tribulation also shows no hint of a pretribulational rapture. He writes specifically that the antichrist will persecute the church during his three-and-a-half-year reign and that believers' hope to see their Lord appear from heaven will be fulfilled after the reign of the antichrist. See *On the Antichrist* 61 (*ANF* 5:217); 64 (*ANF* 5:218).

59. Lea, "Survey," 177.

premillennialism functioned in the context of the early church's exposition of its overall faith. It has mentioned that premillennialism was part of the polemic against gnosticism and that the tribulation was the final proving ground for believers, but has not developed these ideas at any length. Thus it has given an incomplete (and, one could argue, a somewhat distorted) picture of chiliastic eschatology in the early church. For a conclusion, I would like briefly to complete the picture by setting patristic discussions of eschatology in their proper context.

As mentioned previously, at the heart of gnosticism lies a profound dualism between the spiritual and the material. This dualism surfaces in four crucial ways. First, it leads to the sense that the material world is evil and unredeemable and thus that salvation applies only to the soul, not to the body. Second and closely related, it leads to a denigration of history: if the physical universe is unredeemable, then the panorama of history played out in this physical world is of little consequence. Third, it leads to a distinction between two competing gods—the lesser, material god of the Old Testament and the higher, spiritual God of the New Testament. Fourth, as an outgrowth of the third point, it leads to a docetic view of Christ, in which he (the spiritual representative of the New Testament God) only appears to be human and fleshly. The church's greatest battle in the second and early third centuries was against gnosticism, and the church fathers who led this battle—Irenaeus and Tertullian—used their premillennialism as a primary weapon.[60] A brief retrospect on the passages by Irenaeus already considered in this essay will make this point clear.

As stated earlier, for Irenaeus, the hermeneutical question of how to integrate the Old and New Testaments leads him to identify Israel and the church, which inclines him against pretribulationism and toward what is today called historic premillennialism. The concern that lies behind this is his desire to demonstrate that there is a single God, who wrote a single, united Bible for a single, united people of God. The concern to demonstrate the unity of Scripture is what drives him into the details of Daniel and Revelation, and behind this concern lies his insistence that the same God inspired both books. Furthermore, behind Irenaeus's treatment of an earthly kingdom lies the concern to refute the gnostic denigration of the material world. In his mind, nothing could be

---

60. As Wood ("Eschatology of Irenaeus," 38) points out: "It ought also to be borne in mind that the strong emphasis of Irenaeus on the literal fulfillment of the prophecies concerning the Millennium were no doubt conditioned to some degree by the fact that he was contending against the gnostic heretics, who denied the redeemability of the material. The millennial teaching of Irenaeus must not be isolated from the rest of his theology. It is all of a piece with it, and Irenaeus was the first to formulate (however embryonically) a millennial—indeed premillennial—system of interpretation."

more appropriate for the God who created the world and redeemed humanity through earthly history than to conclude his work with an earthly kingdom as a transition to an eternal kingdom that will also be on a refurbished earth. In Irenaeus's mind, moreover, anyone who denies such an earthly kingdom as overly sensuous and not "spiritual" enough is denying the goodness of the physical universe and thus the goodness of the God who chose to create it and to crown it by making human beings the only beings in the universe who are both spiritual and physical. Furthermore, behind Irenaeus's idea that the tribulation is a vehicle that God uses to prepare his people for eternity is his bedrock conviction that God uses all the events of this world, however evil they may be in themselves, for the good of his saints. Behind Irenaeus's belief that the tribulation (with the terrifying reign of the antichrist) will not be the last event of human history but will give way to the millennial kingdom lies the conviction that the God who created history will ultimately triumph—and be seen by all to have triumphed—in human history in this world.[61]

As a result, for Irenaeus (and for other writers of the early church), eschatology's importance does not lie exclusively, or even primarily, in the question of what will happen at the end of the world. And furthermore, studying eschatology is not exclusively, or even primarily, a matter of identifying what a certain scriptural passage means. Rather, eschatology's significance lies in the way it testifies to the unity of Scripture, the unity of God's purposes, and ultimately the unity and goodness of the God we worship. In the mind of Irenaeus and most of the church prior to Origen, an earthly kingdom following the return of Christ is not merely what Revelation 20 teaches. It is also a central tenet of the faith because it functions to reinforce the central truths of Christianity—that there is one God who in love has created this world for us and us for it, who has personally entered this world in order to redeem us for a future in this world, and who will ultimately triumph in this world over the forces that are arrayed against him.

Such a vision of the *function* of eschatology is not correct simply because Irenaeus and the early church held to it, just as such a vision of the *details* of eschatology is not correct simply because they held to them. Ultimately, our conclusions about eschatology, as about all other matters, will be based on our understanding of Scripture. But we have much to learn about Scripture from the way Christians such as Irenaeus and Tertullian have handled it. One could

---

61. A reading of Irenaeus's entire description of eschatological questions in *Against Heresies* 5.23–36 makes clear how central these issues are in his polemic against gnosticism. See also the excellent summary of the function of Irenaeus's premillennialism in Brian Daley, *The Hope of the Early Church: A Handbook of Patristic Eschatology*, new ed. (Peabody, MA: Hendrickson, 2003), 29–34.

argue that the battle against gnosticism was not merely the greatest battle of the second and third centuries but the greatest battle the church has ever faced, a battle that the church has still not decisively won. Perhaps part of the reason we have not won it is that we have forfeited the use of one of the greatest biblical/theological weapons in this battle—eschatology. Have we overspiritualized the hope held out to Christians and thus essentially conceded to the gnostics among us that the material world is not ultimately important? Have we treated eschatology as a looking glass into the future, whose primary purpose is to assuage the thirst of the curious? If we have, then it is no wonder that latent gnosticism still flourishes in our churches. In such a case, Irenaeus and the early church should serve as our wake-up call, our reminder that eschatology is part and parcel of our understanding of God himself and of our place in his purposes. They believed that the eschatology that best reinforces the Bible's teaching on God is one that we today label posttribulational premillennialism. Their conclusion and the reasons they held to it constitute a challenge to us today not only to take this eschatological option seriously but also to give eschatology its proper place near the center of Christian truth.

7

Toward the Reformed and Covenantal Theology of Premillennialism

A Proposal

Sung Wook Chung

Introduction

As is well known among theological scholars, the Reformed tradition has been almost unanimous in advocating amillennialism in interpreting the account of the millennial kingdom in Revelation 20:1–6.[1] Among the prominent representatives of amillennialism in the Reformed tradition are such great theologians of the church as John Calvin, Abraham Kuyper, Herman Bavinck, Louis Berkhof, and Benjamin B. Warfield.[2]

The Reformed tradition's interpretation of Revelation 20:1–6, however, has been seriously problematic. In particular, my conviction is that we should interpret Revelation 20:1–6 more literally if we accept the covenantal structure and unity of the entire Scripture. On the basis of this initial insight, a theology of premillennialism from a Reformed and covenantal perspective is here proposed.

1. A few Reformed theologians have advocated postmillennialism. Jonathan Edwards (1703–58) is a prominent example.
2. Gordon R. Lewis and Bruce A. Demarest, *Integrative Theology* (Grand Rapids: Zondervan, 1996), 3:372.

A Critical Evaluation of the Traditional Reformed Covenant Theology

Reformed tradition recognizes the importance of a covenantal reading of the entire Bible. According to traditional Reformed federal/covenant theology, God established the covenant of works with Adam in the garden of Eden.

> In the covenant of works or Edenic covenant God, the moral Governor of the universe, submitted Adam as a free moral agent to a test of obedience in Eden. The *parties* of the covenant of works were God and Adam, Adam being representative head of the race. The *promise* God made to Adam (and to humanity in him) was eternal life and favor. The *proviso* was obedience to God's command relative to the tree of knowledge, and the *penalty* for disobedience was physical and spiritual death. The seal connoting ratification of the covenant of works is identified as the Tree of Life. The covenant of works is said to remain binding for all unsaved persons.[3]

The failure of humankind in Eden broke this covenant of works. God, however, extended his grace to humankind by establishing the covenant of grace.

> The *parties* to the covenant of grace are God and the chosen "seed." The *promise* is eternal life and favor. The *proviso* is faith in Christ, albeit a faith given by God himself. And the *penalty* for covenant-breaking is death. The covenant of grace, made with the elect, is a particular covenant. Moreover, it is unconditional in the sense that God will not violate the covenant, but conditional in the sense that individual faith is required for its fulfillment. Covenant theologians maintain that although the covenant of grace and the truth revealed in it is one, it includes several dispensations or differing modes of administration.[4]

It is important to appreciate that Reformed covenant theology has definite merits in promoting "the unity of the covenant of grace, being essentially *the same from Genesis 3:15 through Revelation 22:21*."[5] It also has strengths in affirming "a unity of soteriological purpose. Both Testaments set forth identical promises, the same spiritual life, and the same means of salvation, namely, faith in God's promises."[6] But Reformed covenant theology as it has been traditionally upheld by Reformed theologians has serious problems. First of all, on account of its overemphasis on the soteriological dimension of the covenant of grace throughout the Bible, Reformed covenant theology has not paid deserved attention to the kingdom dimension of God's work within history.

3. Ibid., 3:308; italics in the original.
4. Ibid., 3:309.
5. Ibid.
6. Ibid.

Second, Reformed covenant theology's overemphasis on the soteriological dimension of the covenant of grace has also led many Reformed theologians to spiritualize key passages of the Bible that must be interpreted more literally from the kingdom perspective. For example, many Reformed covenant theologians have taken Revelation 20:1–6 as a metaphorical account, denying the fulfillment of the physical millennial rule on the earth. In a similar vein, many Reformed covenant theologians have argued that the promise of physical blessings to Israel in the Old Testament was not fulfilled "physically" but rather "spiritually" in and through the church, which is the spiritual Israel. Furthermore, according to Gordon Lewis and Bruce Demarest, Reformed covenant theology's view of the kingdom of God has been too much spiritualized: "Covenant theology views the kingdom as a broader concept than either Israel or the church. The kingdom signifies the rule of God, as a spiritual and invisible reality, initially over believing Israel and subsequently over the New Testament community."[7] Third, by overly focusing on the covenant of works in Genesis 2:15–17, Reformed covenant theology has not correctly understood the significance of Genesis 1:26–28 for the reality of God's kingdom in general and the millennial rule of Jesus Christ in particular.

An Alternative Covenantal Reading of Genesis 1 and 2

An alternative covenantal reading of Genesis 1 and 2 will help us overcome the demerits of traditional Reformed covenant theology in relation to the biblical motif of the kingdom of God and the notion of the physical fulfillment of the millennial rule of Jesus Christ on the earth before the advent of the new heavens and the new earth. I believe that Genesis 1 and 2 should be read from a covenantal perspective. Granted, the two chapters do not mention the word "covenant" and, further, do not have all the factors of a full-fledged covenantal document. But this does not necessarily mean that the chapters cannot be taken as a covenantal document.

Genesis 1:26–28 as a Covenant of Promise/Blessings

Genesis 1:26–28 can be interpreted as the archetype of the covenants of promise/blessings found in later sections of the Old Testament.[8] In the Old Testament context, the covenants of promise/blessings were unconditional

7. Ibid.
8. Prominent examples are the Noahic covenant (Gen. 9), the Abrahamic covenant (Gen. 12), and the Davidic covenant (2 Sam. 7).

covenants that God established in order to grant land or some other benefits to his people. The grant was normally permanent and not based on the merits of God's people. In other words, the grant was given to God's servants on the basis of his own sovereign pleasure.[9] The best example of the covenant of blessings is God's covenant with Abraham. For example, in Genesis 12:2–3, God promises Abram that he will make Abram into a great nation and a channel through which all peoples on earth will be blessed. This promissory covenant is renewed and confirmed through the more formal covenants throughout Abraham's life and beyond.[10]

In Genesis 1:26–28, God, as the King of kings, creates his viceroys, his subject kings. "Then God said, 'Let us make man in our image, in our likeness, and let them rule over the fish of the sea and the birds of the air, over the livestock, over all the earth, and over all the creatures that move along the ground.' So God created man in his own image, in the image of God he created him; male and female he created them" (Gen. 1:26–27). God creates man and woman on the basis of his own free determination. Nothing forces God to create humankind. In creating his vice-regents, God manifests his absolute sovereignty and freedom. And God's creation of humankind is an action of God's sheer grace. In addition, God's action of creating man and woman in his own image and likeness means that God wants to have his representatives in physical form. "The image is a physical manifestation of divine (or royal) essence that bears the function of that which it represents; this gives the image-bearer the capacity to reflect the attributes of the one represented and act on his behalf."[11] The major task of these representatives is to rule over the whole creation as God's vice-regents. Lordship and dominion over the entire creation are given to man and woman unconditionally on the basis of God's sovereign grace.

In Genesis 1:28, God gives Adam and Eve, his servants, a grant of descendants, land, and lordship over the creation unconditionally. The unconditional

---

9. Some Old Testament scholars view the covenant of promise/blessings as an example of royal-grant covenants, which were popular in the ancient Near East. See Dennis J. McCarthy, *Old Testament Covenant: A Survey of Current Opinions* (Atlanta: John Knox, 1972); idem, *Treaty and Covenant: A Study in Form in the Ancient Oriental Documents and in the Old Testament*, 2nd ed. (Rome: Biblical Institute, 1978); George E. Mendenhall, "Covenant Forms in Israelite Tradition," *Biblical Archaeologist* 17 (1954): 50–76; Moshe Weinfeld, "The Covenant of Grant in the Old Testament and in the Ancient Near East," *Journal of the American Oriental Society* 90 (1970): 184–203; idem, "Addenda to *JAOS* 90 (1970), p. 184ff.," *Journal of the American Oriental Society* 92 (1972): 468–69.

10. Gen. 17:2–8; 22:16–18; 26:3–5, 24; 28:3–4; 35:11–12; 48:3–4.

11. John H. Walton, *Genesis*, NIV Application Commentary (Grand Rapids: Zondervan, 2001), 131.

character of this covenant is made conspicuous by God's action of sovereign blessing upon Adam and Eve: "God blessed them and said to them, 'Be fruitful and increase in number; fill the earth and subdue it. Rule over the fish of the sea and the birds of the air and over every living creature that moves on the ground.'" By blessing Adam and Eve, God gives them a kingdom that represents the ultimate kingdom and reign of God on the earth. As vice-regents of the ultimate King, they are to represent the King and his attributes in their action of ruling over the creation. Traditional Reformed covenant theology has failed to grasp the covenantal significance of Genesis 1:26–28. Along with Abraham Kuyper, many Dutch Reformed theologians have interpreted Genesis 1:28 as the "cultural mandate."[12] But this interpretation is misleading. Rather, we should take Genesis 1:28 as the "kingdom mandate" or the "statement of the covenant blessing," which gives humankind dominion over the whole creation.

Genesis 2:15–17 as a Covenant of the Law

In the context of God's unconditional and unilateral blessing upon Adam and Eve, we need to understand Genesis 2:15–17 from a covenantal perspective as well: "The LORD God took the man and put him in the Garden of Eden to work it and take care of it. And the LORD God commanded the man, 'You are free to eat from any tree in the garden; but you must not eat from the tree of the knowledge of good and evil, for when you eat of it you will surely die.'" This passage should be interpreted to be the archetype of the covenants of the law or conditional covenants found in later sections of the Old Testament.[13] The covenants of the law, as the Mosaic law clearly demonstrates, regulate God's relationship with his people. Therefore the covenants of the law usually include regulations on how God's people worship God and how they act before God. G. K. Beale argues that Israel's earthly tabernacle and temple are reflections and recapitulations of the first temple in the garden of Eden.[14] According to Beale, the garden of Eden is the unique place of God's presence

12. Millard J. Erickson, *Christian Theology* (Grand Rapids: Baker Academic, 1985), 510.

13. Some Old Testament scholars (Mendenhall, McCarthy, and Weinfeld) view the covenant of the law as an example of the suzerain-vassal covenant, which was common in the ancient Near East. Prominent examples are the Sinaitic covenant (Exod. 19–24) and the Deuteronomic covenant (Deuteronomy).

14. G. K. Beale, *The Temple and the Church's Mission: A Biblical Theology of the Dwelling Place of God*, New Studies in Biblical Theology 17 (Downers Grove, IL: InterVarsity, 2004), 66–80. Beale depends heavily on Gordon Wenham, "Sanctuary Symbolism in the Garden of Eden Story," in *I Studied Inscriptions from before the Flood*, ed. Richard S. Hess and David T. Tsumura (Winona Lake, IN: Eisenbrauns, 1994), 19–25.

and the first place for the first priest, Adam. This means that "part of Adam's function was to worship God"[15] as the representative priest of all the creation. In other words, "he was the archetypal priest who served in and guarded (or took care of) God's first temple."[16]

According to Beale's fresh insights, Genesis 2:16–17 can be regarded as the first "torah."

> Hence, it follows naturally that after God puts Adam into the Garden for "cultivating/serving and keeping/guarding" (v. 15) that in the very next verse God would command Adam to keep a commandment: "and the Lord God commanded the man . . ." The first "torah" was that "From any tree of the Garden you may eat freely; but from the tree of the knowledge of good and evil you shall not eat, for in the day that you eat from it you shall surely die" (Gen. 2:16–17). Accordingly, Adam's disobedience, as Israel's, results in his being cut off from the sacred land of the Garden. This is an indication that the task of Adam in Genesis 2:15 included more than mere spadework in the dirt of a garden.[17]

In Genesis 2:16–17, God plays the role of the great King who establishes a conditional covenant of the law with his people. Adam plays the role of the priest who must demonstrate his faithfulness and loyalty to the great King as the representative of his progeny. On the condition that Adam obeys God's commandment not to eat of the tree of the knowledge of good and evil, he can enjoy the freedom to eat from any tree in the garden. Furthermore, on the condition of his obedience, he can enjoy abundant life in the garden. If he disobeys the great King, he will die. This means that he will lose his enjoyment of freedom and life. When he loses his freedom and life, he loses even the blessing of dominion over the creation.

Genesis 2:16–17 plays a role as the constitution of the kingdom in Eden.[18] As the constitution of the Edenic kingdom, these verses regulate the relationship between God and his people. Furthermore, the Edenic constitution regulates which values the Edenic kingdom must promote. According to the Edenic constitution, the core values of the Edenic kingdom are to be freedom within the context of obedience. In other words, freedom and responsibility are to be celebrated as the cultural ethos of the Edenic kingdom.

15. Beale, *Temple and the Church's Mission*, 67.
16. Ibid., 68.
17. Ibid., 68–69.
18. N. T. Wright (*The Climax of the Covenant: Christ and the Law in Pauline Theology* [Minneapolis: Fortress, 1993], 26) states, in relation to the role of the Torah for the people of Israel, "They [Torah and wisdom] form the charter for Israel's national life *precisely* as the way of life of God's true humanity."

The Character of the First Adam's Rule

In a nutshell, the character of the dominion that God wanted Adam to exercise was both spiritual/priestly and physical/kingly. Adam was blessed to rule over the whole creation, including its spiritual/priestly and physical/institutional dimensions. Adam's rule was anticipated to be extended to the entire creation beyond the boundary of the garden of Eden. Unless he fell, Adam should have ruled over the entire creation physically as well as spiritually.

What is meant by Adam's physical/kingly dominion? According to Walton, Adam's physical dominion "concerns exercising authority that has been granted and acknowledged," including domestication of animals, utilization of natural resources, harnessing of the earth's energy, and the like.[19] In other words, Adam's physical dominion over the creation meant that Adam had political and physical authority over the whole creation as vice-regent for God. This authority, however, did not allow Adam to "legitimize slaughter, abuse, or neglect"[20] but was to be characterized by stewardship, or taking good care of the creation.

What about Adam's spiritual/priestly rule? His spiritual rule was characterized by his priestly service in the presence of God. According to Beale, when God put Adam in the garden to work it and take care of it, God gave Adam a priestly task to guard the garden as the sanctuary, which means to "maintain the upkeep and order of the sanctuary."[21] In sum, Adam was blessed and commissioned by God to rule over the whole creation as king and to worship God as priest in the sanctuary of the garden of Eden. "Adam's kingly and priestly activity in the garden was to be a beginning fulfillment of the commission in 1:28 and was not to be limited to the garden's original earthly boundaries but was to be extended over the whole world."[22]

The Fall: Adam's Loss of Kingly Rule and Priestly Privilege

Adam lost his lordship over the whole creation by obeying Satan and disobeying God. Through his transgression against God, he lost both his spiritual headship as the representative priest for the whole creation and physical dominion over the entire creation. As Beale has argued, Adam permitted "entrance into the Garden to an antagonistic and unclean being. . . . Adam did not guard the Garden but allowed entrance to a foul snake that brought sin, chaos and disorder into the sanctuary and into Adam and Eve's lives. He

19. Walton, *Genesis*, 132.
20. Ibid.
21. Beale, *Temple and the Church's Mission*, 68.
22. Ibid., 83.

allowed the Serpent to 'rule over' him rather than 'ruling over' it and casting it out of the Garden. Rather than extending the divine presence of the garden sanctuary, Adam and Eve were expelled from it."[23]

Ever since the fall of Adam, the whole creation, including humanity and the natural order, has been in subjection to chaos, vanity, cursedness, and death. The apostle Paul depicts dramatically the current condition to which the creation is subjected: "The creation waits in eager expectation for the sons of God to be revealed. For the creation was subjected to frustration, not by its own choice, but by the will of the one who subjected it, in hope that the creation itself will be liberated from its bondage to decay and brought into the glorious freedom of the children of God. We know that the whole creation has been groaning as in the pains of childbirth right up to the present time" (Rom. 8:19–22).

Through the fall, Adam lost his kingly dominion over the entire creation as well as his priestly privilege to guard the sanctuary, obey God's commandment in freedom, and worship God. Ever since the fall of Adam, Satan has been ruling over the creation not only spiritually but also physically. Satan's rule is spiritual and invisible because he is a spiritual and invisible being. As a spiritual ruler, Satan has enslaved humankind and led it to worship him or other idols. Satan's rule is also physical because his spiritual and invisible power makes a great impact upon the physical dimension of the current world system. Spiritual and physical dimensions are distinct from each other but cannot be separated. Satan's spiritual rule has physical/institutional effects and consequences.

Genesis 3:15 as the Promise to Restore the Lost Dominion

Right after the fall of the first Adam and in the context of rebuking the serpent, God promised to send the woman's seed, who would be the second Adam and the last Adam. "And I will put enmity between you and the woman, and between your offspring and hers; he will crush your head, and you will strike his heel" (Gen. 3:15). The seed of the woman would come to crush the head of the serpent. "He who does what is sinful is of the devil, because the devil has been sinning from the beginning. The reason the Son of God appeared was to destroy the devil's work" (1 John 3:8). Since the devil's work is not only spiritual in its character but also physical and institutional in its effects, we should interpret Genesis 3:15 as God's promise to restore not only Adam's spiritual rule but also his physical rule on earth and in time before

23. Ibid., 87.

the advent of the new heavens and earth, which will be eternal. Clearly, this dominion will be exercised not by the first Adam but by the second/last Adam as the representative of a new kind of humanity.

Adamic Covenants and Jesus Christ as the Second Man and the Last Adam

God established two covenants with Adam. One was an unconditional covenant of blessing, and the other was a conditional covenant of the law. The two covenants were together geared to establish the Adamic kingdom over the entire creation in accordance with God's will and purpose. Furthermore, this kingdom dominion was supposed to have a physical and institutional form. Through Adam's fall, God's original plan appeared to be thwarted. But by promising to send the seed of the woman right after the fall of Adam, God guaranteed that his original purpose and plan would stand firm and be fulfilled ultimately. It was God's original purpose and plan that humanity exercise dominion over the entire creation not merely spiritually but also physically in time and space. In other words, "God's ultimate goal in creation was to magnify his glory throughout the earth by means of his faithful image-bearers inhabiting the world in obedience to the divine mandate."[24]

Jesus Christ, as the seed of the woman, came to the world as the image of God. In Jesus Christ's person and work, God's original plan and purpose began to be fulfilled. First of all, Jesus Christ is not merely a bearer of God's image but the very image of God: "He is the image of the invisible God, the firstborn over all creation" (Col. 1:15); "The Son is the radiance of God's glory and the exact representation of his being" (Heb. 1:3). As God's image, Jesus Christ represents God's authority, dominion, glory, and honor. But as the Son of Man, Jesus Christ represents all humanity before God as well. He is the head of a new kind of humanity. Second, as the promised Messiah, Jesus Christ embodies three offices of king, priest, and prophet. He came to the world as the King of kings, the Prophet of prophets, and the High Priest. Third, Jesus Christ came to the world as the second/last Adam: "Adam . . . [was] a pattern of the one to come" (Rom. 5:14); "So it is written: 'The first man Adam became a living being; the last Adam, a life-giving spirit. . . . The first man was of the dust of the earth, the second man from heaven'" (1 Cor. 15:45, 47).

Whereas the first Adam failed to fulfill the commission and mandate that God gave him through the two Edenic covenants, Jesus Christ, as the last Adam, began to fulfill both the covenant of blessing and the covenant of the law that

24. Ibid., 82.

were originally given to the first Adam. First, while he was on earth, Jesus Christ as the King of kings exercised dominion over the entire creation. His dominion was demonstrated primarily by his miracles. For example, when he calmed the ferocious sea, he showed his absolute sovereignty over the natural order. When he raised dead people to life, he demonstrated publicly his mighty dominion over the power of death. Through the exercise of his dominion over the creation, the last Adam began to fulfill what the covenant of Genesis 1:26–28 required and anticipated of the first Adam and all humanity. Second, Jesus Christ as the High Priest loved God with all his heart, all his mind, all his soul, and all his power. His love for God was demonstrated through his perfect obedience to the Father's will, even up to death on the cross. Whereas the first Adam obeyed Satan and disobeyed God, the last Adam obeyed God and rejected Satan's temptations. Through his love for, and obedience to, God, the last Adam began to fulfill what the covenant of Genesis 2:16–17 required not only of the first Adam but also of all humanity. By beginning to fulfill what the original two covenants anticipated, the last Adam began to succeed in reestablishing the kingdom of God among humankind. As the Prophet of prophets, the Lord Jesus delivered faithfully the message of God the Father about the eternal kingdom of God and the salvation of sinners. Jesus Christ revealed God's plan and will for the redemption of fallen humanity and the restoration of cursed cosmos.

Adamic Covenants and the Millennium

Why does Jesus Christ have to reign with all believers alive at the parousia for a thousand years? Why is the millennium necessary? In order to answer these significant questions, we need, first of all, to understand the relationship between the Adamic covenants and the millennium. As already pointed out above, Adam's kingly rule has both a spiritual/priestly dimension and a physical/institutional dimension. Through the first coming of Jesus Christ, the last Adam began to restore and fulfill both the spiritual and the physical dimensions of the first Adam's kingly rule. The first Adam's kingly rule has, however, not yet been completely restored and fulfilled. In particular, although Satan's head was crushed by the cross, he is still making a great impact upon the physical/institutional dimension of the world system. Therefore, by establishing the millennial kingdom, Jesus Christ, as the last Adam, will restore and fulfill not only the spiritual/priestly dimension but also the physical/institutional dimension of the first Adam's kingdom.

Revelation 20:6 demonstrates that those who will reign in the millennial kingdom will be both kings and priests: "Blessed and holy are those who have part in the first resurrection. The second death has no power over them, but they will be priests of God and of Christ and will reign with him for a thousand years." As the first Adam was a priest-king and the last Adam was also a priest-king, those who will reign with Christ will be priest-kings as well. The first Adam's priest-kingly activity, which was thwarted by the fall, will be fulfilled in the millennial kingdom. Therefore the millennial kingdom will be a restoration and fulfillment of the Edenic kingdom on the earth.

Another reason God establishes the millennial kingdom on the earth is that God's covenants and promises must be fulfilled. In other words, by establishing the millennium, God demonstrates his unswerving faithfulness to his covenants. Our God is the God of faithfulness and truthfulness. Our God cannot deceive or deny himself. Our God cannot lie: "God is not a man, that he should lie, nor a son of man, that he should change his mind. Does he speak and then not act? Does he promise and not fulfill?" (Num. 23:19); "He who is the Glory of Israel does not lie or change his mind; for he is not a man, that he should change his mind" (1 Sam. 15:29); "God did this so that, by two unchangeable things in which it is impossible for God to lie, we who have fled to take hold of the hope offered to us may be greatly encouraged" (Heb. 6:18). God's faithful character brings his covenant and promise to fulfillment. Since the Edenic covenants of blessing and the law were given in the context of this earth, they must be fulfilled on this earth before its entrance into the eternal and transformed state of the new heavens and earth. The major difference between the millennial kingdom and the new heavens and earth is that the millennial kingdom is not an eternal kingdom whereas the new heavens and earth are eternal in character. The major continuity between the millennial kingdom and the new Jerusalem in the new heavens and earth is that both will have priest-kings who will reign with Jesus Christ. In this sense, we may say that the millennial kingdom is the penultimate realization of the kingdom promise/blessing in the context of the current world, whereas the new Jerusalem in the new heavens and earth is the ultimate realization of the kingdom promise/blessing in the context of the eternally transformed cosmos. As Lewis and Demarest have stated:

> Scripture promises a distinct, future reign with Christ on earth. . . . Jesus said that those who stood by him in his trials would "eat and drink at [his] table in [his] kingdom and sit on thrones, judging the twelve tribes of Israel" (Luke 22:30). To the early churches Paul said, "Do you not know that the saints will judge the world?" (1 Cor. 6:2). Again: "If we endure, we will also reign with him" (2 Tim. 2:12). John taught that those who now suffer with Christ will in the future "reign [with him] on the earth" (Rev. 5:10). Note that the reigning takes

place on the "earth"; the new heavens and earth are not in this context. Christ's present redemptive rule mediated through Christians in various spheres does not preempt a more direct, universal rule of Christ following this return.[25]

In sum, the covenantal unity of the entire Bible demands that the millennial kingdom should be materialized on this earth before the beginning of the new heavens and earth.

The Abrahamic Covenant and the Millennial Kingdom

Another covenant that has significant implications for the millennial kingdom on earth is the Abrahamic covenant. God called Abram and promised him blessings. More than anything else, God promised to make Abram a great nation and to bless all the families on earth through him: "I will make you into a great nation and I will bless you; I will make your name great, and you will be a blessing. I will bless those who bless you, and whoever curses you I will curse; and all peoples on earth will be blessed through you" (Gen. 12:2–3). God's promise of blessings upon Abram and his descendants is not only spiritual but also physical. As God's blessing upon Adam had a specific physical shape and was given in the context of the current world of time and space, so God's blessing upon Abram had a physical orientation. Reformed theologians who interpret this passage purely spiritually are in the wrong. Their understanding of God's blessings is distorted by their unwitting gnostic tendencies, which disregard and ignore the importance and value of the physical in God's eyes.

God's promise to make Abraham into a great nation was fulfilled in the history of Israel. God's promise to give Abraham numerous descendants was fulfilled by the Israelites' being fruitful and multiplying in the land of Egypt (Exod. 1:1–7). God's promise to give Abraham's descendants a land was fulfilled by Joshua's conquering the land of Canaan. And God's promise to give Abraham's descendants many kings (Gen. 17:6) was fulfilled through David and his royal line.

When the apostle Paul interprets the Genesis account of the Abrahamic covenant, he says that Abraham received a promise that he would be an heir of the world: "It was not through law that Abraham and his offspring received the promise that he would be heir of the world" (Rom. 4:13). The problem, however, is that the Genesis account of the Abrahamic covenant does not explicitly mention this inheritance. We may solve this problem by appealing to

25. Lewis and Demarest, *Integrative Theology*, 3:408.

later passages of the Old Testament that promise the inheritance of Abraham and his offspring. For example, Psalm 37:9–11 reads, "For evil men will be cut off, but those who hope in the LORD will inherit the land. A little while, and the wicked will be no more; though you look for them, they will not be found. But the meek will inherit the land and enjoy great peace." It is undeniable that this passage signifies that Abraham's descendants will inherit the land, which means the world.[26] In the New Testament, Jesus reinforces this by declaring, "the meek . . . will inherit the earth" (Matt. 5:5), alluding to Psalm 37:11. And the writer of the book of Hebrews states that God appointed the last Adam heir of all things: "but in these last days he has spoken to us by his Son, whom he appointed heir of all things, and through whom he made the universe" (Heb. 1:2).

Hence we may argue that through his first coming, Jesus Christ, as the seed of Abraham, has already begun to fulfill this promise but the ultimate realization of his inheritance will come in the future. Considering the physical and material character of the promise, the fulfillment must be similarly physical and material. When Abraham's descendants, that is, all believers alive at the parousia, rule over the earth in the millennium with their Messiah, God's promise of blessings will be materialized physically on this earth. Since the Bible stresses this point, we should not spiritualize it. The millennial kingdom will signify the completion of the Lord's redemptive program on *this* earth.[27] After that, we will have the new heavens and new earth, which will last eternally.

Concluding Remarks

As discussed above, the Reformed tradition has not been successful in grasping the covenantal significance of Genesis 1:26–28. This is so mainly because it has overly concentrated on Genesis 2:16–17, interpreting it as the covenant of works. The Reformed tradition's concentration on the covenant of works has led many Reformed theologians to spiritualize the plain teaching of Revelation 20:1–6 and to advocate amillennialism. I propose that the Reformed tradition should give up its time-honored covenantal reading of Scripture on the basis of the idea of the covenant of works in the garden of Eden. The Reformed tradition should acknowledge that Genesis 1:26–28 must be taken as an account of the covenant of blessings/promise and Genesis 2:16–17 must be taken as an account of the covenant of the law. This alternative covenantal reading of

26. Ps. 37:22, 29, 34 conveys the same message.
27. Lewis and Demarest, *Integrative Theology*, 3:408.

the first two chapters of the book of Genesis will lead us to recognize premillennialism as the only viable and valid way of interpreting Revelation 20:1–6. Right after the Lord Jesus Christ comes again to the earth, he will establish the millennial kingdom and reign with all believers alive at the parousia on this earth, physically as well as institutionally.[28]

28. Special thanks go to Craig Blomberg and Richard Hess, my colleagues at Denver Seminary, for their helpful comments on this article.

8

Premillennial Tensions and Holistic Missiology

Latin American Evangelicalism

OSCAR A. CAMPOS

Before evangelicalism was ever known in Latin America, Catholicism was referred to as the only officially recognized "religion" in the area.[1] Traditional Catholicism, with its understanding of the mission of the church as the expansion of the visible institutional church, and of the church as the kingdom of God, conquered Latin America and imposed its rule.[2] It was not until the nineteenth century that non-Catholic Christianity began to make its way into Latin America.[3] Of special historical significance is the growing twentieth-century movement known as evangelicalism, particularly its understanding and praxis of the mission of the church, derived from its founding American missionary movement, which was inspired by premillennialism.

1. "Religion" is a popular, nonformal, but legal designation of Catholicism in Latin America.

2. For extended research on these issues, see Oscar A. Campos, "The Mission of the Church and the Kingdom of God in Latin America" (PhD diss., Dallas Theological Seminary, 2000).

3. José Míguez-Bonino, "Roman Catholic–Protestant Relations," in *The Religious Situation: 1969*, ed. Donald R. Cutler (Boston: Beacon, 1969), 135. Míguez-Bonino mentions that there was already a Protestant presence, though limited, since the time of the emancipation movements and that it was welcomed by liberal and anticlerical politicians in Latin America.

American Premillennialism and Evangelicalism in Latin America

Latin American evangelicalism was born in direct relationship with the faith missions movement, which is basically a North American phenomenon that emerged at the end of the nineteenth and early twentieth centuries and still functions today.[4] This movement was influenced by two main features: premillennial theology and fundamentalism.[5] These elements, carried from North America to Latin America by faith missions, shaped the identity and missiological approach of evangelicalism.[6]

Although there is some controversy about the originating or determining factor of the faith missions, it seems that the first surge of interest came with the influence of premillennialism.[7] Missionaries and donors were convinced of the urgency to preach the gospel before the second coming of the Lord. They "overflowed the insufficient denominational missionary structures."[8] Dana L. Robert describes the situation as a "mission revival."[9] Robert's thesis is that the faith missions movement originated with a "premillennialist mission theory" adopted by denominational leaders such as A. T. Pierson, A. J. Gordon, A. B. Simpson, and others who became the fathers of the faith missions.[10] The concepts

4. J. Herbert Kane, *Understanding Christian Missions*, 3rd ed. (Grand Rapids: Baker Academic, 1982), 160. See also Pablo A. Deiros, *Historia del cristianismo en América Latina* (Buenos Aires: Fraternidad Teológica Latinoamericana, 1992); Clayton L. Berg and Paul E. Pretiz, *The Gospel People of Latin America* (Monrovia, CA: MARC, World Vision and Latin American Mission, 1992).

5. Cf. Emilio A. Núñez and William D. Taylor, *Crisis and Hope in Latin America: An Evangelical Perspective*, rev. ed. (Pasadena, CA: William Carey Library, 1996), 401–6.

6. Oscar A. Campos, "La misión de la iglesia y el reino de Dios en el evangelicalismo tradicional," *Kairós* 21 (July–December 1997): 51–70.

7. Ernest R. Sandeen (*The Roots of Fundamentalism: British and American Millenarianism, 1800–1930* [Chicago: University of Chicago Press, 1970]) proposes a well-documented thesis that by the second half of the nineteenth century, it was millenarianism that gave life to fundamentalism and not the opposite.

8. Edwin L. Frizen Jr., *75 Years of IFMA, 1917–1992: The Nondenominational Missions Movement* (Pasadena, CA: William Carey Library, 1992), 69.

9. Dana L. Robert, "'The Crisis of Missions': Premillennial Mission Theory and the Origins of Independent Evangelical Missions," in *Earthen Vessels: American Evangelicals and Foreign Missions, 1880–1980*, ed. Joel A. Carpenter and Wilbert R. Shenk (Grand Rapids: Eerdmans, 1990), 29.

10. Ibid., 30. See also Klaus Fiedler, *The Story of Faith Missions* (Oxford: Regnum, 1994), 272–81. Fiedler identifies the influence of premillennialism in A. B. Simpson and consequently in the Christian and Missionary Alliance, James Hall Brooks and the Gospel Missionary Union, C. I. Scofield and the Central American Mission, and Paul Fleming and the New Tribes Mission, among others. The Christian and Missionary Alliance would be later related to the pentecostal movement, especially the Assemblies of God—a major evangelical force in Latin America. See Gary B. McGee, *"This Gospel . . . Shall Be Preached": A History and Theology of Assemblies of God Foreign Missions to 1959* (Springfield, MO: Gospel Publishing House, 1986), 57–67. Cf. Pablo A. Deiros and Carlos Mraida, *Latinoamérica en llamas* (Miami: Caribe, 1994).

of "rapture" and "dispensations" were also introduced within premillennial-ism. This "dispensational futuristic premillennialism" was an outgrowth of the teachings of John Nelson Darby[11] and the Niagara Bible Conference movement. These teachings were collected by C. I. Scofield in *The Scofield Reference Bible*[12] and became popularly known as dispensationalism.[13] The main feature of inter-est here regarding dispensationalism, however, is its particular premillennialist view, especially as it relates to missiology in Latin America.

Dispensational premillennialism is foundational in the missiological prac-tices of most evangelical groups in Latin America related to North American faith missions. Even the popular and fast-growing pentecostal and charismatic movements are generally so identified. About 70 percent of all evangelicals in Latin America are pentecostals or charismatics and are related to dispensa-tional premillennialism and fundamentalism.[14] Since these groups represent the majority of evangelicals, the popularity and influence of traditional dis-pensational evangelicalism in Latin America cannot be denied.[15]

11. Darby was an Anglican minister who left the Church of Ireland to help found the movement known as the Plymouth Brethren and later became an itinerant missionary teaching prophecy from a dispensationalist perspective. See Mark A. Noll, *A History of Christianity in the United States and Canada* (Grand Rapids: Eerdmans, 1992), 376. For a comprehensive study on Darby, see Larry V. Crutchfield, *The Origins of Dispensationalism: The Darby Factor* (Lanham, MD: University Press of America, 1992).

12. C. I. Scofield, ed., *The Scofield Reference Bible* (Oxford: Oxford University Press, 1909). In the introduction to the 1909 edition, Scofield mentions that his work is the result of the last thirty years of biblical studies and relates them to the Bible studies and conference movement. This introduction was printed also in the following editions of this Bible.

13. Craig A. Blaising, "Dispensationalism: The Search for Definition," in *Dispensationalism, Israel, and the Church: The Search for Definition*, ed. Craig A. Blaising and Darrell L. Bock (Grand Rapids: Zondervan, 1992), 19–21.

14. See Douglas A. Oss, "The Hermeneutics of Dispensationalism within the Pentecostal Tradition" (paper presented at the annual meeting of the Dispensational Study Group of the Evangelical Theological Society, November 21, 1991), 2: "Historically Pentecostals have con-sidered themselves to be dispensationalists. Early Pentecostals were influenced significantly by dispensationalism and American fundamentalism. The *Scofield Reference Bible* was endorsed by official Assemblies of God publications, and the denomination's chief organ, *The Pentecostal Evangel*, commonly affirmed the dispensational stance of the movement." Oss is a professor at Central Bible College, Springfield, MO. David Stoll also comments, "Dispensationalists did not approve of the new manifestation. . . . But many pentecostals took up dispensationalism anyway, reshaped it, and organized their own, more enthusiastic variant of fundamentalism" (*Is Latin America Turning Protestant? The Politics of Evangelical Growth* [Berkeley: University of California Press, 1990], 48–49). See also Donald W. Dayton, *Theological Roots of Pentecostalism* (Peabody, MA: Hendrickson, 1987), 145–47. Cf. Deiros and Mraida, *Latinoamérica en llamas*, 49–70; Deiros, *Historia del cristianismo*, 161–80.

15. This topic was documented and brought to international attention through the well-known studies of David Martin and David Stoll. See David Martin, *Tongues of Fire: The Explosion of Protestantism in Latin America* (Cambridge, MA: Blackwell, 1990); Stoll, *Is Latin America*

The influence of dispensational premillennialism went beyond particular mission agencies because of the popularity of *The Scofield Reference Bible*, and this Bible's missionary intention carried on.[16] This premillennialist missiological approach, with its emphasis on evangelism, interconnected with fundamentalism very well. American fundamentalism is a larger phenomenon that would require a separate study.[17] Here it is at least important to differentiate between "the fundamentalist movement" and "the fundamentalist controversy."[18] Still, both of them influenced the dispensational premillennialism carried into Latin America by faith missions. The North American fundamentalism that was taken to Latin America by faith missions had experienced what some writers have called "the Great Reversal" regarding social issues. That experience affected fundamentalist missionary theology and praxis, which avoided all social concern. "The 'Great Reversal' took place between 1900 and 1930, when all progressive social concern, whether political or private, became suspect among revivalist evangelicals and was relegated to a very minor role."[19]

The faith missions movement reflected both the premillennialist fervor and the theological zeal and culture of fundamentalists who were against modern-

---

Turning Protestant? Cf. José Míguez-Bonino, *Rostros del protestantismo latinoamericano* (Buenos Aires: Nueva Creación, 1995), 54, 65, 76.

16. Robert ("Crisis of Missions," 44) explains, "Other late-nineteenth-century premillennialists who contributed to the origin of independent evangelical missions also should be mentioned here . . . [including] Cyrus Ingerson Scofield. . . . What is almost never mentioned about the *Scofield Reference Bible* is that its purpose was not to codify a theological system but to be a one-volume reference work for missionaries who had no access to theological libraries." Noll (*History of Christianity*, 378) agrees with Robert about the missionary intention of the *Scofield Reference Bible*, "which he intended as a portable guide for missionaries more than a polished theological system." See also Andrew F. Walls, "The American Dimension in the History of the Missionary Movement," in Carpenter and Shenk, *Earthen Vessels*, 17.

17. E.g., fundamentalism in American evangelicalism is closely related to British evangelicalism. See Ian S. Rennie, "Fundamentalism and the Varieties of North Atlantic Evangelicalism," in *Evangelicalism: Comparative Studies of Popular Protestantism in North America, the British Isles, and Beyond, 1700–1990*, ed. Mark A. Noll, David W. Bebbington, and George A. Rawlyk (Oxford: Oxford University Press, 1994), 333–50. That work proposes the general idea that the relationship between British and American evangelicalism expressed in fundamentalism is also evident in pentecostalism. Martin (*Tongues of Fire*, 19–23) applies a similar idea to Latin American evangelicalism in its direct relationship to American, and consequently to British, fundamentalist evangelicalism.

18. Sandeen (*Roots of Fundamentalism*, ix–xix) explains that to understand that millenarianism gave life to fundamentalism and not the reverse, it is necessary to separate the fundamentalist movement from the fundamentalist controversy. Fundamentalism existed before, during, and after the controversy of the 1920s.

19. George M. Marsden, *Fundamentalism and American Culture: The Shaping of Twentieth Century Evangelicalism, 1870–1925* (Oxford and New York: Oxford University Press, 1980), 86. Cf. Charles van Engen, *Mission on the Way: Issues in Mission Theology* (Grand Rapids: Baker Academic, 1996), 129.

ism within and outside different denominational settings.[20] This combination of elements led to a different way of financing and organizing missionary efforts. Denominations lacked funds for the increasing missionary forces that were motivated by premillennialism while being "affected" by modernism.[21] Berg and Pretiz explain this situation in identifying some of the mission agencies representing this evangelicalism in Latin America:

> With a loss of confidence by many in the theology of the mainline denominations and their respective missions, thousands of more conservative Christians found a vehicle for their missionary outreach in such societies as CAM International (originally the Central American Mission, founded by C. I. Scofield of the dispensational Scofield Bible) or TEAM (The Evangelical Alliance Mission). The first CAM couple went to Central America in 1891. A greater number of "faith missionaries" arrived when the modernist-fundamentalist controversy peaked in the 1920s and 1930s. . . .
>
> Despite failures and set-backs, however, the faith mission wave touched the length and breadth of Latin America. One mission specialized in radio. The World Radio Missionary Fellowship established the first missionary radio station, HCJB, in Quito, Ecuador, when the country had only a handful of people with receivers. Another, the Latin American Evangelization Campaign (later, the Latin America Mission) began in 1921 by conducting citywide united evangelistic campaigns. Wycliffe Bible Translators and New Tribes Mission reached Indian populations in the jungles and in the mountains.[22]

Dispensational premillennialism and fundamentalism were combined into a very conservative evangelicalism. This was the kind of evangelicalism most often carried to Latin America by faith missions.[23]

20. E.g., Chester E. Tulga, *The Foreign Missions Controversy in the Northern Baptist Convention, 1919–1949: 30 Years of Struggle* (Chicago: Conservative Baptist Fellowship, 1950), 9. Here Tulga mentions the controversy within the Northern Baptist Convention that was manifested in their convention in Denver in 1919, which led to the formation of the Fundamentalist Fellowship of the Northern Baptist Convention in 1920, later named the Conservative Baptist Fellowship of Northern Baptists: "The modernists had captured most of the colleges and seminaries and attained to a large influence in others. The new interest in social reform and world reconstruction had taken on the terminology of the Gospel. Modernists, who had been hostile to missions as carried on by the orthodox, now became enthusiastic about the foreign missionary enterprise. The Great Commission was being interpreted in social terms, the old evangelical words were being invested with liberal meanings, the new missionary candidates were coming from liberal schools, the evolutionary philosophy of history guaranteed a better return from human effort than the individual Gospel message, so hostile modernism had become a missionary modernism."

21. Frizen, *75 Years of IFMA*, 69–70.

22. Berg and Pretiz, *Gospel People*, 47.

23. The opinion of Kane is that Latin American evangelicalism is very unusual because of "an abnormal number of conservative missionaries" who have ministered there and that

Dispensational Premillennialism and the Mission of the Church
in Latin America

Dispensational premillennialism was the theological framework that supported the missiological approach of the dispensational evangelicalism that
went to Latin America through the faith missions movement.[24] Torrey M.
Johnson explains,

> The supreme task of the Church of Jesus Christ is to evangelize the world as
> quickly and as effectively as possible. . . . By "evangelize" we do not mean to
> educate, to cultivate, to Christianize. . . . By "evangelize" we mean to announce,
> to proclaim, and to witness to the saving grace of the Lord Jesus Christ. . . .
>
>   The Word of God is very specific in teaching that the present age will end in
> great cataclysm, ushering in the return of our Lord Jesus Christ who will then
> set up His kingdom and establish righteousness and peace on earth.[25]

In this missiological approach, premillennialism provides the theological
framework, and at the practical level, the "future kingdom" becomes the
goal of missions. Charles van Engen, describing the Great Commission and
the coming millennium as the two overriding motifs for evangelical missions
during the 1940s and 1950s, adds,

> Focusing on Matthew 24:14, the premillennialists thought that once the church
> had preached the gospel of the kingdom to every nation, the millennium would
> begin. Their hopes for the second coming of Christ and the new kingdom he

---

"consequently the churches they brought into existence are among the most conservative in
the world." He also says that about "95% of the Protestants in Latin America are conservative
evangelicals" (*Understanding Christian Missions*, 230–31).

   24. Samuel Escobar, referring to dispensationalism as a pessimistic view of the kingdom of
God, considers this position "the most popular one among active evangelical missionary societies. . . . There has been an arrogant attitude (bordering on intolerance) among pre-millennialist
dispensationalists who have tried to equate their particular view with orthodoxy. This position
being the most popular one among active evangelical missionary societies, it is sometimes believed
that missions-mindedness can only come from pre-millennialism" ("The Return of Christ," in
The New Face of Evangelicalism: An International Symposium on the Lausanne Covenant, ed.
C. René Padilla [Downers Grove, IL: InterVarsity, 1976], 262).

   25. Torrey M. Johnson, "Missions," *Central American Bulletin* 289 (March 1950): 1–2
(the *Bulletin* is the journal of the Central American Mission). In a similar way, Roger S.
Greenway explains, "The Social Gospel emphasized Christian obligation to respond to
physical need and oppression, the priority of social action and the task of establishing the
kingdom of God on earth now through human efforts. Fundamentalists rejected these and
emphasized spiritual need, evangelism, and the future heavenly aspects of the kingdom of
God. Theological conservatives began to rigidly dichotomize evangelism and social concern,
word and deed" (*Together Again: Kinship of Word and Deed* [Monrovia, CA: MARC, World
Vision, 1998], 15).

would establish on earth lent a strong, almost desperate urgency to gospel proclamation.[26]

From this perspective, evangelization is carried out so that the kingdom may come. It ushers in the kingdom. The transition is one from mission to kingdom.[27] The return of Christ and the establishment of the kingdom depend on the preaching of the gospel. "This kind of eschatology creates the closest interconnection between eschatology and missiology."[28] It makes evangelization the most important aspect of the mission of the church.

> Here then, is a divine utterance and program. And simply speaking, it sets forth the following facts in the following order: first, a present work of grace in which God visits and gathers out, preeminently from the Gentiles, a people for His name; second, the return of Christ; third, the restoration and establishment of the Jewish theocratic kingdom with its attendant worship; and fourth, the salvation in the kingdom-age of the "residue" of the Jews, and of "all" the Gentiles upon whom God's name shall be called. . . . God is visiting the nations, and Christians have the high privilege of visiting them with Him. He goes forth, in the persons of the missionaries, not to convert all the world—since not all men will accept Him—but to gather out from it a willing people, heavenly in quality and innumerable in quantity, which shall be to the glory of His name throughout eternity. And, manifestly, this preparatory work will bring to pass the event which is described as following it, that is, the coming of Christ. This then is the final and consummating motive which God sets before Christians, namely, to go forth everywhere, preaching the good tidings to every creature, in order that the Church may be made complete and that the King and the Kingdom may come.[29]

Furthermore, the dispensational view of the eschatological kingdom of God is related to the idea, popular among dispensationalists, of the "postponement" of the kingdom. "Because the King was rejected, the Messianic, Davidic kingdom was (from a human viewpoint) postponed. . . . Christ was never designated

26. Van Engen, *Mission on the Way*, 130.

27. Many Baptist theologians in the United States, including George E. Ladd, supported this view, which is also held by premillennialists and dispensationalists in Latin America. Cf. Oscar A. Campos, "The Kingdom of God and the Mission of the Church: A Survey of the Baptist Approach" (paper submitted for course 4599, Independent Doctoral Study in Theology, Dallas Theological Seminary, 1993).

28. Cf. Fiedler, *Story of Faith Missions*, 274–76.

29. Henry W. Frost, "What Missionary Motives Should Prevail?" in *The Fundamentals: A Testimony to the Truth* (Chicago: Testimony, 1910), 12:91–92. Frost was the first president of the Interdenominational Mission Association, and *The Fundamentals* is a reference work for fundamentalism.

as King of the church. . . . Though Christ is a King today, He does not rule as King. This awaits His second coming."[30]

The idea of the postponed kingdom, shared by most traditional dispensationalists (both classical and revised), also carries the missiological implication that evangelization will bring Jesus's kingdom.[31] This representative theology of missions also has been held within dispensational evangelicalism in Latin America.[32] It emphasizes urgency and "rapid evangelization" because, "like the early church, they believed that Jesus' Second Coming was just around the corner."[33] Thus premillennial dispensational evangelicalism brought its evangelistic zeal to syncretistic Catholic Latin America.[34]

The emphasis of this missiology has been on the individual spiritual conversion to the gospel presented by the *evangélicos* in contrast to common Catholic practice in Latin America.[35] Evangelism has been directed at an experience of

30. Charles C. Ryrie, *Basic Theology* (Wheaton: Victor Books, 1986), 259. This work has been translated into Spanish as *Teología básica*, trans. Alberto Samuel Valdéz (Miami: Unilit, 1993). See also J. Dwight Pentecost, *Eventos del porvenir: Estudios de escatología bíblica* (Miami: Vida, 1984), 351–53, originally published as *Things to Come* (Grand Rapids: Zondervan, 1977).

31. Ryrie (*Basic Theology*, 397–99) believes in a present but spiritual kingdom related to spiritual salvation, which is similar to George Ladd's view. Ryrie's idea is that evangelization will bring the future kingdom or expand the present spiritual kingdom.

32. This is still the case in the growing evangelical missionary movement in Latin America represented by COMIBAM Internacional. See Rodolfo (Rudy) Girón, "La evangelización y la misión mundial," in *CLADE III* (Buenos Aires: Fraternidad Teológica Latinoamericana, 1992), 756–65; Federico A. Bertuzzi, "El esfuerzo misionero en y desde América Latina," ibid., 355–67; and idem, *El despertar de las misiones* (Miami: Unilit and COMIBAM Internacional, 1997), in which one of the subheadings is "The Second Coming Is Conditioned." See also Jonatán P. Lewis, ed., *Misión mundial: Un análisis del movimiento cristiano mundial*, vol. 1, *Las bases bíblicas e históricas*, 2nd ed. (Miami: Unilit, 1990); Anne Motley Hallum, *Beyond Missionaries: Toward an Understanding of the Protestant Movement in Central America* (Lanham, MD: Rowman & Littlefield, 1996), 47.

33. Robert, "Crisis of Missions," 45.

34. For a view of evangelism as one of the distinctive characteristics of evangelicalism, see Lewis Sperry Chafer, *Grandes temas bíblicos*, rev. ed. by John F. Walvoord, trans. Emilio A. Núñez and Nancy Fernández (Grand Rapids: Outreach Publications, 1976), 279–80; idem, *Teología sistemática*, tomo 2, vol. 4, trans. José María Chicol, M. Francisco Liévano R., and Rodolfo Mendieta P. (Dalton, GA: Publicaciones Españolas, 1974), 21, 45, originally published as *Systematic Theology* (Dallas: Dallas Seminary Press, 1948), 4:21, 44. The final authority of the Bible is a very important characteristic of evangelicalism in Latin America as well. Within the scope of this essay, however, evangelism is the one element most related to the mission of the church.

35. See Orlando Costas, "Conversion as a Complex Experience: A Hispanic Case Study," *Latin American Pastoral Issues* 16 (January 1989): 8–32. See also Lewis Sperry Chafer, *El evangelismo verdadero*, trans. Evis Carballosa (Cherokee, NC: Spanish Publications, 1971), 23–47, originally published as *True Evangelism; or, Winning Souls by Prayer*, rev. ed. (Wheaton: Van Kampen, 1919). Cf. idem, *Salvación*, trans. Emilio Antonio Núñez (Miami: Spanish Publications, 1968), originally published as *Salvation* (Wheaton: Van Kampen, 1917).

spiritual transformation called "the new birth," in reference to John 3:3–8. This experience stresses the spiritual nature of the gospel. Surely, the spiritual element is the *primary* aspect of the gospel, but more often within dispensational evangelicalism it has been the *only* aspect.[36]

Within dispensational evangelicalism, this emphasis is on the individual who is spiritually and morally transformed, without regard to his or her social context.[37] It is an individual spiritual salvation.[38] Thus the mission of the church, according to the thought and practice of dispensational evangelicalism in Latin America, is to save people (or "to save souls") from eternal damnation.[39] For this reason, the material, physical, and earthly affairs of the individual were secondary; any social involvement was of little importance.[40]

According to Samuel Escobar, because of the influence of pietism at the origin of the evangelical missionary movement, "the finality of the mission came to be more and more understood as 'the conversion of individual persons to the gospel of Jesus Christ'" ("Católicos y evangélicos en América Latina frente al desafío misionero del siglo veintiuno," *Kairós* 14–15 [1994]: 72 [my translation]).

36. Costas, "Conversion as a Complex Experience." Cf. Lewis Sperry Chafer, *He That Is Spiritual*, rev. ed. (Grand Rapids: Zondervan, 1967; repr., 1983), 20. C. Norman Kraus, commenting on the British and American Plymouth Brethren movement and its influence on the teaching of mission as evangelization, added, "They conceived salvation as a heavenly and spiritual reality almost to the exclusion of its physical, psychological, and social dimensions. They held that the primary task of the church is evangelism, that is, the verbal proclamation of the Word" ("Introduction: Evangelism, Missions, and Church Growth," in *Missions, Evangelism, and Church Growth*, ed. C. Norman Kraus [Scottdale, PA: Herald, 1980], 20).

37. Costas, "Conversion as a Complex Experience." Cf. Kraus, *Missions, Evangelism, and Church Growth*; J. Dwight Pentecost, *Marchando hacia la madurez espiritual*, trans. Francisco Adrover and Milton Portugal, 2nd ed. (Grand Rapids: Outreach, 1985), 263–74, originally published as *Designed to Be Like Him* (Chicago: Moody, 1966).

38. For comments on the Pietist and Puritan background of the evangelicalism taken to Latin America, see Wilton M. Nelson, *Protestantism in Central America* (Grand Rapids: Eerdmans, 1984), 52–53. It also seems that part of the reason for this emphasis comes from a strong dualistic view of humanity: spiritual versus material. Cf. Chafer, *Salvación*; Kraus, *Missions, Evangelism, and Church Growth*.

39. Van Engen, *Mission on the Way*, 131. Cf. Chafer, *Grandes temas*, 281–83. Writing about CAM International's doctrinal basis, Dorothy Martin notes, "The Founders constantly emphasized that the Mission's purpose was to carry the Gospel to every creature in Central America. It was not established to plant churches or schools. Those institutions were important, of course, but the men felt they would follow as a natural outgrowth of evangelization" (*100 . . . and Counting: A Centennial History of CAM International* [Dallas: CAM International, 1990], 6). Cf. Chafer, *Evangelismo verdadero*; P. E. Burroughs, *Ganando almas para Cristo: Un estudio en evangelismo*, trans. Elías M. Ruiz (El Paso: Casa Bautista de Publicaciones, n.d.).

40. This is illustrated by Charles C. Ryrie's defense of "Christian priorities" in *La responsabilidad social: Lo que todo cristiano debe saber* (Puebla, Mexico: Las Américas, 1990), 7, 12, 134–35, originally published as *What You Should Know about Social Responsibility* (Chicago: Moody, 1982). Cf. Peter Kuzmic, "Historia y escatología: Perspectivas evangélicas," in *Al servicio del reino: Compendio de artículos de autores no latinoamericanos sobre la misión integral de la iglesia*, ed. José María Blanch (San José, Costa Rica: Visión Mundial Internacional, 1992).

This limited understanding of the mission of the church in Latin American traditional evangelicalism derived from its North American source, traditional dispensationalism.[41]

It should be recognized, however, that some dispensationalists, motivated by Christian compassion, have been involved in social work. Nevertheless, when this occurred, it was normally a means of evangelistic outreach and not necessarily the result of their theological framework, as their focus was on individual salvation rather than social transformation.[42] Incorporating social concerns was sometimes considered a negative influence on the primarily spiritual aspect of the mission of the church. Along this line, some contemporary social and missiological issues have been viewed as "forces against world evangelization." Frizen, speaking of contextualization and of what he calls a "neo-social gospel," illustrates this situation:

41. See Justo L. González, "In Quest of a Protestant Hispanic Ecclesiology," in *Teología en conjunto: A Collaborative Hispanic Protestant Theology*, ed. José David Rodríguez and Loida I. Martell-Otero (Louisville: Westminster John Knox, 1997), 80–97:

> As Protestant Latinos and Latinas we have inherited a theology in which ecclesiology plays a very secondary role. This can be explained by a number of factors. First, the Protestantism that was brought to us, both in Latin America and in much of the United States, was a Protestantism that centered on personal salvation. . . . What was important was one's own individual faith, rather than the faith of the community. . . . You had to be born again individually. . . . Within that theological framework, the church is at best a vehicle for the preaching of the gospel, and a source of support and assurance for those who have been born anew. . . . Second, when transplanted into a predominantly Roman Catholic environment, that individualistic form of Protestantism became even more anti-church. (p. 80)

Russell D. Moore recognizes that "dispensational ecclesiology has always been somewhat problematic in relation to the construction of a meaningful socio-political ethic." Citing Michael D. Williams ("Where's the Church? The Church and the Unfinished Business of Dispensational Theology," *Grace Theological Journal* 10 [1989]: 166–80), Moore refers to Scofield and Chafer's "otherworldly strain" because they conceived Christians as "'heavenly citizens' who are merely passing through the created order on their way to eschatological bliss. . . . Citing Chafer's conception of the church as a 'missionary society' created to train witnesses for Christ, Williams sees the root of dispensationalism's weak ecclesiology in an eschatological grid which anticipates an apostate institutional church in the last days. As such, dispensationalists have had to locate the primary work of the Spirit within the individual" ("Till Every Foe Is Vanquished: Emerging Socio-political Implications of Progressive Dispensational Eschatology" [paper presented at the annual meeting of the Evangelical Theological Society, November 17, 1999], 19–20).

42. Hallum, *Beyond Missionaries*, 29–30. Cf. Robert A. Pyne, "The New Man in an Immoral Society: Expectations between the Times" (paper presented at the annual meeting of the Dispensational Study Group of the Evangelical Theological Society, Santa Clara, CA, November 20, 1997), 3–10; M. Daniel Carroll R., "Broadening Horizons, Redirecting Focus: A Response to Robert Pyne on Progressive Dispensationalism and Social Ethics" (paper presented at the annual meeting of the Dispensational Study Group of the Evangelical Theological Society, Santa Clara, CA, November 20, 1997), 2–3; Núñez and Taylor, *Crisis and Hope*, 384–86; Moore, "Till Every Foe Is Vanquished."

Contextualization can be good. However, there are dangers in attempting to make theology culturally relevant. . . . In trying to make the gospel message relevant, Christians are open to political interpretations of the gospel, which, they believe, will solve the grave social problems of the world. . . .

There appears to be a growing tendency among some evangelicals toward a neo-social, or holistic, approach to the gospel. There is an increasing emphasis on hunger, health, living conditions, development, and justice. Some evangelicals are equating this to the gospel message of salvation . . . that the mission program must minister to the whole man in every aspect of his life and relationships.[43]

Differing biblical interpretations were viewed as a denial of biblical authority, and a "holistic gospel" was considered an error. These missiological concerns within faith missions are related to the fundamentalist attitudes that led to the "Great Reversal" on social issues. As already mentioned, the controversies between fundamentalism and modernism have been carried to the mission fields. Consequently, these controversies have also influenced dispensational evangelicalism and its missiology in Latin America. Núñez, commenting on Marsden's exposition of the topic, observes,

No wonder that pioneer American evangelical missionaries in Central America were afraid of falling into the trap of liberalism as they got involved in social work. They wanted to be loyal, and rightly so, to their spiritual vocation. They did not want to betray the gospel message and preach instead the improvement of the individual by means of the improvement of society. Their hope was not in human progress, but in the Lord's return. They preferred not to invest time, money, and human resources in establishing big institutions. The experience of some historical Protestant denominations, which dedicated their main efforts in the mission field to institutional work with little success in the area of church growth, was a negative lesson to the pioneers working under faith missions.[44]

At the same time, Núñez indicates that dispensational premillennialism has been "used and abused" within evangelicalism and that it is "no wonder that this eschatological view has been described by some of its critics as pessimistic, fatalist, and excessively futuristic." In specific reference to Latin America, he adds, "We in the Third World have inherited the use and abuse of that system of biblical interpretation."[45]

Norberto Saracco critically exposed this dispensationalist theological framework for missions before one of the largest gatherings of Latin American

43. Frizen, 75 Years of IFMA, 382–83.
44. Núñez and Taylor, Crisis and Hope, 404–5.
45. Ibid., 402–3.

evangelical leaders and theologians: "Unfortunately, contemporary evangelicals, especially in Latin America, have been influenced by a dispensationalist theology that has given them a Gospel without Kingdom, and by a western worldview that has deprived them from a holistic understanding of human beings and the world."[46]

Saracco's critique shows the relationship between the premillennial theological framework and the missiological approach of traditional dispensational evangelicalism in Latin America.[47] In this regard, his accusation is that understanding the eschatological kingdom of God exclusively as a future historical event has made dispensational missiology indifferent to concern for the present social context. Therefore priorities in relation to society become clearly evangelistic in nature, focused on individualistic spiritual salvation. Sociopolitical contexts, earthly affairs, and material, physical dimensions will be transformed for good when every person and every thing is surrendered to Christ in "the future kingdom of God."[48]

Although this missiological approach is changing now, most dispensational evangelicals have shared this common understanding of the mission of the church: to seek, at the present time, individual spiritual salvation. Thus they seek to spread the gospel about Jesus Christ the Savior in order that sinners may repent and receive forgiveness from God and prepare for the coming of the Lord to establish his "future" kingdom. This future kingdom of God is the physical, earthly, "millennial" kingdom, which stands in contrast to the present spiritual activity of God (or present salvific manifestation of God). Latin American dispensational evangelicalism has supported its nonholistic missiological approach with its futuristic premillennialist theology of the kingdom of God. It has a limited view and praxis of the mission of the church

46. Samuel Escobar, "Report: The Whole Gospel for the Whole World from Latin America," *Transformation* 10.1 (1993): 30–32. The gathering was CLADE III, the third Latin American Congress on Evangelism, sponsored by the Latin American Theological Fraternity (LATF) and celebrated in Quito, Ecuador, from August 24 to September 4, 1992.

47. This relationship has also been exposed by others in Latin America. Cf. Emilio A. Núñez, "La naturaleza del reino de Dios," in *El reino de Dios y América Latina*, ed. C. René Padilla (El Paso: Casa Bautista de Publicaciones, 1975), 17–36; Kuzmic, "Historia y escatología," 73–106; Stoll, *Is Latin America Turning Protestant?* 48–49.

48. Cf. Charles C. Ryrie, *Las bases de la fe premilenial*, trans. Santiago Escuain (Terrasa, Spain: Portavoz Evangélico, 1984), 17, 99, 122, originally published as *The Basis of the Premillennial Faith* (Neptune, NJ: Loizeaux Brothers, 1953); idem, *Síntesis de doctrina bíblica* (Barcelona: Publicaciones Portavoz Evangélico, 1979), 72, 182. See also Cyrus I. Scofield, *Dividiendo bien la palabra de verdad* (Los Angeles: Casa Bíblica de Los Angeles, n.d.), 20, originally published as *Rightly Dividing the Word of Truth* (Chicago: Bible Institute Colportage, n.d.); Lewis Sperry Chafer, *Dispensationalism*, rev. ed. (Dallas: Dallas Seminary Press, 1936), 57–65; J. Dwight Pentecost, *Profecías para el mundo moderno* (Miami: Logoi, 1973), 85–97, originally published as *Prophecy for Today* (Grand Rapids: Zondervan, 1961).

(individualistic spiritual salvation) because of a limited view of the kingdom of God (a future millennium), among other factors (e.g., fundamentalism).

Premillennialism and Holistic Mission in Latin American Evangelicalism

The evangelical holistic missiology that developed in Latin America during the second half of the twentieth century reveals a transitional movement within evangelicalism. It is a transition from the nonholistic missiology represented by traditional dispensational and fundamentalist evangelicalism into the holistic missiological approach of an emergent "contextual evangelicalism" in the region.[49] Contextual evangelicalism has also been called in Latin America "new evangelicalism."[50]

Contextual evangelicalism and its holistic missiology also represent an evangelical reaction to the challenges posed by liberation theology, especially regarding its concerns for the social realities of the Latin American context.[51]

49. The designation "contextual evangelicalism" is preferred because of the conscious intent of this movement to contextualize its theology. It was indeed this intent that originated the movement. See Samuel Escobar, *De la misión a la teología*, ed. C. René Padilla, Colección FTL (Buenos Aires: Kairós, 1998), 9; Núñez and Taylor, *Crisis and Hope*, 331–71; Emilio A. Núñez, "Testigo de un nuevo amanecer," in *Hacia una teología evangélica latinoamericana: Ensayos en honor de Pedro Savage*, ed. C. René Padilla (San José, Costa Rica: Caribe, 1984), 108. Cf. Orlando E. Costas, *Liberating News: A Theology of Contextual Evangelization* (Grand Rapids: Eerdmans, 1989), originally published as *Evangelización contextual: Fundamentos teológicos y pastorales* (San José, Costa Rica: SEBILA, 1986). There is a conceptual difference between a contextual theology (e.g., liberation theology) and a contextualized theology (contextualization). Contextual evangelicalism represents a contextualized theology of mission, a theology that, soundly based on Scripture, seeks to be relevant to social context but is not determined by it (contextual theology).

50. The term "new evangelicalism" was used to highlight an existing relationship with the American (US) movement likewise known as new evangelicalism. It was also a term identified with a departure from some of the most conservative missiological elements of fundamentalism, which included traditional dispensationalism, as described earlier. For these reasons, Míguez-Bonino and Deiros, well-known and respected Latin American writers, also use the term "new evangelicalism" to identify this movement in Latin America. They are, however, uncomfortable with the expression. Therefore Míguez-Bonino suggests as an alternative designation "evangelical renovation"; and Deiros, simply "conservatives" instead of ultraconservatives. See Míguez-Bonino, *Rostros del protestantismo latinoamericano*, 54; Deiros, *Historia del cristianismo*, 803. Cf. Alberto F. Roldán, "Los caminos de la teología protestante en América Latina," *Kairós* 14–15 (1994): 142–62; Samuel Escobar, "Mission Studies, Past, Present, and Future," *Missiology* 24 (January 1996): 7.

51. This reaction came as a later development mostly for reasons of theological maturity, rather than of chronology. Contextual evangelicals were still formulating their positions on the mission of the church while liberation theologians were already impacting the world with their theology. See Pius Franz Helfenstein, *Evangelikale Theologie der Befreiung: Das Reich Gottes in der Theologie der 'Fraternidad Teológica Latinoamericana' und der gängigen*

"In Latin America, the theological and exegetical work of liberation theologians has served to spur evangelicals to reconsider how they read the biblical text and mine from this study the foundations of their conception of what it means to be the church in such a needy continent."[52]

Emilio Antonio Núñez also explains this theological development as a work of a reactive nature:

> Generally speaking, we conservative evangelicals in Latin America have been behind schedule in our theological work. . . . Some of us have finally become interested in doing theology; but we are reacting to some challenges that we cannot avoid any more in our social and ecclesiastical context. Our theology is a theology of reaction. We did not take the initiative to produce an evangelical theology on the basis of the Scriptures in response to our social situation. We have been forced to enter into the theological arena by the social turmoil in which we live and by the non-biblical or anti-biblical answers that some theologians are giving to the problems of the Latin American people.[53]

Contextual evangelicalism, mostly represented by the Latin American Theological Fraternity, represented a middle-ground missiology. It stood at the center of the tensions produced by the opposing missiological positions behind

---

Befreiungstheologie, ein Vergleich [Evangelical Theology of Liberation: The Kingdom of God in the Theology of the Latin American Theological Fraternity and the Current Liberation Theology, a Comparison] (Zurich: Theologischer Verlag, 1991). Helfenstein sees the LATF as a movement almost parallel to liberation theology. One of the reasons is that liberation theology was officially born with the Latin American Bishops Conference celebrated in Medellín in 1968 (in the aftermath of Vatican II) and the LATF was born in 1970 in relation to the Latin American Congress on Evangelization (CLADE I) celebrated in 1969. These two events were chronologically close to each other, but in theological development, liberation theology was far ahead. Helfenstein is right, however, in presenting similarities between the two movements, such as that both developed from a concern for social context, for doing a Latin American theology, and for taking the perspective of the kingdom of God as the foundation for their theologies. His book was originally a doctoral dissertation, at the University of Basel, on the LATF.

Helfenstein wrote his dissertation in 1989. With a similar approach, Dieumeme E. Noelliste had written "The Church and Human Emancipation: A Critical Comparison of Liberation Theology and the Latin American Theological Fraternity" (PhD diss., Northwestern University, 1987). He compared liberation theology and the LATF as movements of social change. He discussed their differences and limitations and proposed their self-correction by mutual cooperation.

52. M. Daniel Carroll R., "Context, Bible and Ethics: A Latin American Perspective," *Themelios* 19 (May 1994): 9.

53. Núñez and Taylor, *Crisis and Hope*, 347. Núñez was one of the founding members of the LATF and with Taylor has been part of contextual evangelicalism in Latin America, representing dispensational evangelicalism in this missiological dialogue. See also Emilio A. Núñez, *Liberation Theology*, trans. Paul E. Sywulka (Chicago: Moody, 1985).

liberation theology and traditional dispensational evangelicalism in Latin America.[54]

Contextual evangelicalism also represented a middle-ground theology of the kingdom of God. It rejected the opposite views held by liberation theology and traditional dispensational evangelicalism on the kingdom of God. Samuel Escobar in 1976 discerned that "if the teaching about the Kingdom of God and the return of Christ is determined heavily by either of these two alternatives—panic or utopianism—we find ourselves with a very poor substitute for Christian hope."[55] Therefore, in order to support its holistic missiology, contextual evangelicalism incorporated a corresponding theological framework that included a present and active manifestation of the eschatological kingdom of God even while expecting its future consummation.

The writings surrounding the LATF's second theological consultation all focused on the topic of the kingdom of God.[56] This was not a surprise. The challenges of liberation theology and of contemporary biblical scholarship led to a consensus that a treatment of the biblical theme of the kingdom of God was needed in order to support a holistic missiology.[57] Furthermore, after the LATF had started its discussion on the mission of the church, it needed to determine its corresponding foundational biblical-theological framework.

54. Deiros said that contextual evangelicals "would be considered as 'liberals' by the extreme 'right' of the fundamentalists, and as 'fundamentalists' by the extreme 'left' of the liberationists" (*Historia del cristianismo*, 803). Cf. Núñez and Taylor, *Crisis and Hope*, 353–54.

Carroll's comments describing the role of fundamentalist missionaries as evangelical leaders in Latin America illustrate this tension as well. He recognizes that "for many the threat from Liberation Theology raised the stakes even higher, and anything attempting to interact in new and creative ways with socio-political issues was met with suspicion and even hostility. Happily, in spite of these pressures, some evangelicals did move ahead and their impact is growing. I am thinking here particularly of the contributions of the 'Fraternidad Teológica Latinoamericana'" ("Broadening Horizons," 4). Helfenstein (*Evangelikale Theologie der Befreiung*, v), while comparing the LATF with liberation theology, also referred to the reaction (*Reaktion*) of the fraternity to Western theology and especially to its North American ecclesiological and theological ties and its action (*Aktion*) in relation to Latin American social problems. See also Samuel Escobar, "Mañana: Discerniendo el Espíritu en América Latina," *Kairós* 20 (January–June 1997): 7–28.

55. Escobar, "Return of Christ," 261.

56. C. René Padilla, "La segunda consulta de la F.T.L. en Lima," *Boletín teológico* 4 (February 1973): 1–4; Emilio A. Núñez, "El reino de Dios," *Boletín teológico* 5 (May 1973): 1–2; Oscar Pereira García, "El reino de Dios en la Biblia," *Boletín teológico* 6 (September 1973): 1–6; Padilla, *Reino de Dios*.

57. A focus on the kingdom of God for a holistic missiology has become a conscious and common theological framework within liberation theology, conciliar or ecumenical theology, and new evangelicalism as well, among others.

The biblical theme of the kingdom of God seemed to be the most appropriate place to begin.[58]

Escobar related the lordship of Christ to the historical presence of the kingdom of God in order to determine the mission of the church. Because Jesus is the Lord of the universe, he is the Lord of history.

> To state, then, that Jesus Christ is the Lord of History is also to state the truth that the lordship of Christ is the reason for the missionary task of the church, that the way by which his lordship is affirmed is also the extension of his kingdom—the fact that it becomes a reality evident in the lives of people from all nations, races, colors and classes of the world. This historical and universal dimension of the lordship of Christ becomes the essence of the missionary task: *The church exists for mission!*[59]

Escobar also asserted, "The wholeness recognizes the need of a personal experience of the salvific grace of God, but at the same time it recovers the biblical vision of the human being as a social being whose transformation is lived out in the first place in the context of a community that is in itself an expression of the kingdom of God and an announcement of the new creation."[60] Esco-

58. The LATF moved quickly on these issues. To move on from the topic of the mission of the church to the topic of the kingdom of God in order to support its theology of mission took the LATF just a few years compared with what it took for liberation theology to do the same. It might be because the kingdom topic was already part of the LATF's theological preunderstanding. Cf. C. René Padilla, *Mission between the Times: Essays on the Kingdom* (Grand Rapids: Eerdmans, 1985), originally published as *Misión integral: Ensayos sobre el reino y la iglesia* (Buenos Aires: Nueva Creación, 1986); idem, *Discipulado y misión: Compromiso con el reino de Dios*, 2nd ed. (Buenos Aires: Kairós, 1997); idem, "La misión cristiana en las Américas: Una perspectiva latinoamericana," in *Misión en el camino: Ensayos en homenaje a Orlando E. Costas* (Buenos Aires: Fraternidad Teológica Latinoamericana, 1992), 67–94; idem, *Reino de Dios*; J. Norberto Saracco, "El evangelio de poder," in *CLADE III*, 157–66; Fraternidad Teológica Latinoamericana, "Declaración de Quito," ibid., 853–61; Washington Padilla, *Hacia una transformación integral* (Buenos Aires: Fraternidad Teológica Latinoamericana, 1989); Valdir R. Steuernagel, ed., *Al servicio del reino en América Latina: Un compendio sobre la misión integral de la iglesia cristiana en Latinoamérica* (San José, Costa Rica: Visión Mundial, 1991), 13; idem, ed., *La misión de la iglesia: Una visión panorámica* (San José, Costa Rica: Visión Mundial, 1992), 11; Pedro Savage, "La iglesia como comunidad discipuladora del reino," in *Conversión y discipulado*, ed. Mariano Avila and Manfred Grellert (San José, Costa Rica: Visión Mundial, 1993), 87–120; Roberto J. Suderman, *Discipulado cristiano al servicio del reino* (Guatemala City: SEMILLA, 1994); Emilio A. Núñez, *Teología y misión: Perspectivas desde América Latina* (San José, Costa Rica: Visión Mundial, 1996), 34.

59. Samuel Escobar, "Jesus Christ: Lord of the Universe," in *Jesus Christ: Lord of the Universe, Hope of the World*, ed. David M. Howard (Downers Grove, IL: InterVarsity, 1974), 28.

60. Samuel Escobar, "Entender a la América Latina en el nuevo milenio," *Apuntes pastorales* 17 (January–March 2000): 18 (my translation). Cf. idem, *Evangelizar hoy* (Buenos Aires: Certeza ABUA, 1995), 9.

bar's contribution to the topic was very important but limited. He needed to develop further the relationship between the lordship of Jesus, the kingdom of God, and the mission of the church.[61]

Orlando Costas addressed the kingdom topic more directly.[62] According to Costas, "the kingdom serves as the frame of reference for the mission of God." He explained in a general way that the mission of the church is a concrete announcement of the kingdom now:

> To participate in the mission of God is to announce the good news of the kingdom. This is an all-embracing and dynamic activity that is not limited to a predetermined set of verbal propositions. . . . Announcing the kingdom is considered a part of the new life and not an isolated occurrence divorced from reality. The proclamation is always contextual, presented in new Spirit-filled words and by means of a dynamic transforming witness.[63]

Costas and Escobar both referred to the kingdom of God as the framework for developing the mission of the church. They saw the kingdom as a concrete present reality connected to the mission of the church. They understood the kingdom as manifested in the totality of present history, the lordship of God over all.

> The goal of evangelization is not simply to promote growth of the church or merely to help individuals come to salvation. Rather, the all-encompassing goal of evangelization is to make known God's kingdom as embodied in Jesus Christ and made present by the Holy Spirit. In so doing, evangelization prepares the way for the revelation of the kingdom of glory. . . .
>
> Through evangelization the church leads women and men to confess Jesus as Messiah and Son of God. To confess Christ is to believe in the kingdom. . . . In

61. Besides, as Georg F. Vicedom had already explained, "the justification of the mission by means of the lordship of God is nothing new" (*The Mission of God: An Introduction to a Theology of Mission*, trans. Gilbert A. Thiele and Dennis Hilgendorf, Witnessing Church Series [St. Louis: Concordia, 1965], 12).

62. Cf. Priscilla Pope-Levison, *Evangelization from a Liberation Perspective*, American University Studies, Series 7, vol. 69 (New York: Peter Lang, 1991), 133–45, for a good and compact analysis of Orlando Costas. In her book, which came out of her doctoral dissertation, Pope-Levison shows that Catholic and Protestant liberation theologies developed into theologies of "holistic evangelization" clearly related to the "reign of God" theme that both Catholics and Protestants have worked on. Orlando Costas is one of the ecumenical Protestant theologians whom she studied in order to demonstrate this. She presents Costas as an evangelical committed to liberation theology, which comes into Protestantism through the conciliar or ecumenical movement.

63. Orlando E. Costas, *Christ outside the Gate: Mission beyond Christendom* (Maryknoll, NY: Orbis Books, 1982), 91–92. See also idem, *The Integrity of Mission: The Inner Life and Outreach of the Church* (San Francisco: Harper & Row, 1979), 5–8.

the resurrection of the crucified Jesus, God his Father revealed the liberating rule of the kingdom and thus inaugurated a new order of life. The kingdom involves both the present anticipation of that new order and its final consummation in glory. The Lordship of Christ stands for that rule and that order. . . .

Through evangelization the church builds itself up—but only as a sign and an instrument of the kingdom. The church is the community of those who have confessed Jesus as the Christ and the Son of God.[64]

In his last works, Costas showed a more detailed and refined theology. He also referred to a present and future aspect of the kingdom. The kingdom is ruled according to the lordship of Christ. He explained that the church as sign and instrument of the kingdom is built up through evangelization.[65]

Andrew Kirk, another LATF theologian, addressed the kingdom topic from an ethical perspective. He worked on the "kingdom ethics" of the mission of the church. According to Kirk, the church in its mission should follow the kingdom ethics of Jesus, who is our model.[66] Later Kirk would be more specific about the topic:

The kingdom of God is an eschatological event in the sense that God's final purpose to create all things new, abolishing sin, suffering, sorrow and death, is already a reality in the ministry of Jesus Christ and the life of the early church.

The kingdom breaks onto the world scene as a new creative power in the midst of an order of decay, deceit and disruption. . . .

The kingdom spells out a tension between real but limited change now and total change in the future. This eschatological tension between realism and hope is in itself a powerful challenge to be committed to change.[67]

Kirk, from an ethical perspective, followed a kingdom theology similar to that of other LATF theologians. He focused especially on the tension between the present and the future aspects. Mervin Breneman also contributed to this discussion. He explained that the biblical tension was not only between the "already" and "not yet" aspects of the kingdom, that there is

64. Costas, *Liberating News*, 82–83.
65. Ibid.
66. Andrés [J. Andrew] Kirk, *Jesucristo revolucionario*, trans. Ana Poliak (Buenos Aires: Aurora, 1974), 33–46.
67. J. Andrew Kirk, *Theology and the Third World Church*, Outreach and Identity: Evangelical Theological Monographs 6 (Downers Grove, IL: InterVarsity, 1983), 42. See also idem, "Missio Dei; Missio ecclesiae," in *Contemporary Issues in Mission*, ed. J. Andrew Kirk, Department of Mission Occasional Series 1 (Birmingham, UK: Department of Mission, Selly Oak Colleges, 1994), 1–16.

also a tension in relation to the historical continuity and/or discontinuity of the kingdom.[68]

This tension, according to Breneman, affects how the kingdom is defined or understood at the present time. It can be either (1) a monist history where the kingdom is the action of God in the whole world (like the liberation theology in Gustavo Gutiérrez and Hugo Assman) or (2) a dual history where the kingdom is expressed in the community of God's people (like traditional Catholicism, where the church is the kingdom).[69] He suggested a combination of both positions: that the church is the concrete expression of the kingdom and that it has a responsibility to society. He also said that in the New Testament the kingdom is related to the sovereignty of God, the lordship of Christ. Therefore the church is the paradigm of the kingdom with its kingdom ethic of justice.[70]

Núñez is another LATF theologian who advocates holistic missiology in connection with his understanding of the kingdom of God. A founder of the LATF, he has been a pioneer of holistic missiology among Latin American dispensationalists. Although he shares the holistic emphasis of the LATF, his theology differs because of his dispensationalist stance, which influenced his kingdom theology.[71]

There are common denominators in the theological positions of LATF members presented here, but not complete agreement. Since the consultation on the kingdom of God, different approaches have been presented. It was René Padilla, however, who best and most comprehensively articulated what seems to have become the most commonly accepted LATF approach to kingdom theology. Since the beginning, Padilla's theology of the kingdom of God seemed to occupy the standard position within the LATF.[72] The holistic

68. J. Mervin Breneman, "Apuntes sobre la continuidad y/o discontinuidad entre el reino de Dios y la historia," *Boletín teológico* 5 (May 1973): 2–8. See also Helfenstein, *Evangelikale Theologie der Befreiung*, 62–66.

69. Breneman, "Apuntes sobre la continuidad," 2. This explanation shows again that the LATF was reacting to liberation theology and that LATF theologians (Escobar, Costas, Kirk, and others) focused their understanding of the kingdom of God on its present and concrete reality.

70. Ibid., 2–8.

71. Núñez stands between traditional and progressive dispensationalism. But he is definitely part of contextual evangelicalism.

72. Other LATF theologians in later publications have often repeated what Padilla expressed about the kingdom of God. This is not necessarily due to his particular influence within the LATF (although he is very influential) but to a common understanding coming from contemporary biblical theology (e.g., Ladd and Cullmann). At the same time, his theology of the kingdom seemed to correspond better to the thoughts and goals of LATF members. See Padilla's delayed publication in English: C. René Padilla, "The Kingdom of God and the Church," *Theological Fraternity Bulletin* 1–2 (1976): 1–23. See also Padilla, *Mission between the Times*, 186–99.

mission of the church within the LATF has been basically seen as determined by the "ethic of the kingdom." The mission is to follow the example of Christ in life and ministry. It is submission to his lordship in the world at the present time and in the future consummation of his glorious rule.[73]

Latin American contextual evangelicalism through the LATF has focused on the present aspect of the kingdom of God in order to support its holistic missiology. It was Padilla who first stated that in Christ the kingdom of God is a present reality and that the kingdom is "the basic presupposition of the mission, and the central theme of Jesus' preaching."[74] It was also Padilla who, since the beginning of the LATF, would echo Oscar Cullmann and George Eldon Ladd to explain the tensions of the "already" and "not yet" aspects of the kingdom[75] and, most important, apply them to holistic missiology.

Padilla stated that "the mission of the church can be understood only in light of the kingdom of God" and that to define the relationship between the kingdom and the church and the relationship between the kingdom and the world separately would be incomplete.[76] They are related. The kingdom of God is "an eschatological reality that is both the starting point and the goal of the church."[77] In this sense, the church is related to the kingdom as the "new society," the community of the kingdom. The church is "the community of the kingdom in which Jesus is acknowledged as Lord of the universe and through which, in anticipation of the end, the kingdom is concretely manifested in history."[78] This eschatology called for a revision of Latin American ecclesiology, a revision that can be found in later publications.[79]

According to Padilla, the present manifestation of the eschatological kingdom of God provides the framework for a holistic missiological approach. The "paradigm," the model for the mission of the church, is Jesus: Jesus pro-

73. The universal lordship of Christ is central to the theology of mission in the LATF. Cf. Helfenstein, *Evangelikale Theologie der Befreiung*, 62.

74. Padilla, "Segunda consulta de la F.T.L.," 3.

75. This is also a reference made by Héctor Darío Olivares, "Acerca del reino de Dios," *Boletín teológico* 4 (November 1972): 7–8; and Breneman, "Apuntes sobre la continuidad."

76. According to Padilla, to understand the mission of the church in the world, we should not see the relationship of the kingdom either to the world or to the church as a separate issue.

77. Padilla, *Mission between the Times*, 186.

78. Ibid., 189–90.

79. See C. René Padilla and Tetsunao Yamamori, eds., *La iglesia local como agente de transformación: Una eclesiología para la misión integral* (Buenos Aires: Kairós, 2003); Juan Driver, *Imágenes de una iglesia en misión: Hacia una eclesiología transformadora* (Guatemala City: Semilla, 1998); Humberto Bullón et al., *Postmodernidad y la iglesia evangélica* (San José, Costa Rica: IINDEF, 2000); In Sik Hong, *¿Una iglesia posmoderna? En busca de un modelo de iglesia y misión en la era posmoderna* (Buenos Aires: Kairós, 2001); Arturo Piedra, Sidney Rooy, and H. Fernando Bullón, *¿Hacia dónde va el protestantismo? Herencia y prospectivas en América Latina* (Buenos Aires: Kairós, 2003).

claimed the gospel, the good news of the kingdom, and presented the signs of the kingdom. Padilla presents at least three facets of Jesus's life that believers should interpret and follow: (a) the example of his incarnation (involvement in the real situations of people), (b) the example of his ministry (proclaiming the gospel of the kingdom especially to the poor, teaching "all the things that Jesus commanded" and serving people in their physical needs), and (c) the example of his death and resurrection (the cost of complete sacrifice).[80]

Washington Padilla, summarizing René Padilla's teaching on the subject, also explains that the purpose of what Jesus did was

> to *transform* human life *holistically*: to create a new world where God is supreme and human beings relate to each other according to his original purpose of love and justice, that is to say, the kingdom of God. And for this he created the new movement that the New Testament calls *the church*. It is called to fulfill at least three functions in society:
>
> (1) a function of opposing the established order and the "kingdom of darkness" . . .
>
> (2) . . . a function of demonstrating before the world what God wants for all humanity . . .
>
> (3) . . . a function of penetrating society by means of oral preaching but also by means of silent influence.[81]

Conclusions

Contextual evangelicalism developed its missiology under the rubric that the mission of the church is evangelism *and* social responsibility, a holistic mission. The LATF applied a corresponding premillennial theology in order to support their holistic missiology. The LATF's kingdom theology was based on the tension of the "already" and "not yet" aspects as seen in other contemporary kingdom theologies. As already mentioned, however, it was the present manifestation of the eschatological kingdom of God that supported LATF's holistic missiological approach. According to Padilla, "the gospel is good news concerning the kingdom, and the kingdom is God's rule over the totality of life."[82]

---

80. W. Padilla, *Hacia una transformación*, 12–17.

81. Ibid., 15–16 (my translation); italics in the original.

82. Padilla, *Mission between the Times*, 198. Here Padilla, commenting on the Lausanne Covenant, adds: "Because of his death and resurrection, Jesus Christ has been enthroned as Lord of the universe. The whole world, therefore, has been placed under his Lordship. The church . . . is called to 'share his concern for justice and reconciliation throughout human society and for the liberation of men from every kind of oppression' (Lausanne Covenant, par. 5)" (p. 199).

Since this essay has focused on the nonholistic missiology of dispensational evangelicalism due to its futuristic view of the eschatological kingdom of God, it is only fair to at least mention some of the work of progressive dispensationalism in the last twenty years and its different stance on the issues of the kingdom of God and, consequently, holistic missiology. We should not put together all dispensationalists but at least distinguish between two large classifications: traditional (preclassical, classical or Scofieldian, and revised or essentialist) and progressive.

Progressive dispensationalism still is part of the popular dispensational tradition related to Latin American evangelicalism (as already mentioned), but it has developed a biblical theology of the eschatological kingdom of God that includes the elements necessary to support a holistic missiology such as that developed by Latin American contextual evangelicalism. Therefore progressive dispensationalism is relevant not only for American premillennialism but also for Latin American dispensational evangelicalism in its quest for a biblical framework that would provide theological support for its holistic view of ministry (missiology).

Progressive dispensationalism not only accepts an already inaugurated messianic kingdom (with Jesus's first advent fulfilling initially and partially the promises of the old dispensation) even as it expects its millennial and final consummation (a third dispensation initiated at the second coming); it also proposes a concept of holistic redemption and a similar understanding of the nature of the church and its mission, reflecting the present aspect of the messianic kingdom.[83] We can end these thoughts with Blaising's presentation

---

83. Moore ("Till Every Foe Is Vanquished," 4–5) made an important statement in this regard that illustrates the nature of progressive dispensationalism and its missiological potential:

> Recent years have seen large sectors of evangelical theological traditions coalesce around the concept of inaugurated eschatology, the idea that biblical eschatology includes both an "already" of initial fulfillment and a "not yet" of future consummation. . . . Interestingly, this inaugurated eschatology has also been adopted by a growing number of dispensational premillennialists dissatisfied with traditional dispensationalism. This new movement, dubbed "progressive dispensationalism," has upset classical eschatological categories by combining an inaugurated eschatology and a unitary understanding of the people of God with a vigorous defense of a premillennial hope for the restoration of national Israel. This emergence of progressive dispensationalism may foreshadow pivotal developments in the construction of an eschatologically informed evangelical socio-political ethic.

See also, among others, Blaising and Bock, *Dispensationalism, Israel, and the Church*; Craig A. Blaising and Darrell L. Bock, *Progressive Dispensationalism: An Up-to-Date Handbook of Contemporary Dispensational Thought* (Wheaton: BridgePoint Books, 1993); Oscar A. Campos, "El dispensacionalismo y la tradición dispensacional," *Vox Scripturae* 7.2 (June–December 1997): 101–13; Robert L. Saucy, *The Case for Progressive Dispensationalism: The Interface between Dispensational and Non-dispensational Theology* (Grand Rapids: Zondervan, 1993).

of some of the contents of progressive dispensationalism and his explanation of this term:

> They believe that the Bible reveals one divine plan of holistic redemption for all peoples. This holistic redemption is progressively revealed and affirmed in Old Testament promises of blessings, the New Testament proclamation of the gospel, and the biblical hope of the future coming of Christ. This same holistic redemption is likewise partially and progressively realized in biblical history through a succession of divine-human dispensations and will be ultimately fulfilled when Christ returns and completes the final resurrection. The term *progressive dispensationalism* is taken from this notion of progressive revelation and accomplishment of one plan of redemption.[84]

84. Craig A. Blaising, "Contemporary Dispensationalism," *Southwestern Journal of Theology* 36 (1994): 11.

Conclusion

There is no doubt considerable irony in the fact that this volume perpetuates the trend Tim Weber so poignantly notes in chapter 1. Throughout the resurgence of premillennialism over the last two centuries, *historical* premillennialism has been promoted mainly through seminaries and Christian colleges and in works of nonfiction written for a reasonably theologically literate audience. This collection of essays is no different. It emerged from an academic conference at a theological seminary, and the essays presented there and commissioned subsequently preserve that level of academic rigor. As explained in the introduction, this volume is part of an ongoing series of publications resulting from the annual conferences, at Denver Seminary, of the Denver Institute of Contextualized Biblical Studies. If there is to be a popular, populist contextualization of these essays at the simplest level for the complete theological novice, someone else will have to create it. If there are to be novels, works of science fiction, movies, DVDs, or other media to disseminate historical premillennialist convictions, they will have to be created by people with greater skills in those areas than we have.

On the other hand, Weber also rightly points out that classic dispensationalism has dwindled considerably in its presence and impact even within dispensationalist circles. With a few exceptions, the next generation of dispensationalists, mainly "progressive" as they are, will not be inspiring (unless unwittingly, against their intentions) a new round of end-times novelists, date setters, doomsayers, and the like. The twenty- and thirty-somethings of today among whom we minister have, for the most part, very little time or patience for the eschatological debates of even just a generation ago, and they are so put off by the "Left Behind" kind of literature that it can take quite a bit of persuasion to convince them that eschatology in all but its broadest contours is even a major doctrine of the Christian faith worth elevating to a fundamental or studying in any detail. But present them with a compelling case for historic premillennialism while agreeing with them that it should not be a doctrine that in any way divides them from fellowshipping and working together in ministry with those of different eschatological perspectives, and they can see its value and cogency.

Perhaps this is the case nowhere more clearly than in the area of social ethics. The logical corollary of classic dispensationalism is that the world is going to hell in a handbasket and the most we can hope to do is save souls before the end is upon us and we have no further opportunity to do so. Postmillennialism, followed consistently, engenders an unbridled optimism in what God wants to do in Christianizing the earth through his Spirit-filled followers, an optimism that is hard to mesh with humanity's experience in any prolonged period of world history. Amillennialism and historic premillennialism both acknowledge the "already but not yet" inaugurated kingdom of God, and both allow for God to still want to do great good on this earth through his people and for the devil to still wreak great havoc. We should never be surprised, after a 9/11 or a tsunami, or their cataclysmic equivalents in any era, of the depths of evil displayed by some people and the heights of goodness and altruism in others. The Christian doctrines of both the pervasiveness of sin and the image of God in all humanity, however marred, account for these extremes in human behavior as no other world religion, ideology, or even other branches of Christian eschatology can.

But historic premillennialism would appear to still be "one up" on amillennialism by insisting that God will fully vindicate his purposes for *this* universe, even before the eternal state. The millennial vision of the Bible cannot adequately be accounted for by the best of the "church age" now, nor can it be equated with the eternal state because of the lack of full eradication of the potential for rebellion still present in it. Historic premillennialism also arguably gives the most realistic and thus inspiring vision of the amount of continuity and discontinuity between the successive phases of cosmic history. To some degree, only hinted at in the Scriptures, all our God-guided efforts to make this world a better place (as the Scripture defines "better") will not be in vain but will come to fruition in the millennium. God will not have to start again from scratch, ignoring our contributions, nor is this age as good as it will get, nor may we naively look forward to completely creating the kingdom of God on earth without the incredible impetus caused by Christ's visible and public return to reign on earth. Now there is a vision that can keep us hopeful in the bleakest of times and humble in the most joyous. We invite all our readers to embrace a similar vision for as long as the Lord delays in his return and to allow him to use it to motivate us and work through us for his glory and for the good of all his creation. Amen!

List of Contributors

Craig L. Blomberg, distinguished professor of New Testament, Denver Seminary, has served on the seminary faculty since 1987. Previously he taught at Palm Beach Atlantic College in West Palm Beach, Florida. Holding a doctorate in New Testament from the University of Aberdeen in Scotland, he has written on a broad range of topics, especially in Gospels Studies.

Oscar A. Campos, professor of theology in the Seminario Teológico Centroamericano in Guatemala City, Guatemala, since 1997, received his doctorate in theology from Dallas Theological Seminary in Texas. His writings have focused on the history and effects of premillennialism in Latin America, the topic of his contribution to this volume.

Sung Wook Chung, associate professor of Christian theology, Denver Seminary, joined the faculty in 2005. He previously taught at King College in Bristol, Tennessee. He holds a doctorate in systematic theology from the University of Oxford. He has published widely in both Korean and English, particularly on the thought of Karl Barth and on world religions.

Hélène Dallaire, associate professor of Old Testament, Denver Seminary, joined the faculty in 2006. Previously she taught at Hebrew Union College–Jewish Institute of Religion in Cincinnati, where she also earned her doctorate in Hebrew and cognate studies (comparative semitics). She is well known for her pioneering research on Hebrew pedagogy, and she is currently a member of the CoHeLet project (Communicative Hebrew Learning and Teaching).

Donald Fairbairn, professor of historical theology, Erskine Theological Seminary, Due West, South Carolina, earned his doctorate in patristics from the University of Cambridge. He has taught widely in both Western and Eastern Europe, especially at the Evangelische Theologische Faculteit, Leuven, Belgium. His publications have focused on patristic Christology and on Eastern Orthodoxy today.

Richard S. Hess, Earl S. Kalland Professor of Old Testament and Semitic Languages, Denver Seminary, joined the faculty in 1997. He previously taught at International Christian College in Scotland and Roehampton University in London. He earned his doctorate from Hebrew Union College in Cincinnati and has published extensively in his two fields.

Don J. Payne, associate dean and assistant professor of theology and ministry, Denver Seminary, obtained a doctorate in systematic theology from the University of Manchester, England. His published work centers on the life and thought of J. I. Packer, theological reflection, and mentoring. He joined the faculty of Denver Seminary in 1998 after serving in the pastorate for a decade.

Timothy P. Weber, senior consultant at EFL Associates, an executive search firm, in its higher-education practice, received a doctorate in church history from the University of Chicago. He taught at Denver Seminary from 1976 to 1992 and then served in administrative and teaching roles at three other seminaries. His writings have focused on American premillennialism.

Scripture and Ancient Writings Index

Subject Index

Abraham, covenant with, 144–45
Acts, tribulation in, 72
Adam, covenant with, 134–44
Adventists, 7–8
afterlife, the, 38–39, 42–60, 85. *See also* resurrection, bodily
Against Heresies (Irenaeus), 112–13, 118–19, 120–21, 125–28, 129–31
allegory, 29–31, 119–20
American Bible and Prophetic Conference. *See* prophetic conferences
amillennialism, xii–xiii, 3, 65–67, 85, 172
Amos, Book of, 27
Antiochus Epiphanes, 53–54
arithmetic, millennial, 7
Augustine, 116–17
authority, biblical. *See* Scripture, theology and

Beale, G. K., 137–38
Believers' Meeting, 12
Bible, the. *See* Scripture, theology and
Blaising, Craig, 96–97, 168–69
Blessed Hope, The (Ladd), 19
blessings, covenant of, 135–37
body, resurrection of. *See* resurrection, bodily
Breneman, Mervin, 164–65
Brethren, Plymouth. *See* Plymouth Brethren
Brookes, James H., 12, 15

Cameron, Robert, 13
Catholic Apostolic Church, 9
Chafer, Lewis Sperry, 21, 63
chiliasm. *See* premillennialism, defined

Christ, Jesus the, 140–45, 167
Chrysostom, John, 124–25
church, the
  early, 105–31
  individual conversion and, 156n41
  in Revelation, 75–77, 81–82
  theology and, 94, 97–98
City of God, The (Augustine), 116–17
classic premillennialism. *See* premillennialism, defined
Classic Reformed theology. *See* covenant theology
common-sense realism, 98–100
complex marriage, 6
Constantine, Emperor. *See* Rome, theology and
contextual evangelism, 159–69. *See also* kingdom, the; social issues, mission and
conversion, individual, 154–56, 158–59. *See also* salvation, emphasis on
Costas, Orlando E., 163–64
covenant theology, xv, 133–46
creedal theology. *See* tradition, theology and
Crucial Questions about the Kingdom of God (Ladd), 19

Daniel, Book of, 27, 52
Darby, John Nelson, xiii, 9–11, 13, 62–63, 101–2
David, King, 48
death, life after. *See* afterlife, the
dispensationalism
  development of, 10–22, 101–2
  missions and, 149–59